FISHER OF MEN: A LIFE OF JOHN FISHER, 1469–1535

Fisher of Men: a Life of John Fisher, 1469–1535

Maria Dowling
Senior Lecturer in History
St Mary's, Strawberry Hill

BX
4700
.F34
D68
1999

First published in Great Britain 1999 by
MACMILLAN PRESS LTD
Houndmills, Basingstoke, Hampshire RG21 6XS and London
Companies and representatives throughout the world

A catalogue record for this book is available from the British Library.

ISBN 0–333–74670–8

First published in the United States of America 1999 by
ST. MARTIN'S PRESS, INC.,
Scholarly and Reference Division,
175 Fifth Avenue, New York, N.Y. 10010

ISBN 0–312–22367–6

Library of Congress Cataloging-in-Publication Data
Dowling, Maria, 1955–
Fisher of men : a life of John Fisher, 1469–1535 / Maria
Dowling.
   p.   cm.
Includes bibliographical references and index.
ISBN 0–312–22367–6 (cloth)
1. Fisher, John, Saint, 1469–1535.   2. Christian saints—England–
–Biography.   I. Title.
BX4700.F34D68   1999
282'.092
[B]—DC21   99–10939
                                                  CIP

This book is printed on paper suitable for recycling and made from fully managed and sustained forest sources.

10   9   8   7   6   5   4   3   2   1
08   07   06   05   04   03   02   01   00   99

Printed and bound in Great Britain by
Antony Rowe Ltd, Chippenham, Wiltshire

For Joan Henderson in friendship, and in cheerful memory of Terry Dowling

Contents

Note and Acknowledgements

Spelling and punctuation have been modernised in all quotations from and references to documents of the fifteenth and sixteenth centuries. All dates are new-style. Biblical quotations are taken from the Douai version, as being in time and style closest to Fisher's own language. Quotations from sources in foreign languages have been given in English. Where possible, I have used and acknowledged published translations. Where these fail I have translated the documents myself. I have used two translations of Erasmus' letters; Rouschausse's edition of his correspondence with Fisher, and that of the University of Toronto for the whole correspondence.

Citations from a publication called *The Eagle* may seem puzzling. This was the college magazine of St John's, Cambridge, which printed documents from the archive there between 1889 and 1913. R.F. Scott republished these extracts in three series, as *Notes from the College Records*. As these were not repaginated as a new edition but simply reprinted under their old pagination the easiest way to locate a particular document is to look for the issue in which it first appeared. I hope this is helpful.

I am grateful to the British Academy for a grant for research in the Vatican archive and library, and to St Mary's, Strawberry Hill for research support. I would like to thank the staff of the following archives and libraries: the British Library and Public Record Office, London; the Bodleian Library, Oxford; Cambridge University Library; the archive and library of the Vatican; the Folger Shakespeare Library, Washington, DC; the National Széchenyi Library, Budapest; and the Muniment Room and Library, Westminster Abbey.

Especial thanks for co-operation, helpfulness and patience are due to Mrs Janet Barnes and the staff of Dr Williams's Library, London; Dr Thomas and the staff of the Haus,-Hof,-und Staatsarchiv, Vienna; and Mr Malcolm Underwood, archivist of St John's College, Cambridge. As ever, the Institute of Historical Research, University of London has provided both an extremely useful library and an invaluable forum for discussion. I would like to thank the staff, past and present, most warmly.

Indeed it is a pleasure to thank so many scholars for their interest and assistance. A.G. Dickens has always been generous and enthusiastic in discussion of my work. The late L.R. Gardiner helped greatly in the early stages of this project by his scholarship and encouragement. I am grateful to Conrad and Elizabeth Russell for both encouragement and the opportunity to discuss Fisher, as I am to Patrick Collinson. Edmund Green has provided invaluable technical assistance as well as sensible ideas about the historical evidence. I am most grateful to Alasdair Hawkyard for preparing the index, and to Andrew Plaa who once rescued a valuable set of notes. I must also thank Christopher and Jill Hebron for kindly showing me round their part of Fisher's palace at Rochester. My colleagues, past and present, in the History Programme at Strawberry Hill have been most supportive. In particular, I am indebted to the guidance and critical comment on the work of Christopher Harper-Bill. As always, my parents have been a constant source of strength.

Two people in particular are owed a debt of gratitude. Susan Wabuda, by her friendship and scholarship, has sustained this study over the years. Joan Henderson has helped many generations of scholars at the Institute of Historical Research, including myself, by encouragement, positive criticism and her own considerable scholarship. It is most fitting that this book should be dedicated to her.

Conventions

Arch. Cant. *Archaeologia Cantiana*

ASV *Archivio Segreto del Vaticano*

Bradshaw and Duffy *Humanism, Reform and the Reformation: the Career of Bishop John Fisher*, ed. Brendan Bradshaw and Eamon Duffy, Cambridge, 1989

BL British Library, London

Bridgett, *Life of Fisher* T.E. Bridgett, *Life of Blessed John Fisher*, 2nd edn, London, 1922

CM *Calendar of State Papers, Milan, Volume I, 1385–1618*, ed. Alan B. Hinds, London, 1912

CSP *Calendar of State Papers, Spanish*, ed. G. Bergenroth, P. Gayangos, M.A.S. Hume, 8 vols, London, 1862–1904

CUL Cambridge University Library

CV *Calendar of State Papers, Venetian, Volume IV, 1527–1533*, ed. Rawdon Brown, London, 1871

The Eagle College magazine of St John's, Cambridge, reprinted as *Notes from the Records of St John's College, Cambridge*, ed. R.F. Scott, 3 series, privately printed, 1889–1913

Early Life, I, II *'Vie du Bienheureux martyr Jean Fisher, cardinal, évêque de Rochester'*, ed. F. Van Ortroy, *Analecta Bollandiana*, Vol. X, pp. 121-365 (1891), Vol. XII, pp. 97–283 (1893)

EETS Early English Text Society

English Works *The English Works of John Fisher*, ed. J.E.B. Mayor, EETS extra series 27, London, 1876

Episcopal Register Fisher's register as bishop of Rochester, in Kent County Archives Office, Maidstone. Reproduced on microfilm as 'Church Authority and Power in Medieval and Early Modern Britain: The Episcopal Registers, Part 8', Brighton, 1987

Erasmi Epistolae *Opus Epistolarum Des. Erasmi Roterodami*, ed. P.S. and H.M. Allen, H.W. Garrod, 11 vols, Oxford, 1906–47

Erasmi Epistolae (Rouschausse trans.) *Erasmus and Fisher: Their Correspondence*, ed. Jean Rouschausse, Paris, 1968

Erasmi Epistolae (Toronto trans.) *Correspondence of Erasmus*, trans. Wallace K. Ferguson, R.A.B. Mynors, D.F.S. Thomson, Alexander Dalzell, 11 vols, Toronto, 1974–94

1526 Sermon *A sermon had at Paul's . . . by John the bishop of Rochester upon Quinquagesima Sunday, concerning certain heretics . . .*, London, 1526

Foxe John Foxe, *Acts and Monuments*, ed. S.R. Cattley, 8 vols, London, 1837

Hall's Chronicle Edward Halle, *The Union of the Two Noble Families of Lancaster and York*, London, 1550, facsimile reprint Menston, 1970

L & P *Letters and Papers, Foreign and Domestic, of the Reign of Henry VIII*, ed. J.S. Brewer, J. Gairdner, R.H. Brodie, 21 vols, London, 1862–1932

Lamb, *Cambridge Documents A Collection of Letters, Statutes and Other Documents, from the MS Library of Corp. Christ. Coll., Illustrative of the History of the University of Cambridge*, ed. John Lamb, London, 1838

Lewis, *Life of Dr Fisher* John Lewis, *The Life of Dr Fisher*, ed. T. Hudson Turner, 2 vols, London, 1855

Opera R.D.D. Ioannis Fischerii, Roffensis in Anglia Episcopi, Opera, Würzburg, 1597

PRO Public Record Office, London

Reynolds, *Life of Fisher* E.E. Reynolds, *Saint John Fisher*, London, 1955

Rouschausse, *Vie et Oeuvre* Jean Rouschausse, *La Vie et Oeuvre de Jean Fisher*, Nieuwkoop, 1972

SJC Archive of St John's College, Cambridge

STC *Short-Title Catalogue of Books Printed in England, Scotland and Ireland, and of English Books Printed Abroad, 1475–1640*, 2 vols, ed. A. Pollard and G.R. Redgrave, Bibliographical Society, London, 1926; 2nd edn ed. W.A. Jackson, F.S. Ferguson, Katharine F. Pantzer, Bibliographical Society, London, 1976, 1986

St. P   State Papers . . . *King Henry the Eighth,* 11 vols, London, 1830–52

Treatise of Prayer   A Treatise of Prayer, and of the Fruits and Manner of Prayer, by the most reverend Father in God John Fisher, trans. R.A.B., Paris 1640, facsimile reprint Menston, 1969

Two Fruitful Sermons   Here after ensueth two fruitful sermons, made & compiled by the right reverend father in God John Fisher, doctor of Divinity and Bishop of Rochester,[?] 2nd edn, London, 1532

Vienna   Haus,-Hof,-und Staatsarchiv, Vienna

Introduction

> I have often had thoughts of writing his life myself, but I will confess to you I dare not venture upon it, lest I should give offence; for I would rather do him right, or nothing at all.[1]

Thus in the eighteenth century the historian of St John's, Cambridge wrote to John Fisher's current biographer about the difficulty of the task the latter had undertaken. All biographers of Fisher have faced a number of related problems, stemming from the nature of the historical sources and from historiographical considerations.

The first factor is Fisher's standing as a canonised saint of the Roman Catholic Church. This has meant that most biographies of Fisher – certainly, the best of them – have actually been hagiographies. While no one would doubt the serious scholarship of T.E. Bridgett, E.E. Reynolds and Jean Rouschausse,[2] it has to be said that hagiography has a purpose different from that of objective historical study. It aims to stir the devotion of the faithful by reciting the lives and deaths of good men and women. As such, it is a perfectly legitimate medium; but its purpose does necessarily affect the approach of the writer to his subject. John Fisher was canonised because he suffered martyrdom in defence of the Church Catholic. He had a reputation for virtue and holiness long before his troubles with Henry VIII began; but whether he would have been canonised had he died in his bed in 1527 is highly questionable. What this means for the hagiographer is that the life is shaped and conditioned by the death, the subject's righteousness confirming that he died in a just cause. Thus the bulk of most lives of Fisher is taken up with his struggle with the king over the divorce and royal supremacy.[3]

The pattern for hagiographies of Fisher was set by the earliest, Elizabethan biography, hereafter referred to as the *Early Life*. Though it might be expected that a life of a martyr would devote most space to his passion and death, it seems that lack of documentary sources also affected the balance of this work. As the present study uses the earliest biography quite extensively it is as well to say something here about its provenance and veracity.

All the surviving manuscripts of the *Early Life* – which exists in quite different English and Latin versions – were collated and edited

1

by the Bollandist François Van Ortroy. The editor was careful to obtain corroboration of statements in the biography, and where he was dubious about any of them he was honest enough to say so. Van Ortroy's is the only edition of the *Early Life* which can be used with confidence, as it is the most critical and comprehensive. Above all, the authentic Elizabethan biography should not be confused with the embroidered version composed by Thomas Bayly in the seventeenth century. Doubtless for the best of reasons, this author added many pious and unnecessary interpolations in order to strengthen the sanctity of his subject's character. Therefore while it is interesting as an example of reformation hagiography it is worthless as a historical source.

What of the *Early Life* itself? There are indications that it emanated from Cambridge, possibly from Fisher's own college of St John. The assiduous, anonymous author prepared for his task by sending out questionnaires to men who had known or at least known of Fisher in his lifetime. However, he was hampered by the limits of human memory and longevity. Two answers to one of these forms should show the problem succinctly. Firstly, the respondent 'cannot devise how you should find where he was made priest, it is so long ago'. Secondly, 'Of his notable acts I have no knowledge, for I was but a yo[ung] scholar of St John's college when he died'.[4] Thus material for Fisher's youth and middle years was scarce in comparison to that available for the end of his life.

The shape of the *Early Life* was also affected by the nature of the surviving historical evidence about Fisher. Naturally enough, Fisher appears much more often in the state papers during the last years of his life, as he was one of the king's most eminent and most feared opponents. The divorce period, too, saw an increase in ambassadorial reports from and to the English court, and Fisher often figured in despatches. Yet this does not explain why there should seem to be a comparative dearth of documentation prior to the late 1520s. Some sources, indeed, have inexplicably disappeared. Internal evidence from the correspondence of Erasmus shows that he and Fisher exchanged numerous letters, yet only a handful of these are extant. Nothing at all seems to have survived of Fisher's correspondence with Reuchlin. As far as concerns England, Tudor censorship accounts for the loss of some sources. A proclamation of December 1535 commanded surrender of Fisher's printed works. This was part of the campaign to obliterate his memory. His private library was broken up by Cromwell, his motto and device removed from the chapel of St John's College, his empty tomb thrown out of the chantry and left in a courtyard. Even as late as the reign of Edward VI the authorities would seem to have feared Fisher still. His earliest biographer took the testimony of the aged parson of Cuxton.

It hath been reported by a good old priest called Master Buddell, who in his life wrote many of his books for him, that there came to him on a certain time, in the foresaid King Edward's days, a minister by authority of him that then occupied the see of Rochester, and took from him as many written books and papers of this holy man's labours and travails as loaded a horse; and carrying them to his master, they were all afterward burned.[5]

Fear of the authorities also caused the destruction of evidence.

it was once told me by a reverend father that was dean of Rochester many years together, named Master Phillips, that on a time in the days of King Edward VI, when certain commissioners were coming towards him to search his house for books, he for fear burned a large volume which this holy bishop had compiled, containing in it the whole story and matter of the divorce. Which volume he gave him with his own hand a little before his trouble.[6]

While Catholic hagiographers have paid more attention to Fisher's martyrdom than his ministry, Protestant writers have shown Fisher scant sympathy or even attention. (Though John Bruce felt that Fisher was the victim of a miscarriage of justice, and should never have been executed.)[7] Some of them have regretted the paradox that a man of such qualities should have persisted in error.

For his learning and other virtues of life this bishop was well reputed and reported of by many, and also much lamented by some. But whatsoever his learning was, pity it was that he, being endued with that knowledge, should be so far drowned in such superstition; more pity that he was so obstinate in his ignorance, but most pity of all, that he so abused the learning he had, to such cruelty as he did.[8]

Some authors have been ready to do justice to a man of good life though wrong opinions. John Lewis gave a judicious account of Fisher's life and death, though he could not resist some digression into theological discourse to prove him erroneous.

Most significantly, Fisher's reputation has suffered through the

'Whiggish' school of thought which sees history as a series of pro-gressive steps; to be on the losing side in an event like the English reformation is to be wrong, and results in marginalisation.[9] As late as the 1960s, Michael Macklem's popular biography saw Fisher as a medieval relic, increasingly irrelevant, isolated, and un-English in the modern Tudor state.[10] Truly, Fisher can be described as the great missing figure of the period.

Attempts have been made to remedy this. E.L. Surtz's magis-terial work explored Fisher's thought in detail. More recently, Richard Rex has analysed Fisher's theology most thoroughly.[11] (Thus there is no separate chapter in this book on Fisher as theologian; it seemed pointless to duplicate work already done. My debt to Rex, and to scholars such as Stephen Thompson and Malcolm Underwood in other spheres, will be evident in the notes to the text.) Most honour-ably, Cambridge University produced a commemorative volume of essays following the 450th anniversary of Fisher's death. Mean-while, Cecilia Hatt is working on a critical edition of Fisher's English works.

The present volume aims to give a more rounded view of Fisher than has hitherto been presented in a full-length study. It is poss-ible to do this using archival and other materials which were not available to the Elizabethan or even more recent biographers. The form chosen is that of a thematic study, rather than a conventional biography following Fisher from his cradle in Beverley in 1469 to his uncertain grave in London in 1535.[12] Such an approach might lead to a somewhat fragmented picture of Fisher. However, a sum-mary here of his career, with some comments on his personality, ought to serve as a unifying element.

John Fisher was born in 1469 to a merchant family in Beverley in Yorkshire. Evidently destined for the priesthood, he went up to Cambridge in 1483 where he gained the degrees of BA, MA and DD. He was ordained priest in 1491, while still under the canonical age.

At Cambridge he was master of Michaelhouse, 1496–98, and president of Queens', 1505–8. His association with Margaret Beau-fort involved him in the practical work of founding her colleges, Christ's and St John's. Fisher also held university posts, ending as chancellor from 1504 to 1535. During the same period he was Bishop of Rochester.

As a humanist scholar Fisher undertook the difficult study of Greek and Hebrew, when he was comparatively advanced in years. He numbered among his friends and associates such humanist luminaries as Erasmus, Reuchlin, Colet and More. The advent of the Protestant reformation turned his talents towards polemical theology, and he wrote against Luther, Oecolampadius and other reformers. He also found time to be an assiduous preacher and a writer of devotional works and plays. From 1527 he was engaged in opposition to Henry VIII over the divorce and royal supremacy. He was executed for treason on 22 June 1535. Some weeks before his death he was created cardinal.

So much for the bare bones of Fisher's career. His personality has proved somewhat elusive to biographers. He is usually presented as the archetype of an austere, unworldly bishop. Catholic iconography, based on Holbein's drawing of Fisher in old age, confirms his image as something of a tomb effigy. Above all, invidious comparisons have been made with Thomas More. As E.E. Reynolds put it: 'One was, first and last, a preacher. By nature he was not socially inclined, nor had he an ever ready sense of humour. The other was an active lawyer and statesman and the centre of a happy family.'[13]

A few references to Fisher's literary works and other records will show him in a more human light. His sermons are full of emotion: anger and sorrow at heresy and sin; compassion for physical suffering and fear for sinners in hell; joy in the beauty of created nature and in the love of God. He was not devoid of humour. Sometimes this was heavily sarcastic, as when he wondered at the 'miracle' of Luther's wife giving birth just six weeks after her marriage. He could be tactless and impulsive, as when he apparently accused the members of the reformation parliament of lack of faith. His relations with Cambridge were not always smooth, possibly because of his highhanded nature.

His spirituality was charismatic and emotional. Often he wept while celebrating mass. His favourite phrase when describing devotion was 'the fervour of charity', and his stress on the mutual love of God and man runs as a *leitmotif* through his sermons and devotional works.

Writers have contrasted the warm family life of More to the lonely austerity of Fisher's existence. It is true that Fisher was abstemious in food and drink, though it seems that ill-health, particularly digestive complaints, was at least partly the cause of this. Certainly he kept a good table for others.[14] He seems to have been on good terms with his family. His brother Robert was steward of his household, his half-sister Elizabeth was a nun at Dartford in Rochester diocese. The children and grandchildren of his mother's second marriage to a man named White benefited from his generosity. His nephews filled the two Fisher scholarships at St John's, Cambridge. His half-brothers visited him in prison, and owed him money at his death. Naturally a bishop was expected to provide for his kindred; yet the impression given is of a degree of family closeness. It is interesting that Margaret Beaufort gave Fisher's mother a gift of money when he became bishop.

Thomas More has been celebrated for his wit on the scaffold. Fisher, too, was capable of gallows humour. When a rumour arose of his imminent execution his cook did not bother to prepare his dinner that day. When no meal appeared Fisher reproached him: 'take this for a general rule: make rea[dy] my dinner at my due hour. And if thou see me dead before, then eat it thyself. If myself be alive, I will never eat one bit the less'. At the same time, he prepared for his end with fitting dignity and piety.

after rising he put on all his best apparel very curiously [carefully], and caused his hose to be trussed round, and his head combed etc. An [d when] his servant said: 'Sir, I marvel that ye are so curious in trimming yourself this day, seeing ye shall put all off again before noon': he answered again: 'What, man! Do you not know that [this is] our marriage day? I must be gay this day for honour of the mar[riage].'

It is hoped that the chapters which follow will 'do right' to 'this worthy prelate, neither dumb in preaching, nor idle in writing, neither cold in devotion, nor ambitious in aspiring'.[15]

1 Cambridge

Come ye after me, and I will make you to be fishers of men
(Matthew 4:19)

John Fisher's association with the University of Cambridge is well
known, despite Henry VIII's attempts to obliterate his memory there.
He is especially remembered and honoured as the man who chan-
nelled Margaret Beaufort's charitable piety in the direction of
university patronage. He was also a considerable benefactor to
Cambridge in his own right, both in terms of material endowment
and in the promotion of humanist studies. Fisher's aim in all this
was quite straightforward; the university and its colleges should
educate young men in piety, learning and virtue, so that they could
teach and preach to the people on the one hand and add to the
lustre of Christian scholarship on the other.

The chief events of Fisher's career at Cambridge can be summarised briefly. Probably he went up in 1483 at the age of 14, having
learned Latin grammar in his native town of Beverley. A student
at Michaelhouse, he was BA in 1488 and MA in 1490–91, when he
also became a fellow of his college. He was senior proctor in 1494–
95, and in 1496–97 was paid for lecturing by the university
congregation. In 1501 he became Doctor of Divinity, and was also
vice-chancellor. In 1502 he was the first of Lady Margaret's lectur-
ers in theology. In 1504 he was elected university chancellor for
the first time, and was re-elected annually until 1514.[1]

Some traces remain of Fisher's studies at Michaelhouse and of
his continued connections with the college. One of the informants
for the Elizabethan biography, questioned as to where Fisher went
to school and his age on going up to Cambridge, answered: 'To
that point as yet I can learn nothing. But in Cambridge he was in
Michael's house under Dr Melton and continued h[is] whole study
there, as appeared by the study which he dressed there, which was
the fairest in Cambridge'.[2] A vignette of Fisher as a young student
is provided by John Bouge, a Carthusian of Axholme. Writing almost
50 years later he recalled: 'we were scholars together in Cambridge,
of one form and of one parish; and for a little pastime I might
speak to him out of my chamber window into his chamber window'.[3]
It is pleasant to find that the young Fisher had his frivolous side.

Fisher's tutor was William Melton, fellow of Michaelhouse from about 1485 and master of the college from 1495 to 1496. Melton was a theologian, gaining his BD in 1490 and his DD in 1496. Fisher refers to his early studies with Melton in his book against Oecolampadius of 1527.

> My master, William Melton, chancellor of York, a man eminent both for his holiness and for every kind of erudition, used often to admonish me when I was a boy and attended his lectures on Euclid, that if I looked on the least letter of any geometrical figure as superfluous, I had not seized the true and full meaning of Euclid. But if the disciple of Euclid must be careful in points of geometry, certainly the disciple of Christ must weigh well each word of his divine master, and be thoroughly convinced that there is not a word without its purpose.[4]

Melton may be classed as a reform-minded humanist, and that not solely because of his association with Fisher; indeed, it seems likely that his was a formative and continuing influence on his pupil. His famous sermon to ordinands of about 1510 warned the prospective priests against imitating the sins of unlearned, immoral and negligent clergy. It seems to mirror Fisher's concern with the provision of well-educated and effective priests and preachers.[5]

Melton's will of 1528 reveals his humanist interests and connections. Among his books were works by schoolmen, Greek and Latin classical and patristic writers, and modern humanist authors. There are several copies of the new testament inclusing Erasmus' Greek edition. There is also mention of *Roffensis contra Lutherum*. Melton himself is credited with writing against Luther, though his work is not known to have survived.[6]

The *Early Life* states that Fisher was elected to succeed Melton as master of Michaelhouse when the latter became chancellor of York. There seems to be no archival proof of Fisher's mastership, though links between that college and St John's occur in financial documents. In 1516, for example, John Riplyngham gave £100 to Fisher and Henry Hornby as executors of Margaret Beaufort to found two scholarships at St John's for natives of Yorkshire. The lands they bought with part of this sum were to revert to Michaelhouse in default of the election of scholars. When Fisher himself founded four scholarships at St John's in 1521 he stipulated that failure to elect scholars would cost the college twenty shillings a month, to be paid to himself, his brother Robert and Michaelhouse.[7]

The *Early Life* states that Fisher left Cambridge to serve Margaret Beaufort as chaplain: 'she ceased not still [sic] she had procured him out of the university to her service: by mean whereof he resigned the mastership of Michaelhouse and left the university for that time'.[8] While it is not entirely true that Fisher severed his connections with Cambridge on entering Margaret's household, it was quite in character for that imperious lady to have demanded that he resign the mastership. Fisher never forgot Michaelhouse, however. When he was settling his affairs in Rochester prior to his last journey to London in spring 1534 he made Michaelhouse a gift of £100, 'which was after paid to the college in gold'.[9] In 1546–47 Michaelhouse was merged into Henry VIII's new college, Trinity. Whether there was anything left of Fisher's legacy for the king and his executors to enjoy is not known.

The other Cambridge college of which Fisher was sometime head was Queens', where Margaret Beaufort acted as patron after the death of Elizabeth of York in 1503.[10] In 1505 she secured the resignation of Thomas Wilkinson as president so that Fisher could succeed him.[11] Her primary purpose in advancing Fisher was not the welfare of Queens'; rather, she wished to provide a lodging for him in Cambridge so that he could supervise the building of her new foundation, Christ's. As for Fisher himself, the modern historian of Queens' is not far from the truth in saying that 'His commitment to Queens' was largely a token one.' He did not try to introduce major reforms at the college, and he was only resident there during the royal visits of 1506 and 1507.[12] None the less, there are occasional records of Fisher's activity as president. The fellows sometimes went to consult him at Rochester, and he issued a number of licences for study abroad as well as transacting other college business.[13] It is noteworthy that when Fisher went to Cambridge in 1516 for the formal opening of St John's College, Queens' made its former president a gift of sweet hypocras wine and 'sugarplate and suckettes', spending a total of 4s 2d.[14] Tradition holds that Erasmus resided at Queens' between 1511 and 1514 because of Fisher's association with the college.

In 1508 Fisher made known his desire to resign the presidency of Queens', citing the fact that he was non-resident, showing his concern at holding so many offices, and voicing his wish to spend more time on diocesan matters. Queens' expressed satisfaction at having had him for its head, balancing against his non-residence his integrity of life, great learning and fame.[15] The college's letter to Lady Margaret on the occasion contains rather more than formal regret at the loss of Fisher.[16]

If Fisher was merely dutiful in fulfilling his responsibilities towards Queens', he certainly worked hard at the business for which Margaret had appointed him president there; the foundation and building of Christ's College. Before considering his labours there it might be useful to consider the origins and nature of his association with Margaret.

Fisher first met the king's mother in 1495 when, as senior proctor, he was sent to her on university business. His accounts laconically state his expenses and the fact that he dined with the lady mother of the king.[17] As Margaret's modern biographers have commented, Fisher clearly made a great impression at this initial meeting. When she renewed her vow of chastity before him some years later she declared: 'I avow to you, my lord of Rochester, to whom I am and have been, since the first time I see you admitted, verily determined to owe my obedience'. As for Fisher, he wrote much later of the debt he felt he owed Margaret from the beginning of their relations: 'I freely admit that once she had adopted me both as her confessor and her moral and spiritual guide, I learned more of what leads to an upright life from her rare virtues than I ever taught her in return.'[18]

Fisher probably entered Margaret's service about the year 1498, though when precisely he became her confessor cannot be known. Margaret's household accounts contain a number of references to him, as well as the note of a 'reward' of 6s 8d given to his mother in November 1508, presumably to celebrate his elevation to the episcopal bench.[19]

The relationship between the two was certainly close, based on mutual respect and, it would seem, affection. Fisher preached the Church's traditional month-mind or memorial sermon for Margaret's soul soon after her death in 1509. This is redolent of a warmth which is lacking in the funeral sermon for Henry VII he had delivered some months previously; yet in terms of patronage he was more bound to the king than to her.

Fisher's regard for Margaret persisted throughout his life. He was at pains to establish the commemoration of her anniversary at Cambridge. By his private statute of foundation for St John's, the Fisher fellows were bound to remember Margaret at their masses as the woman to whom the bishop was as much bound as to his natural mother. In 1529 the university offered to celebrate exequies for Fisher at St John's as a mark of respect for its chancellor. He replied modestly that he would be happy if they would merely link his name with Margaret's in their prayers; he had just been her agent, advising her as her confessor to leave some of her wealth to educate young men in virtue and learning so that they could preach the gospel. Finally, as Lord Morley told Queen Mary some years later:

> I do ensure your highness that Dr Fisher, then bishop of Rochester, being her ghostly father, showed me not long before his death that he had written her life, which I suppose to be in your grace's hand; then if it be so, O good Jesu how joyous would it make me to see and to read it, written by so good a man and so divine a clerk as that bishop was.[20]

It is a great loss to studies of both Fisher and Margaret that this biography seems not to have survived.

It is generally asserted that Fisher must be credited with directing Margaret's charitable impulses towards education and away from the simple endowment of monastic chantries. While this is broadly true, some qualifications must be made to the assumption.

In the first place, some credit must go to Margaret herself, who was intelligent and (for an Englishwoman of the fifteenth century) well-educated. She shared Fisher's concern with regeneration of the Church through improved education and training of the clergy. Secondly, Erasmus' praise of Margaret's munificence has possibly caused misunderstanding of her and Fisher's purpose. Erasmus was concerned to vaunt educational endowment at the expense of chantry foundation. Thus the epitaph on her tomb which he composed (and Fisher possibly commissioned) commemorates her in rather concise terms for founding a grammar school at Wimborne, two divinity lectures at Oxford and Cambridge, a preachership at the latter university and two Cambridge colleges, Christ's and St John's. In 1535 he praised her and Fisher's educational work in the preface to the preaching manual which Fisher had commissioned from him: rather than bequeath rich revenues to build monasteries Margaret and Fisher had preferred to endow university colleges where true preachers would be trained.[21]

Besides Erasmus' deliberate omission of Margaret's monastic patronage (he was notoriously averse to monks and monasticism), the foundation of chantries for the good of one's soul and the promotion of clerical education were not necessarily two separate issues.

University colleges were meant to be both learned societies and intercessory institutions, with scholars and fellows bound to pray for the souls of founders and benefactors. Indeed Fisher, working with Margaret, was following in the episcopal tradition of bishops like Wykeham and Fleming in seeking to renew the Church through education of the clergy as well as acquiring personal spiritual benefits.

Finally, while Jones and Underwood see Margaret's concentration on the patronage of Cambridge as due to Fisher's influence, they point out that he was not the only university scholar in her household. In particular, they describe the academic career and administrative work of Henry Hornby, and mention also Hugh Oldham (effective co-founder of Corpus Christi, Oxford), John Fotehede (fellow and then master of Michaelhouse), Robert Bekensaw (Fisher's chosen successor at Queens'), and Hugh Ashton. Many of these kept up their university connections, especially with Cambridge. Some, too, were concerned as practical men of affairs with the foundation and organisation of Margaret's Cambridge colleges. Thus while Fisher was probably the greatest single influence on Margaret in matters of educational endowment, 'he did not labour in isolation'.[22]

Margaret Beaufort's first benefactions to the universities were public divinity lectures at Oxford and Cambridge and a preachership at Cambridge alone; given his marked interest in the preaching ministry, this last foundation undoubtedly shows Fisher's influence. Margaret obtained licences to found the lectures in 1497, though they were not officially established until 1502. She was permitted to endow them to the value of £20, and Westminster Abbey was responsible for paying the readers £13 6s 8d a year. According to the charter of 1502 the first Cambridge reader was Fisher himself, and indeed he received payments as Lady Margaret Professor.[23]

The Cambridge preachership was established in 1504. The preacher was to be DD or at least BD and a fellow of some college; later, preference was given to fellows of Christ's. The preacher was to give six sermons a year, one in London and the others at specified places which had connections of patronage with Margaret. He was to receive the generous stipend of £10 a year. The first Lady Margaret preacher was John Fawne of Queens'.[24] It might seem odd that Fisher himself did not fill the post, but it must be remembered that he was promoted to the see of Rochester very shortly before the foundation deed was drawn up, in November 1504.

Margaret Beaufort founded Christ's College in Cambridge in 1506.

Christ's was actually a refoundation of Godshouse, a medieval teacher-training college initially favoured by Henry VI. The foundation of Christ's was most definitely Margaret's own work; she gave close and personal supervision to the drawing up of the statutes, and between 1505 and 1509 spent the prodigious sum of £1,625 on the college. None the less she relied considerably on the experience and expertise of Fisher, by now chancellor of Cambridge, as a university administrator. In 1525 Christ's itself credited Fisher with having urged Margaret to found the college, while Jones and Underwood have discerned Fisher's hand in the foundation and organisation of Christ's.[25]

Fisher was active in the affairs of Christ's both as visitor and as Lady Margaret's executor, it would seem. His visitor's injunctions of July 1510 survive, and they cover such routine matters as the compulsory speaking of Latin within the college precincts by fellows and scholars; the rendering of half-yearly accounts; safe-keeping of the college seal; the residence of scholars; nightly closing of the college gates; and the exclusion of dogs.[26]

Christ's College requested Fisher's financial help from time to time. An undated letter shows the master and fellows asking to borrow money from him; that they were successful is attested by a receipt of £40.[27] In another letter Henry Hornby asked Fisher for assistance for Christ's.

> since my last writings unto you the master of Christ's hath desired me to pray your lordship that he may receive of you money to finish divers works in the said college necessary to be done.... I perceive by the said master he hath no money of the college's to perform the premises. Wherefore, good my lord, I heartily beseech you to deliver unto him such money at this time for the intent abovesaid as ye shall think convenient.[28]

Hornby may have been requesting money from Margaret's estate rather than from Fisher's own purse; it is often difficult to distinguish one source from another.

Certainly, Fisher made a considerable benefaction to Christ's when he decided to have his anniversary commemorated there by mass and prayers for his soul and those of his family. He gave the college £43 to buy land worth 40s a year. On the occasion the master was to receive 16d, the fellows 12d each, and the scholars 4d or 2d depending on whether or not they were BA. In addition, 5s 4d would be spent on a feast or dinner that day.[29]

However, there is evidence that negotiations between Fisher and Christ's were not always smooth. Fisher liked to have his own way, as is shown by a letter from his chaplain Richard Sharpe to Nicholas Metcalfe, master of St John's. Sharpe said that Christ's would not go forward unless it submitted fully to Fisher's will. The bishop had said they would make no statute for him, he would devise the agreement himself. Thus Sharpe asked Metcalfe to advise the fellows to 'put the matter wholly to my lord and the master'. Payments of varying amounts seem to have been made for keeping the anniversary up to 1535. Fisher also gave the college a trilingual bible. It has disappeared, but presumably it was a copy of the Complutensian Polyglot.[30] While Christ's was not intended by Margaret Beaufort to be exactly the kind of humanist academy that Fisher later made of St John's, it is not to be doubted but that he encouraged the new learning in the first of Margaret's colleges.

Margaret died in 1509, having signalled her intention of founding a second college in Cambridge but without making concrete and practical provision for its establishment. Therefore while her estate partly provided the funds for St John's, the actual execution of her will (in both the literal and the metaphorical sense) fell to Fisher. Thus the new college bore the stamp of his ideas and personality much more markedly than did Christ's.

Fisher's task in relation to St John's was threefold. Firstly, as Margaret Beaufort's executor he was charged with ensuring that her intention was carried out as far as was feasible. His work was made both easier and more difficult by the other executors' resigning their authority in the matter into his hands in March 1516.[31] Previous to that date much valuable work had been done by Fox and Hornby. Secondly, he added to Margaret's bequest a significant private foundation. Finally, he gave the college successive codes of statutes which made provision for humanist studies.

The role of executor to Lady Margaret was not an easy one. Fisher himself drew up an account of his troubles and difficulties in this respect; a copy of this exists in the old register of St John's known as the 'Thin Red Book'.[32] There were three problems. Firstly, Margaret's old servants expected to get a large share of her goods, and were resentful that so much of her property and revenues was being diverted to Cambridge. Secondly, some people who had made promises of patronage or assistance to the living Lady Margaret – a formidable and powerful woman – sought to slide out of their obligations after her death. Thirdly, Henry VIII, while duly pious towards his grandmother's memory, naturally expected to receive the bulk of her estate.

Fisher's account speaks of a 'great storm, the which was stirred by my lady's servants. The occasion was this. When my lady was at the point to depart out of this world unto the mercy of God, I had pity of her poor servants and moved her that such as had done her good service and was but little recompensed, that it would please her they might somewhat be considered, after the wisdom of my lord of Winchester and me'.

Far from being grateful to Fisher for this intercession, the servants intrigued against him at court so as to have their avarice satisfied: 'they made unto the king great surmises that they should have my lady's goods divided amongst them, which put us to a great trouble. For all that they could imagine of evil against me, they gave information unto the king and made him very heavy lord against me'. After Fisher's journey to Rome for the Lateran council was cancelled, Margaret's servants attacked with a new line of strategy: 'they caused us to be called to accounts of all my lady's goods, and to show a cause why we should keep the king's inheritance from him to the value of four hundred pounds yearly'. The executors showed their accounts to Southwell, the king's chief auditor, 'and there I was compelled a long time to give attendance upon him at sundry places and many times. And there straitly our accounts were examined and he well pleased with them, and thought it reasonable that till all things were performed the profits of the said lands should remain unto the college'. Unfortunately Southwell died before he could make a full report to the king, and the executors were summoned to a new enquiry before his successor: 'and then we were more straitly handled and so delayed, wearied and fatigate that we must needs let the land go, notwithstanding all the right that we had thereunto ... there was no remedy but the king's counsel would take profits of these lands for the king'.

Meanwhile Margaret's stepson James Stanley went back on an agreement he had made with her in March 1509. This signified his consent to her turning the decayed hospital of St John in Cambridge into a college of students. She would take Stanley's place as patron of the hospital, though the new college would be subject to the bishop of Ely as visitor. He would rank as co-founder and benefactor (thus benefitting from the prayers of the scholars) and could present three candidates for one scholarship in the college.[33] This was the first of four foundations to be suppressed for the endowment of St John's College. It would, however, be facile to see these suppressions as a prelude to Henry VIII's general dissolution of the monasteries. Unlike that king, Fisher and Lady Margaret were simply redistributing ecclesiastical property within the Church so as to make more efficient use of it.

His stepmother once dead, Bishop Stanley began to wonder what further advantages he could gain by the transaction. Fisher's account speaks feelingly of Stanley's manoeuvrings.

> albeit that he had promised my lady his assent . . . yet because he had not sealed [the agreement] he would not perform his promise, and so delayed the matter a long season till at the last we were fain to agree with him . . . he purposely delayed it for causes which I will not here rehearse.

Stanley's tactics gained him the right to nominate three fellows of the new college and for succeeding bishops of Ely to nominate one. Meanwhile the three remaining brethren of the hospital were proving hard to dislodge, not least because, to Fisher's exasperation, the papal bull procured to dissolve the house proved to be 'of no value, and all by the negligence of our counsel which devised it'. Accordingly a new proposal had to be drafted and sent to Rome.

Stanley promised Hornby that he would use his episcopal authority to remove the brethren to St John's house in Ely, though when he did this is uncertain. Hornby himself sent the brethren a letter of stern warning, accusing them of trying to frustrate Margaret's intention; if they stood in the way of her will the king would take her lands and profits for himself, but if they proved amenable they would be well provided for.[34]

Eventually, on 15 December 1510, Stanley advised the brethren to resign their claims. He had done his best for them, but now 'such bulls be obtained that whether I will or not, means will be found that ye shall be removed from your house'. He arranged a good settlement for them of an annual pension of £7 each with licence from the pope to accept benefices.[35]

None the less the brethren did not leave Cambridge with a good grace. It was not until 15 March 1511 that the official of Ely wrote to Fisher: 'My lord, with great difficulty and labour (as your lordship will be informed in time to come) I have accomplished my lord's commandment and removed the said fellows to Ely.' Doubtless Fisher was glad to see the back of the said fellows. Doubtless, too, he was pleased that Stanley's successor at Ely, and therefore visitor of St John's College, was his fellow-humanist Nicholas West rather then a wily prelate of the Stanley type.

There was also trouble with Henry VIII's aunt, Katherine Courtenay, Countess of Devonshire. Possibly she, like Stanley, had made some promise to Margaret Beaufort of support for the new college. At any rate, Fisher records that when Margaret's lands were lost to the king her executors sought some recompense through negotiations with the countess: 'and so finally my lady Katherine, which bought for her son the young Lady Lisle, for certain sums of money was bounden as strongly as learned counsel could devise the bonds to pay the behove of the said college'. Fisher's mistrust of the lady is evident from his language, and it was not misplaced. The heiress whose wardship and marriage had been bought by the Courtenays died, and they lost the profits of her lands. The countess was 'comforted and counselled' not to pay her obligation to the college. 'They made it a matter of conscience because of the death of that young lady', wrote Fisher bitterly.

Though Fisher was too wise to say so in his written account, the greatest obstacle to the establishment of St John's College was the king. Jones and Underwood give a fair summary of the situation. The codicil to Margaret's will stated that the projected college was to be built and 'sufficiently endowed'; but it did not specify a timescale, nor did it define what was 'sufficient'. Meanwhile Henry's lavish expenditure at court and in warfare and his abandonment of his father's financial policy had depleted the royal coffers and revenues. Plainly he needed to recoup from the profits of his grand-mother's lands; hence Fisher's tedious troubles with the king's two chief auditors. However Henry did make some compensation for the lost revenues by awarding the college a wardship worth £2,800 a year, which was paid until the death of the heir in 1519.[36]

St John's was also granted the decayed royal hospital of Ospringe, Canterbury diocese. This was obtained with the assistance of Wolsey which, as always, proved expensive. Nicholas Metcalfe's accounts as master of St John's show payment of a 'reward' of £40 to Wolsey for his labour in the matter, paid 'through the hands of my lord of Rochester'.[37] Wolsey also helped St John's to acquire the estates of two dilapidated and lax nunneries, Broomhall in Berkshire and Higham in Fisher's own diocese.

The college accounts are full of references to rewards for legal or other assistance in matters such as these, as well as to money expended on fulfilling the obligations of the dissolved religious houses.

In 1526 Fisher's brother Robert received the last instalment of the sum of £17 4s 10d paid for 'presents' given by Fisher to Wolsey; presumably these were in addition to the £40 already mentioned.[38] In Easter term 1525 6s 8d was paid to the judges in exchequer 'for their kindness showed' when sentence was given for Broomhall and Higham. Wine was given to Dr Bright 'to have him good' in the matter of fellowships to be founded by the will of Dr Fell. Sir Richard Southwell was evidently worth sweetening; in Hilary term 1531 the college paid 2s 5d for a bag of comfets and a bottle of wine for him, as well as spending 20d on figs and 22d on a box of caraways. Such sums might be compared with the 12d spent on alms to the poor of Higham.[39]

Perhaps Katherine of Aragon was a more disinterested friend to St John's. She complied with the college's request to remit a payment of £50 due to her, as St John's had just paid the king £500 for Ospringe. The college also asked her for permission to buy lands in Essex from Lord Bergavenny, expressing its gratitude for her cancellation of a debt. An early list of benefactors of St John's compiled after her disgrace and death records that 'Katherine the most gracious queen of England pardoned us of fifty pounds due unto her for the mortising of the lordship of Riddiswell'. The queen may have visited Cambridge in 1518 and 1519 on her way to Walsingham, and was certainly there in February 1521.[40]

To the hard work of negotiating for property and revenues for St John's Fisher added a generous benefaction of his own. One estimate has it that his donations of money and plate to the college amounted to £1,700.[41] It is impossible to determine the exact value of his gifts in money, as varying sums are given in different documents in the St John's archives;[42] certainly it was in excess of £1,000.

There is some confusion as to how much money was Fisher's own and how much was Lady Margaret's which he spent as her executor. Indeed, Fisher was actually accused of passing Margaret's money off as his own by his former protégé Richard Croke. Towards the end of the 1520s Croke began to say that Fisher had misappropriated Margaret's funds in order to promote and enrich his own relatives and to pack the college with Yorkshiremen. Fisher's counter-charges against Croke were that he did not carry out his lecturing duties, failed to eat at the common table, and had formed a clique of favourites whom he treated to private dinner parties. Fisher said that he would leave accounts which would clarify the provenance of monies given to St John's; if he ever drew up such a document it has not survived.[43]

Matters are obfuscated by Fisher's claim that he financed his private foundation at St John's from an unspecified sum which Margaret had given him as a personal gift. He made a statement about this in his private statute for the college, 'lest anyone should think that I have made this large endowment with other people's money', adding somewhat sardonically, perhaps, that it was better to invest the money in St John's than to squander it on his relations.[44]

Given the closeness with which Margaret's accounts were scrutinised by the royal auditors, it seems unlikely that Fisher would have been able to misuse her money. Moreover, a charge of defrauding the king of his inheritance would have been a useful weapon when Fisher was proving difficult about the divorce and supremacy. It is true that the college paid pensions to Fisher's clients, sums ranging from £5 to his brother Robert and half-brother Edward White to 13s 8d to unnamed servitors.[45] It is also true that the two Fisher scholarships were filled by his own nephews. All this might have caused some jealousy and ill-feeling in the college, but does not necessarily mean that Fisher was guilty of dishonesty. On the other hand, the context of the quarrel between Fisher and Croke was the royal divorce; Croke was an eager champion of the king, and it is difficult not to suspect him of hoping to curry favour by casting aspersions on the morality of the queen's most formidable defender.

Fisher's private statute provided a number of places and posts at St John's. There were to be three Fisher fellows from Yorkshire and one from Rochester diocese, as well as two Fisher scholars. The preference for northerners might seem to lend weight to Croke's accusations, but the same bias is found in Margaret Beaufort's statutes for Christ's.[46] Indeed, William Bingham, the founder of Godshouse, had petitioned Henry VI for permission to establish the college because he had found 'no further north than Ripon seventy schools void or more that were occupied all at once within fifty years past, because that there is so great scarcity of masters of grammar'.[47]

At least two of the Fisher fellows were to be priests when elected. There were also to be four examiners in humanities, dialectic, mathematics and philosophy. Most innovatory was Fisher's establishment of lectures in Hebrew and Greek. In making provision for his soul Fisher also took care to help the poorer college members; 24 trentals of masses were to be distributed annually to the most virtuous and most indigent priests at St John's, who would receive ten shillings each. Fisher's obit was to be celebrated by the whole college, when the master would receive 6s 8d, the fellows 3s 4d, and the scholars a shilling.[48]

In addition, Fisher gave St John's his moveable goods by deed of gift, reserving the use of them to himself during his lifetime. The most valuable part of this donation was his 'library of books (which was thought to be such as no one bishop in Europe had the like)'.[49] Unfortunately the college never had the benefit of this important gift, as it was plundered by the king's commissioners who went to Rochester after Fisher's final arrest to inventory his possessions.

> Then they came to his library of books, which they spoiled in most pitiful wise, scattering them in such sort as it was lamentable to behold. For it was replenished with such and so many kind of books, as the like was scant to be found again in the possession of any one private man in Christendom; and of them they trussed up thirty-two great pipes, besides a number that were stolen away ... the poor college was now defrauded of their gift and all was turned another way.[50]

While Cranmer managed to acquire a number of Fisher's books, one of the informants for the *Early Life* identified other destinations for them: 'at his apprehension the lord Cromwell caused all to be confiscated, which he gave to Morison, Plankney of Chester and other that were about him'.[51] The loss of this unique library was a palpable blow to the college, which tried desperately to secure it by approaching likely patrons. St John's was still lamenting its injury in the reigns of Edward VI and Mary I.[52]

Fisher's great commitment and attachment to St John's is shown by his decision to be buried there: 'He founded a chapel beside the high altar of the said college and a tomb of white stone finely wrought where he purposed to have been buried if God had so disposed ... above his chapel and tomb was graved in Roman fair letters this sentence, *Faciam vos piscatores hominum.*'[53] Furniture and altarcloths were embellished with the elements of Fisher's rebus, dolphins (for fish) and ears of corn; the college accounts show, for example, a payment for 30 little dolphins at 2d each.[54]

Great pains were taken after Fisher's death to eradicate all traces of his work at St John's: 'All the stalls' ends in the choir of that college had graven in them by a joiner a fish [sic] and an ear of wheat. But after he had suffered at London, my lord Cromwell then commanded the same arms to be defaced, and monstrous and ugly antics to be put in their places.'[55] The tomb was dismantled, and disappeared until 1773. It was discovered when some old rubbish was being cleared away at the east end of the college chapel. Just before this, Fisher's statutes had been returned to the college from private hands; the antiquarian Thomas Baker remarked that, had they not reappeared, Fisher's benefactions would have remained unknown.[56]

So much for Fisher's private donation. In the broader context of college foundation he and the other executors worked to carry out Margaret Beaufort's intentions. Margaret had said publicly that her projected college should be 'as good and of as good value' as Christ's. Her petition to Henry VIII of 1509 specified that the college should have 50 members.[57] Christ's was roughly the same size, with 12 fellows and 47 scholars.

The beginnings of St John's College were not auspicious. As Jones and Underwood remark, 'The reality until 1515 was a college of five fellows awaiting completion of their buildings, and receiving half as much money for their commons as the former brethren of the hospital were receiving in pensions.' Fisher worked success-fully to increase the strength of the college. In 1515 and 1516 there were at different times between five and eleven fellows and three or four scholars. At the formal opening of St John's on 29 July 1516 31 fellows were elected. Not all of them stayed for long, but thereafter the college had an establishment of at least 20 fellows, and in 1519 there were 26 fellows and 23 scholars.[58]

Besides salvaging part of Margaret Beaufort's legacy, Fisher attracted other patrons to St John's. The list of early benefactors of the college records that bequests and donations from both Cambridge scholars and outsiders bought land to the value of £304 12s 8d.[59] One of the most significant gifts was the Linacre endow-ment. By his will of 1524 the medical humanist Thomas Linacre made provision for a lecture in medicine at each of the universi-ties. St John's received £221 13s 4d in ready money and lands in London worth one shilling a year. The ready money bought land worth £11 a year. All this was to support a professor of medicine who would lecture in the schools. He was to be chosen by the master of St John's and receive a yearly stipend of £12. The first Linacre lecturer, appointed in 1525, was Fisher's protégé George Day.[60]

Fisher regulated study at St John's by three successive codes of statutes he issued in 1516, 1524 and 1530. These contain three unusual, if not unique features. Firstly, Fisher gave mathematics an important place; scholars of St John's had to prove their proficiency before taking the MA or taking up a fellowship. Among the more eminent early mathematicians from St John's were John Cheke, Thomas Smith and Roger Ascham.[61] Secondly, preaching was stressed as one of the most important functions of the college; one-quarter of the fellows was to be engaged in preaching to the people in English. The college accounts show payments for sermons given.[62] Thirdly, Fisher's humanistic interest in the biblical and classical tongues was amply if ambitiously expressed in the statutes.

Theology was the goal to which all other studies led; thus the tongues were the instruments of that study rather than an end in themselves. As was usual in university college statutes, undergraduates were expected to understand and speak Latin before they were admitted. In addition, and more unusually, Greek and Hebrew were to be studied by those the master and seniors thought fit. Two college lectures in these languages were established by the statutes of 1530. The Greek lecturer would teach grammar and literature on alternate days to the junior members of the college. The Hebrew reader was to lecture to the seniors on grammar and the psalter or some other book of scripture. If no Hebrew teacher were available the seniors could have lectures on Scotus instead, provided that the works expounded were turned into better, more humanistic Latin. Meanwhile the Greek reader should study Hebrew so that the college should not lose the benefit of instruction in that tongue. In 1530 Fisher added Chaldee and Aramaic to the list of languages to be studied. This was over-optimistic, given the dearth of teachers of oriental languages, and these subjects were omitted from the royal statutes of 1545.[63]

Fisher's provision of humanist studies at St John's may be compared with the parallel work at Oxford of Richard Fox, who founded Corpus Christi college in 1517. Fox was more combative than Fisher in that he established public lectures in rhetoric, Greek and theology which threw down the gauntlet to the traditionalists. Particularly provoking was his stricture that the theology lecturer should base his work on the Church fathers and not on the schoolmen, 'who, as in time, so in learning, are far below them'. The resultant 'Greeks and Trojans' furore was only ended by the intervention of the king; possibly this was what Fox had intended. Erasmus was full of praise for both founder-bishops, though he did remark that Greek was studied at Cambridge 'in complete tranquillity' because it was Fisher who directed the college at which it was taught.[64]

Numerous references occur in the St John's accounts to books bought at Fisher's command, among them two Hebrew books which cost 40s, a Greek vocabulary at 6s, and a geometry book at 8s.[65] A copy of Sir Thomas Elyot's *Book Named the Governor* was purchased for 20d. Marmaduke Constable spent £8 3s on Latin and Greek books for the college for which he was reimbursed. An astrolabe, a *mappa mundi* and a book of cosmography were also purchased for St John's. Fisher's own scholars and nephews, Edward and Matthew White, received a variety of books. These included Cicero's *De Officiis*, works by Terence, Ovid and Horace, a 'logic', a 'sophistry', a Greek primer and a Greek dictionary.[66]

Fisher himself made the college gifts of books. In September 1511 he donated two missals and some works of scholastic theology; in 1513 he gave a number of canon law books. Also in that year the college purchased books from Wynkyn de Worde. These were mostly works of the Greek and Latin fathers, including Chrysostom, Origen, Cyprian and Jerome.[67]

Fisher made one other contribution to teaching materials. John Smyth of St John's told Metcalfe that if 'our company might have the play that my lord made they would provide to play it'. In a separate letter he said that 'the company would gladly have my lord's play'.[68] This play may well have been one of a number written by Fisher for St John's; it is not extant. Beverley, Fisher's birthplace, was famous for miracle plays staged by the guilds.[69]

Humanists recognised that drama was a useful means of teaching the art of rhetoric as well as pointing a moral. Thus, for example, the boys of Colet's school at St Paul's performed plays and masques at Henry VIII's court.[70] Thomas Watson, a fellow of St John's, was an enthusiast for classical drama. He translated Sophocles' *Antigone* and himself wrote a Latin play called 'Absalom'. A college inventory of the 1540s shows that players' costumes were kept at St John's.[71]

Both Fisher himself and senior members of the college exercised discrimination and discretion when considering candidates for places at St John's. Robert Shorton thanked Fisher profusely for his own promotion to the mastership of the college and commented on some applicants for fellowships.

As for the scholars whom your lordship is moved to take unto your said college, it is so, my lord, that Sir John Weste is thought most able of those three named to your lordship for Lincolnshire.

As for the principal of St Thomas Hostel, although he be competently learned he is nothing personable. I have send unto your lordship here enclosed the names of such persons as is thought good, virtuous and learned men tractable. As for Master Shaas and Master Foster, will not take it.[72]

In October 1515 Sir Marmaduke Constable asked Fisher to be 'good lord' to a priest named Shawe: 'if it would like your lordship to make him a fellow of St John's college of Cambridge, there the aforesaid poor scholar should keep his learning and be able hereafter to be the servant of God and edify himself and other'. This petition was successful, as Shawe had a fellowship by July 1516. Fisher also granted John Huse's request to favour Robert Harry, BA, whom he recommended for a fellowship as a virtuous and well-disposed priest. A less happy case occurs in a letter from John Smyth to Metcalfe. Hugh Ashton had sent Smyth a child whom he wanted to be a scholar at St John's. However the boy did not know Latin and Smyth wondered what to do about him; meanwhile he had put him under the tuition of John Rudde, a fellow of the college.[73]

Politics could play a part in college patronage. Cranmer wrote to Fisher, probably early in 1534 when he was in the Tower, to recommend his kinsman Walter Devenyshe for one of Fisher's own fellowships: 'verily I think he lacketh not of those qualities which should become an honest man to have, over and besides the gift of nature wherewith God hath above the common endued him'.[74] Fisher could scarcely refuse.

The operation of patronage is illustrated by a letter to Metcalfe from John Brandisby, a graduate of Cambridge who was studying in Paris. Brandisby wanted to place his two brothers at St John's.

I spake with my lord of Rochester as I came to Paris. His lordship did give me twenty shillings, and of his own mind (afore I spoke to his lordship) did remember my brethren, and said that he did not forget them, but that they should be the first that should be preferred into St John's college.

Brandisby asked for Metcalfe's help, saying that his brothers 'be very apt and studious and but young; if they might be where great occasion of learning should be, as it is in your college, I do not doubt but they should prove well learned'. James and Richard Brandisby did enter St John's, both graduating BA in 1522 and MA in 1526. Richard Brandisby became a fellow of the college in

1523, and was one of the St John's deputation which visited Fisher in prison.[75]

Of the three masters of St John's in Fisher's lifetime, both Robert Shorton (master 1511–1516) and Nicholas Metcalfe (master 1518–37) were Doctors of Divinity. Shorton had been university preacher in 1507–8, and was later almoner to Katherine of Aragon. Metcalfe was also archdeacon of Rochester, and was important to Fisher in diocesan administration as well as the governance of St John's. The other master (1516–18) was Alan Percy, a son of the earl of Northumberland. Possibly he was chosen as a scion of a noble house who might attract important patronage to the college. His attachment to St John's was sufficiently strong for him to choose to be buried there.[76]

Fisher's work at St John's has been criticised and even denigrated. Croke's accusations have already been mentioned. Roger Ascham wrote to protector Somerset on the college's behalf, complaining of its material losses due to the 'perverse doctrine' which had deprived Fisher of his life and St John's of its riches. He depicted Fisher as a tyrant who governed the college 'absolutely'.[77]

The fact remains that St John's was remarkably loyal to Fisher during his last, troubled years. A deputation of fellows visited him in the Tower. While it is true that its chief purpose was to get him to sign a new code of statutes – something he refused to do unless he could read it thoroughly first – the college accounts show a number of payments for him. Between Hilary term 1534 and Easter term 1535 the college paid for caps and an ivory comb for Fisher and for books to be lent to him. Two sums of £5 and £9 were assigned to him at different times. (St John's was still wise enough, however, to pay 12d for strawberries and 8d for a gallon of wine given to Cranmer when he visited Rochester.)[78]

The college also sent Fisher a remarkable letter of support and consolation. This acknowledged him as teacher, preceptor and lawgiver, prayed God to give him strength, and offered to put the college's wealth at his disposal. Given the circumstances of his death, it is amazing that St John's celebrated his exequies in 1535.[79]

Besides his work of college endowment for and with Margaret Beaufort, Fisher rendered Cambridge 30 years' service as university chancellor. In 1514 he advised the university to offer the position to the increasingly powerful Wolsey. When the cardinal refused the honour Cambridge promptly re-elected Fisher chancellor for life.[80]

Though non-resident like the majority of university chancellors, Fisher was credited by his first biographer with being conscientious in office: 'For knowing indeed what a precious thing learning is in all regiment, and what they were over whom this his authority was to be used, he did not so much esteem the dignity which it contained as well weighed the care thereunto annexed.'[81]

This is consistent with Fisher's own statements about his duties. The same author views him as a university reformer, who 'looked very straitly to the orders and rules of the university: calling every man to his duty, as well in the schools for profit of their learning, as in their churches and colleges for due keeping and observing the service of God'. He was particularly eager to stimulate scholarship: 'Many times, for the encouragement of the younger sort, himself would be present at their disputations and readings, and in disputing among them would bestow many hours together'.[82]

The author, drawing on memories of Fisher's visit of 1521, is perhaps giving a misleading impression of his residence in Cambridge; Christopher Brooke has found but little trace of his presence there, and this is borne out by Stephen Thompson's itinerary for Fisher as bishop. He did go to Cambridge at intervals, but in any case much of his work for it was done at a distance.[83]

Part of the chancellor's role was to persuade patrons to give benefactions to the university. Fisher had some success in this respect with Henry VII. The king was greatly impressed by Fisher's personality, and was directly responsible for his promotion to Rochester; an appointment made, said Henry, on account of Fisher's virtue and learning. Just before this he had made Fisher a present of 46s 8d.[84]

Fisher's technique in extracting patronage is shown in a Latin oration he delivered at Cambridge before the king and his mother in 1507.[85] Its three objectives were to evoke the grandeur of the king, though without resorting to flattery; to show the university's critical situation; and to recall Henry's past benefits to Cambridge.

Fisher began with a comparison of the perilous yet blessed lives of Henry VII and Moses. Both survived the dangers of infancy in a miraculous manner; both had powerful foes who worked to destroy them; both were forced to flee into exile; both returned to authority over their people by the grace of God.

Fisher next gave an account of the ancient history of the university and spoke of the benefits conferred by the king's royal predecessors, in particular Henry VI. (A shrewd touch, given the king's reverence for his namesake.) Henry VI had founded Godshouse for 60 students and had begun work on King's College. He had sent Henry VII's father and uncle to study at Cambridge. But surprised by death (said Fisher, smoothly passing over the Wars of the Roses) he left the work incomplete so that the present king could finish it.

From the fortunate past Fisher moved to the present misfortunes of the university. There were law suits with the town of Cambridge, and chronic plagues had devastated the university; among other victims were ten of the most distinguished and learned doctors. The number of protectors and benefactors was considerably reduced. Things had come to such a pitch that scholars were losing the taste for study and looking for the best way out. Cambridge would have succumbed to despair if the king had not shed the sunlight of his countenance on the university.

Finally, Fisher rehearsed Henry VII's past benefits to the university. The king's interest had been a great stimulus to study. A good example of this was Fisher's own rapid elevation to the see of Rochester. This had caused great astonishment, as he had been a priest for just a few years and had not held a benefice before; but Henry had promoted him to show his goodwill to all men of learning and to encourage them. Not only that, but Henry had visited Cambridge the year before and spent long hours listening to the scholars' disputations, as well as treating the whole university to drink and venison. He had shown himself a loving father and, said Fisher quite bluntly, he could do even more by completing the building of Henry VI's College.

Whether it was Fisher's eloquence or family piety that did the trick, Henry decided to benefit Cambridge. In 1507 he gave 100 marks towards the fabric of the university church, and provided for his anniversary to be kept there for as long as the world would endure for £10 a year.[86] Henry's will, of which Fisher was an executor, mentions a gift of £5,000 given to King's College in pious memory of its founder. It was to be used to complete the building of the chapel.[87]

In the reign of Henry's successor, Fisher worked to find the university friends at court. Thus when Thomas More was knighted and admitted to the king's council Fisher was quick to write to him on behalf of Cambridge, asking him to obtain Henry VIII's munificent patronage. More replied warmly and graciously: 'Whatever influence I have with the king (it is certainly very little) but such as it is, is as freely available to your paternity and all your scholars as is his own house to any man. I owe your students constant gratitude for the heartfelt affection of which their letters to me are the token.'[88]

In terms of university study (as opposed to lectures at St John's) Fisher's greatest achievement was the introduction and encouragement of Greek. While a handful of Cambridge scholars had known and perhaps taught Greek prior to his chancellorship, there was no formal provision for its study in university or college statutes. Fisher is credited with bringing Erasmus to Cambridge in 1511. He lectured on Greek grammar, though he found the audience disappointingly small.

In 1518 Richard Croke, a Fisher fellow of St John's, became the first university Greek professor, at Fisher's expense. Croke was already distinguished, having taught Greek at Leipzig at the age of 26. When the office of university orator was established in 1519 its first holder was named as Croke, 'who first brought Greek literature to us'. How active he was as a Greek lecturer is uncertain. In 1520 the king offered Richard Pace £10 a year to teach Greek at Cambridge, though Pace did not take up the post; possibly this indicates that Croke was either not lecturing at all or not sufficiently to satisfy demand.[89] As has been shown Fisher complained that, among other sins, Croke no longer lectured.

Like Croke, Robert Wakefield was an eminent Fisher protégé who fell out with him over the king's divorce. This gifted Hebrew scholar was granted leave to study abroad by Fisher while retaining his stipend as a fellow of St John's. He continued to be paid up to Hilary term 1532. He took his MA at Louvain in 1519 and taught Hebrew at the trilingual college there founded by Jerome Busleyden. In 1522 he was Reuchlin's successor at Tübingen, where he also taught Greek. Fisher recalled him to teach at Cambridge but it seems unlikely that he did so.[90]

Reformation controversy has obscured Fisher's achievement at Cambridge. The university itself showed gratitude to him, though wisely it sought other friends in his last years. In 1533 it voted Cromwell an annual stipend, and in 1535 it chose him to succeed Fisher as chancellor.[91] What is surprising is that Cambridge did not hasten to distance itself from Fisher in his disgrace, but retained him as its chancellor until his death.[92]

The advent of what Fisher would term heresy, and the onset and progress of the royal divorce, bitterly divided Cambridge. Yet if all confessional bias is laid aside it must be said that, by his work of college foundation, personal patronage of scholars, and pioneering attempt to introduce the study of Greek and Hebrew, Fisher richly deserves Brooke's accolade of being 'the greatest of the benefactors of the university and of all the colleges of that age'.[93]

2 The Humanist

our thoughts and mind, that most admirable creature of God[1]

In general accounts of the early Tudor period John Fisher is not usually portrayed as belonging to the renaissance. Insofar as his scholarship is considered, he is often depicted as a traditionalist rather than a humanist. The term 'humanist' has been used to denote a number of related phenomena associated with the renaissance, as well as (rather sweepingly) to mark off the 'modern' from the 'medieval' mentality. At the same time, it carries the connotation of change or progress, and is often equated with Protestantism. Therefore, it has been argued, John Fisher cannot be regarded as a humanist because he was a defender of doctrinal orthodoxy and papal supremacy.[2]

In reality, humanism had little to do originally with dogma, though its methods would provide both Catholics and Protestants with instruments of biblical exegesis and doctrinal polemic. John Fisher's humanist credentials can be established by considering his attitude to study of the biblical and classical tongues, and to ancient, medieval and modern authors. His friendships with humanists like Erasmus and Reuchlin may also be examined, while scrutiny of his library will reveal the breadth of his interests. Finally, it is constructive to consider the uses to which he put his humanist scholarship.

First, though, it is necessary to attempt a definition of that nebulous word 'humanism'. The present writer would treat it as a blanket term, comprehending a whole range of interests and activities. First in importance among these was appreciation and study of the tongues, Hebrew, Greek and Latin, and of the scriptural bases of Christianity, scripture and the patristic writings. Knowledge of the literature of the classical world was another feature, as was interest in rhetoric, in the purification of Latin and development of vernacular languages. On the pastoral side, there was concern with Church reform, the provision of an incorrupt, educated clergy and a lively preaching ministry. There was also interest in civic virtue and the regeneration of the *res publica* or common wealth. A humanist would be one who sympathised with or practised any – though not necessarily all – of the above, as scholar or patron.

A sure test of an individual's allegiance to humanism is his or her attitude to the sacred and classical tongues. As regards Latin, Fisher wrote fluently in a straightforward, elegant and accessible style. If his polemical works sometimes slide into tedium, the fault lies in the format, with its constant reiteration of evidence, argument and counter-argument.

At the same time, E.L. Surtz has shown that the chief criticism of scholasticism made by humanists was its want of style and eloquence. Here it is pertinent to note Fisher's statute for St John's College concerning the Hebrew lecture; if no Hebrew teacher were available then Scotus might be studied instead, provided that his books were first turned into better Latin. The statute also reveals, of course, the rarity of Hebrew scholars in early Tudor England.[3]

Indeed, Hebrew and Greek were virtually unknown in England before the reign of Henry VIII. Prior to that era a handful of English scholars studied Greek, and one or two may have known some Hebrew. Those who did have access to the tongues usually gained it by study abroad. The youthful John Fisher would have had scant exposure to Hebrew and Greek, and no chance to study them.[4]

It is evident that Fisher appreciated the Greek heritage of Christendom long before he attempted to learn the language. In his sermons he made frequent allusion to the Greek fathers, albeit in the prehumanistic translations and versions which were the only sources available to him for most of his preaching career. It is significant that when Erasmus first tried to attract Fisher's material patronage the bait he used was a translation of a commentary on Isaiah ascribed to Basil the Great.

In September 1511 Erasmus sent part of his translation to the 'best and most learned of prelates', to show him that 'your acts of great kindness and generosity to me have been a challenge to me to show that I am not blatantly ungrateful'. He had used a text from William Grocyn's library, intending to present Fisher with 'a commentary on the most eloquent of prophets by the most eloquent of theologians'. However, Erasmus' labours had convinced him that the work was not really by Basil of Caeserea: 'And this, if you do not entirely disagree, seems unworthy of dedication to your name; unworthy, too, of my bestowing a great deal of care upon it. I give you a tentative sample and, for the rest, will adhere to your decision as if it were that of an oracle.'[5]

Erasmus' next allusion to the project, in a letter to Colet, was much less fulsome.

I have virtually lost interest in translating Basil, not only because certain conjectures suggest that the work is not genuine,
but also because the bishop of Rochester seemed rather unen-
thusiastic after I sent him a sample of my projected translation . . .
also, as I have learned from a friend, he suspects that I am polishing
up a previous version, and not translating from the Greek. What
won't men think of?[6]

It is most significant that Fisher was not uncritical of patristic texts
and their alleged provenance, and that he had no time for indirect
translations. Erasmus also translated the Mass of Chrysostom, apparently intending to dedicate it to Fisher. In the event it was not
published until 1536, after Fisher's death.[7]

From an early date Fisher took a keen interest in Erasmus' labours
on the new testament. In October 1513 Erasmus grumbled to Colet:
'If my Matthew is not in your possession, it must be in the bishop
of Rochester's. This is what I rather guessed anyway. But he failed
to add it to the others because I had given them to him sepa-
rately.' The 'Matthew' was probably some notes on the gospel text;
possibly Fisher wanted to consult them in connection with work on
his own 'harmony' of the gospels, which has not survived.[8]

Certainly, Fisher was eager to see Erasmus' work in progress.
Such was his enthusiasm for the whole project – an improved Greek
text with a fresh Latin version – that Erasmus contemplated
dedicating the work to him. In the event he decided wisely that
the pope would be a more powerful protector of the work and its
editor than the bishop of Rochester. In June 1516 he wrote to Fisher:
'Having originally intended the new testament for you, why I changed
my plan and dedicated it to the supreme pontiff I wrote and explained some time ago, and with your habitual generosity, not to
say wisdom, you will I hope take what I have done in good part.'[9]
Fisher's response was as magnanimous as Erasmus could wish.

Although much impeded with business (for I am getting ready
for a trip to Cambridge, where the college is now at last to be
set on foot), I did not wish your man Pieter to return to you
without a letter from me. I owe you enormous thanks for the
new testament newly translated by your efforts from the Greek,
which you have given me.[10]

Fisher's commitment to Greek studies made him resolve to learn
the language himself, when he was in his late forties. His age and

the complexity of the subject appalled those scholars who were approached to tutor him. August 1516 found a reluctant Erasmus at Rochester, whence he complained bitterly to Andrea Ammonio: 'The bishop of Rochester has driven me by his entreaties to stay with him for ten days, and I have regretted my promise more than ten times over. . . . Meanwhile I am to turn him from a Latin into a Greek – that is the metamorphosis I have undertaken.'[11]

Dismayed at the immensity of the task, Erasmus hastened to pass it on, enlisting Thomas More's help in persuading William Latimer to teach Fisher. Their letters arrived too late; Latimer had already decided to go to Oxford.[12] In January 1517 Latimer sent Erasmus an elaborate letter of excuse. He could not hope to make much progress in the mere month that Erasmus and More had asked him for tuition, though he did not underestimate Fisher's enthusiasm and ability. Erasmus should persuade Fisher to send to Italy for a tutor: 'In this way, it seems to me, you will do more for his future skill in the language than if, while he is still lisping and can barely utter childish cries, you abandon him like a baby in its cradle.'[13]

Erasmus' reply reproached Latimer for his refusal to teach 'that incomparable bishop who wishes to add Greek as a sort of coping-stone to his pyramid of learning'. He did not favour importing a tutor from Italy: 'those who do reach us who are well equipped in the humanities do not always bring with them a character to match. And you know the bishop's high standards'. Erasmus confessed that he had hoped for three months' tuition from Latimer, 'although I have not the face to demand it', and expressed confidence in Fisher's attitude and powers of perseverance.

> such is his passionate desire to learn that I am confident he will by his own resources gain at any rate a working knowledge. And maybe he is content with that, for the only reason why he wishes to learn Greek is to be able to spend his time with more profit and more sound judgment on the scriptures . . . it will be no small encouragement to the young, if they see such an eminent man taking up Greek.[14]

Fisher did manage to make progress in Greek without the benefit of Latimer's tuition. By the summer of 1517 he was sufficiently advanced to notice printers' errors in the new edition of the new testament. While showing off this skill to Erasmus he was full of praise for the work itself.

The new testament, as translated by you for the common benefit of us all, can offend no one of any sense; for you have not only shed light on countless places in it by your scholarship: you have appended an absolutely fresh commentary to the whole work, so that it can now be read and enjoyed by anybody with much more pleasure and satisfaction than before.[15]

Erasmus, possibly moved by a bad conscience, assisted Fisher's studies from a distance. In September 1517, for example, he sent him his new version of the second book of Theodore of Gaza's Greek grammar.[16] By March 1518 he had come to value Fisher's expertise in Greek. Announcing his departure for Venice or Basle to oversee another edition of the new testament, he asked for practical help in the shape of a reliable horse as well as for Fisher's advice: 'I beg you, of your piety, if there is anything of which you think I should be aware, to let me know in a letter by the bearer of this, whom I have sent partly for this purpose and who will return to me without delay. As far as I was able, I have corrected what needed correction.'[17]

In October 1519 he asked again for Fisher's scholarly help.

A fresh edition of the *New Testament* by Froben is impending. Therefore I beg you, for the sake of those sacred studies you love, of your piety befitting a bishop's rank, of our friendship, and in the name of whatever regard you may have for Erasmus, to write down for me at least the notes which you think to be of some account, in case you do not want to read the whole work, dearly though I would like you to do so. . . . Should your occupations prevent you from doing me this service, at least let More handle it, and entreat him if need be.[18]

Thus in a few short years Fisher had progressed from the position of pupil to that of consultant on Erasmus' most important scriptural work. He continued to support and encourage Erasmus. In November 1522 Erasmus told Ferdinand of Bohemia that he was working on a paraphrase of the gospel of John; this was chiefly at the exhortation of the cardinal of Mainz and the bishop of Rochester, 'a man of incomparable holiness and knowledge'. In April 1525, defending his new testament to the Sorbonne, he claimed to have consulted a number of scholars including the bishop of Rochester. All had praised it, and Fisher had thanked him more than once, showing that he had drawn great profit from the work.[19]

If it is surprising that Fisher should study Greek at a comparatively advanced age, it is extraordinary that, in the midst of a busy
life, he should apply himself to Hebrew. His interest in the language
arose from his reading of Pico della Mirandola. Pico had rediscovered
the cabbala, the ancient Hebrew oral tradition of divine wisdom.
Christian cabbalism aimed to harmonise all knowledge, and thus
effect the conversion of the Jews. Fisher came to see the cabbala
as analogous to the apostolic tradition, those 'unwritten verities'
which supplemented and explained the scriptures.[20]

Interest in the cabbala naturally drew Fisher to the greatest
Hebraist of the day, Johannes Reuchlin. In April 1514 Reuchlin
himself prepared the ground by sending a succinct account of his
troubles to Erasmus, then in England. Reuchlin had been attacked
by some Cologne theologians for an opinion on the question of
burning Hebrew books which he had written at the request of the
Emperor Maximilian. When Reuchlin published a defence, *Der
Augenspiegel*, these theologians resolved to burn the book at Mainz.
Reuchlin appealed over their heads to the Holy See, which instituted an inquiry into the matter by the bishop of Speyer. Despite
continued intrigues by the Dominicans this prelate had pronounced
in Reuchlin's favour. Reuchlin now sent a copy of this verdict for
Erasmus to show to his British friends, lest Reuchlin's reputation
had been damaged by the affair.[21]

Erasmus duly showed this to 'several learned friends', who 'were
all smiles'; Fisher and Colet were among these scholars. Fisher's
initial reaction was not uncritical, however. Erasmus thought he
detected 'a certain timidity and almost uneasiness in the bishop's
judgment'. Accordingly he advised Reuchlin to send his book to
England, either to Fisher or to Colet.[22]

Thus Fisher would not give unqualified approval to a book he
had not seen, but plainly Erasmus judged him to be sufficiently
open-minded to read *Der Augenspiegel* without prejudice. Indeed,
Fisher was soon impressed by Reuchlin's learning, as Erasmus
informed him.

> The bishop of Rochester, a most accomplished person, speaks of
> you in a letter to me. 'That you should have thought of me', he
> says, 'and sent me greetings, I take very kindly, and particularly
> that you have given me such a full account of Reuchlin, whom I
> think very highly of although I do not know him ... if he has
> published anything which I may not have here, please have it

sent me. I find his type of scholarship very congenial; in fact, I know no-one else who comes closer to Giovanni Pico.'

Fisher wished to consult Reuchlin about some difficulties in his own studies.

> I wish, my dear Erasmus, you would write and ask him, if you do not happen to meet, where he found the genealogy of the Blessed Virgin Mary which he added to his Hebrew vocabulary; for I very greatly wish to know what authority lies behind it, and at the same time how it can be that, although according to the *Breviarum* of Philo the line of Solomon died out entirely, she is said there none the less to be descended from him. Pray try, dear Erasmus, to see that Reuchlin is so good as to enlighten me on these two points.[23]

This letter of early 1515, besides showing Fisher's critical humanism, may indicate that he was already dabbling in Hebrew. He and Reuchlin entered into correspondence, none of which has survived. In June 1516 Fisher praised Reuchlin to Erasmus: 'He seems to me, in comparison with everyone else whose works I have read so far, to be the best man alive today, especially in knowledge of the recondite field that lies between theology and philosophy and touches on both.'[24]

In a long letter to Reuchlin of that same month Erasmus wrote in detail of Fisher's admiration for him: 'No words of mine can possibly express the enthusiasm and the deep respect felt for you by the bishop of Rochester. . . . He never sends me a letter (and he writes quite often) without making most honorable mention of you.' Fisher had even decided to cross the Channel to visit Reuchlin. Though unable to travel at present he was eager to send a gift, and had asked Erasmus what Reuchlin would like. On the other side, 'I felt that he had a great desire for those Nile reed-pens, the kind of which you gave me three; and so, if you have any, you could make him no more acceptable present.' Finally, Erasmus advised Reuchlin to send his great-nephew to Fisher: 'I assure you, he will be most kindly treated and advanced to a lucrative position, nor will he ever have the chance of more leisure for the pursuit of the humanities.'[25] This youth was Philip Melanchthon; it is intriguing to wonder what might have been the outcome for the reformation if he had studied under Fisher's guidance and patronage.

Erasmus was anxious that Reuchlin should cultivate both Fisher and Colet by writing to them: 'The bishop of Rochester has an almost religious veneration for you. To John Colet your name is sacred.'[26] He also kept Fisher informed of Reuchlin's doings, writing to More in March 1517: 'I send all the Reuchlin pieces in one volume, which please pass on to the bishop of Rochester on the understanding that he reads them and sends them back as soon as he can, for some of them are not to be found elsewhere.' Another letter to More reveals that Erasmus had sent 'Reuchlin's book, translated at my own expense.'[27]

As for Reuchlin, he was somewhat alarmed at Erasmus' zeal on his behalf.

> You speak of that sainted bishop and champion of liberal stud-
> ies the bishop of Rochester, and I should like you to know that
> I regard him, not only with deep respect, as I am bound to do,
> but also no less with affection. But such a warm recommenda-
> tion frightens me, and I do beg you not to let him grow too fond
> of me. You know well enough that distance lends enchantment.
> If he sees me one day close to, and takes a dislike to me, as
> does happen sometimes, the devil will be in it.

At the same time, he wanted to encourage Fisher's interest in the cabbala.

> I told Thomas Anshelm [the Tübingen printer] to send a copy of
> my *Cabbalistica* for each of you . . . together with this letter from
> me. When the books reach you, keep one copy for yourself in
> memory of me, and send the other carefully to my lord of
> Rochester, so that he may know that I have by no means forgotten
> your encouraging words about him.[28]

Some months later Fisher complained to Erasmus that this book had not yet reached him: 'Your dear friend More has sent me his letter, but is still keeping the book, as is his way; this is just what he did long ago with the *Speculum oculare*.' In fact, Colet was the guilty party. Fisher continued:

> I am deeply obliged to you, my dear Erasmus, for many other
> kindnesses, but especially because you make such efforts to have
> Reuchlin bear me so carefully in mind. He is a man whose ac-
> quaintance I heartily welcome; and for the time being, until I
> have read the book and can write to him, please tell him that I
> am as grateful to him as I believe to be possible.[29]

Erasmus continued to act as go-between for the two scholars. In November 1520 he told Reuchlin of Fisher's continued admiration and intention of visiting him in the summer; in November 1521 he was careful to tell Fisher that Reuchlin had moved to Ingoldstadt, where he was teaching Hebrew and Greek. The two never did meet, however. In September 1522 Erasmus told Fisher, 'Reuchlin has gone before us to the powers above. I numbered him among the saints in the *Colloquies* printed last summer.'[30]

Fisher's approval of Reuchlin and appreciation of Hebrew studies put him in the vanguard of humanist thought. In this he outdistanced even some of his eminent contemporaries. Colet, who had been the first to import cabbalistic ideas into England, became disenchanted with them. In 1517 he read Fisher's copy of Reuchlin's *De Arte Cabbalistica* from cover to cover; but he rejected 'Reuchlin's pythagorical and cabbalistic philosophy' in favour of 'the short road to the truth', which was 'the fervent love and imitation of Jesus'.[31] As for Erasmus, he was careful to put a distance between Reuchlin and himself when writing to Wolsey. He said he had derived little from the talmud and cabbala, and that he and Reuchlin were not close; they merely enjoyed a sort of official friendship between learned men.[32]

Fisher probably took lessons in Hebrew at some time between 1515 and 1519. His teacher was his own protégé Robert Wakefield. Richard Rex postulates the existence of a 'Hebrew seminar' organised by Fisher either at Rochester or at Lambeth Marsh, his London house. Certainly, Wakefield had at least one other pupil, Thomas Hurskey, prior of Walton and master of the Gilbertines. In a book published in 1524 Wakefield mentioned other men proficient in Hebrew: William Frisell, prior of Rochester; John Taylor, master of the rolls; James Boleyn, uncle of Anne; and John Stokesley, later bishop of London.[33]

Wakefield, a fellow of St John's, Cambridge, received a considerable amount of patronage from Fisher, who informed the college that 'I have granted him the emolument of his college during the space of two years next ensuing' so that he could study Hebrew abroad.[34]

Wakefield taught Hebrew at Louvain in 1519, where he also took his MA, and Hebrew at Tübingen in 1520, where he succeeded Reuchlin. Fisher recalled him in 1523 to teach Hebrew at Cambridge; Tübingen was so loth to lose him that Fisher was requested to defer his return. Fisher had endowed a Hebrew lecture at St John's, attached to his private chantry, and this, presumably, paid Wakefield's Cambridge salary while he was away.[35]

Relations between Fisher and Wakefield turned sour over the royal divorce. Wakefield had become a royal chaplain in 1523 through the influence of his friend Richard Pace. In 1527 Pace, engaged in justifying the king's case, recommended Wakefield to Henry VIII as another potential propagandist, chiefly because of his skill in Hebrew. Wakefield had actually begun a defence of the queen, possibly at Fisher's behest, but now he found it expedient to change sides. This proved profitable, though Wakefield was so ashamed of his apostasy that he begged Henry to keep it secret. However, he boasted that he would make such an answer to Fisher's book on the case that he would not dare to write anything more.[36]

Wakefield was arrogant in controversy, seeking to humiliate his old patron by calling his learning into question. Fisher had suggested that the Levitical prohibition on which Henry's case largely rested might be an interpolation. It was not found in the Hebrew original, the Chaldaic translation nor the septuagint. Possibly it was a marginal gloss erroneously inserted by a copyist, and if so it should not be taken as holy scripture. Wakefield replied to this somewhat brutally, accusing Fisher of having 'little knowledge of Greek' and of reading Jerome's comments on scripture with insufficient attention. He also denigrated Fisher's skill in Hebrew, alleging his own superiority as his former teacher, and accused him of over-reliance on the schoolmen.[37] Fisher's reply to Wakefield, discovered by Surtz, is severely damaged by fire. However, a fragment of scripture in Greek remains legible: 'No disciple is above his teacher'.[38]

Fisher used his humanist scholarship in a number of studies. His lost harmony of the gospels has already been mentioned. A manuscript commentary on the psalms exists, which Fisher composed at Henry VIII's command, probably in 1525; the king had requested a similar work from Erasmus late in 1524. Fisher also entered into controversy with the French humanist Jacques Lefèvre d'Etaples on the identity of Mary Magdalen.[39] Finally, he engaged in humanistic debate with Pace about the nature of the septuagint. Pace, like Erasmus, Reuchlin and Wakefield, thought of this Greek translation as a purely human product; Fisher felt that it was divinely inspired, like the Hebrew text of the old testament. His work on the septuagint, it has been argued, shows Fisher's humanistic approval of vernacular translations of scripture.[40]

A few references will give an impression of the active use to which Fisher put his learning in Hebrew and Greek. He alludes to Reuchlin in his commentary on Psalm 8 and in his *Assertio* against

Luther. There is a reference to the cabbala in his sermon of 1521 against Luther, and one to the Hebrew etymology of *manna* in the sermon of 1526. It seems that he helped Erasmus with the Hebrew which occurs in Jerome's letters. He makes much use of Greek and Hebrew in his book against Oecolampadius. In the 1526 sermon he appealed to the Greek words of Erasmus' new testament rather than the vulgate, 'for they make better against our enemies'.[41]

Surtz comments that Wakefield's parting shot to Fisher about the schoolmen reveals a sort of generation-gap between older and younger humanists. For scholars like Fisher and Grocyn there was not an insuperable divide between scholasticism and humanism. Indeed, Surtz demonstrates that the attitude of Fisher, Erasmus and More to the schoolmen was one of 'qualified approval and varying compromise'. Rex observes that Fisher's citations from the schoolmen occur chiefly in the divorce writings, while the fathers are used more often in his controversies with reformers, though there is not a rigid division.[42]

Fisher concurred with the general humanist criticism that the schoolmen lacked eloquence and elegance, but he insisted that they did not lack learning. Ideally a theologian should be pious, eloquent and knowledgeable; but piety joined with knowledge was more desirable than eloquence alone. Moreover, divinity students would find the methods of the schoolmen useful.

> Even though they are equipped with the three languages, nevertheless if they lack practice in the scholastic method, they may express the opinion which they have conceived, but when they have expressed it, there is an end to it. They lack the power either to establish their own views firmly or to assail the errors of others strongly.[43]

Some evidence about Fisher's scholarly interests can be gleaned from records of books he owned, borrowed or bought for his scholars. His library at Rochester and its practical organisation was described by a contemporary: 'He had the notablest library of books in all England, two long galleries full. The books were sorted in stalls, and a register of the names of every book hung at the end of every stall.' As has been mentioned, Fisher made a gift of this collection to St John's College, reserving its use to himself in his lifetime. On his second attainder in 1534 the library was treated as Fisher's own property, and thus was forfeit to the crown. Cromwell supervised the packing-up; presumably the bulk of the books went to Henry

VIII, but many were given to Cromwell's own friends and clients. A few extant volumes in various collections have been identified as having belonged to Fisher, but the full extent of his holdings cannot be known.[44]

However, Rex has reconstructed Fisher's library in an ingenious and convincing manner by considering the references in his published works; if Fisher did not actually own all these books, it is at least certain that he read them. Altogether Fisher cited about three hundred works. Only about a dozen of these are by schoolmen. The fathers, Greek as well as Latin, were much more important to Fisher's arguments, and he used about two hundred patristic texts. Among the Greeks he relied on Chrysostom, Origen, Cyril of Alexandria and Cyril of Jerusalem, Gregory Nazianzen and Gregory of Nyssa, John Damascene and Pseudo-Dionysius. Among the Latins he cited Ambrose, Jerome, Cassian, Cyprian, Gregory the Great and Hilary of Poitiers, with Augustine being by far the most frequently used.[45] He also cited medieval and renaissance writers such as Bernard, Francis of Assisi, Petrarch and Pico.

Occasional glimpses of Fisher and his books are afforded by the correspondence of Richard Sharpe, his chaplain, with Nicholas Metcalfe, archdeacon of Rochester and master of St John's. In an undated letter Sharpe told Metcalfe,

> my lord is in good health, loved be Our Lord, and desireth your mastership that by your good means he may have written four sermons of Saint John Chrysostom *contra iudeos*, with certain homilies *de incomprehensibilitate Dei* and other more as they follow in the same book. The book lieth now in the new library [of Cambridge university] (that bishop Rotherham made) and was delivered at the last being of my lord there. For he had borrowed it of the university before.

Sharpe had also written to the master of Christ's College, 'for to help that the foresaid works of Saint John Chrysostom may be written and send to my lord, for it was my lord his mind that I should write to you both for the same thing'. Doubtless this manuscript copy was intended for Fisher's own library. On another occasion Sharpe asked Metcalfe to return two books to John Reynes on Fisher's behalf (*Topica Claudii* and Melanchthon's *Dialectica* et *Rhetorica*), and to ask him to bind another in parchment (*Directorium aureum contemplatiorum*). Other books of Fisher's were with another binder, and 'if your mastership may have any convenient messenger, ye shall do him great pleasure to send him these books'.[46]

The eclectic nature of Fisher's scholarly interests and his ideas about what formed a rounded education may be gauged by the books he supplied to Cambridge institutions and to individuals there. To Christ's College he gave Theophrastus' *De Plantis* and a Greek edition of Aristotle, as well as a trilingual bible. He gave St Catherine's hall an edition of the epistles of Jerome.[47] Metcalfe's accounts as master of St John's provide some detail of expenditure on books both for the college and for Fisher's own scholars. These ranged from Hebrew and Greek books to Latin classics, and included such works as a 'sophistry' and a 'logic' for the undergraduate studies of Fisher's nephew. Fisher's gifts to the college included missals, scholastic works and books of canon law.[48]

Besides collecting books for his own and others' use, Fisher showed some aesthetic interest. He took some trouble over the architecture and adornment of St John's College; a contract with a carpenter of 1516, for example, required the work to be as good or even better than that in comparable parts of Jesus College, Pembroke and King's. As we know from the *Early Life*, he had the choir stalls in the college chapel of St John's embellished with his rebus of a dolphin and an ear of corn, and his motto, *Faciam vos piscatores hominum,* was engraved over his private chantry. After his execution the rebus was removed on Cromwell's orders and the chantry chapel destroyed.[49]

When Fisher's empty tomb was rediscovered in 1773, it was described as 'an old tomb of clunch', with two elegantly-shaped shields at the head and feet which 'seem never to have had anything either carved or painted on them, being as fresh and neat as if out of the workman's hands, and both encircled in a garland or chaplet, exactly like those on the tomb of the foundress of the college'. As for the tomb itself, 'The two sides are ornamented in great taste with figures of boys supporting an entablature, where, no doubt, inscriptions were designed but never executed: and the mouldings at the top and bottom, as also the pilasters, are all finished in a Grecian taste that was in fashion in Henry 7 and 8th's time.' There was also a hollow in which an effigy would have been laid.[50]

The antiquarian Thomas Baker supposed the tomb to have been designed by the Florentine sculptor Pietro Torrigiano, as it was so similar to Margaret Beaufort's in Westminster Abbey. He told his colleague John Lewis that there was polished white marble on the tomb, with the arms of Rochester still visible.[51] Baker's guess about

Torrigiano may have hit the mark. Certainly Fisher commissioned the sculptor to work on Margaret's tomb, and an extant bust of an English churchman by Torrigiano is widely held to be a portrait of Fisher.[52]

Fisher's portrait most definitely survives in a drawing by Hans Holbein; this may have formed the basis of a painting, now lost. The existence of a face-pattern modelled on this drawing may indicate that Fisher intended to have a number of paintings executed, possibly for 'his' Cambridge colleges. Unfortunately there is little documentation of Holbein's work in England, and no trace remains of his contact with Fisher.[53]

Both Richard Sharpe and Erasmus provide brief verbal portraits of Fisher the scholar at work. In 1521 Sharpe depicted Fisher busily engaged in writing against Luther, and somewhat distressed that Richard Pace, who was translating his recent sermon into Latin, had apparently lost part of the English text. Fisher was also asking for his copy of Erasmus' annotations of the new testament, which had been left with a Cambridge binder.[54]

Sharpe praised Fisher for his hard work in writing against heresy; Erasmus, by contrast, reproached him with ruining his health through study. In September 1524 he passed some opprobrious comments on Fisher's working environment.

> The nearby sea and mud which is left at every ebbtide make the atmosphere unwholesome. Your library, too, is surrounded by glass windows on all sides; through the crevices these let in a 'subtle' air and, as the physicians say, a filtered one, pestilential with tiny rare corpuscles. It is no secret to me how unremitting you are in the library, which for you is Paradise. As for myself, if I stayed three hours in such a place, I would be sick.[55]

Erasmus, of course, was notoriously fond of his creature comforts.

While discussing Fisher as humanist it is pertinent to consider his relations with other scholars. These have been the subject of mild controversy, not least because of the desire in some quarters to deny that Fisher was a humanist. There is also a tendency – too ready, given the paucity of documentary evidence – to construct scholarly or literary 'circles', and to suppose that membership of one such group precluded friendly relations with those outside it. In addition, of course, friendship operates in different ways. Fisher's relations with Reuchlin were purely epistolary, yet they wrote affectionately as well as admiringly of each other in letters to their common 'friend' Erasmus.

What was the nature of Fisher's relationship with Erasmus? Germain Marc'hadour has shown that despite their respect for each other their theological opinions differed. Erasmus himself remarked on this several times, and it is true especially in relation to the doctrine of free will. Marc'hadour discovered Fisher's copy of the 1529 edition of Erasmus' *Opus Epistolarum*, which he had annotated heavily. These comments show that while Fisher appreciated Erasmus' elegant and effective use of language he was sometimes highly critical of his theology, especially his thinking on the Eucharist.[56] Whatever Fisher's personal feelings were for Erasmus, he was no undiscriminating admirer.

Furthermore, H.C. Porter has asserted that relations between Fisher and Erasmus, never warm in the first place, grew decidedly chilly at the time of Fisher's controversy with Lefèvre d'Etaples, and never recovered thereafter.[57] A cursory examination of their surviving correspondence would, the present writer believes, both refute this argument and demonstrate the many facets of their relationship.[58]

In the first place, it must be remembered that Erasmus' attitude to his patrons and friends as shown in his letters was inconsistent, and even downright fickle. He was not above flattery, nor shy of complaining about one correspondent to another, particularly where money was concerned. Secondly, it is evident from references in the extant correspondence that many of the letters, in particular those from Fisher to Erasmus, have been lost. Those that do remain show the two collaborating in matters of scholarship, expressing affection (even, on Fisher's part, a somewhat sardonic playfulness), and showing concern and sympathy for each other's health. Despite their critical attitude to each other, their mutual respect is evident.

Turning to the correspondence for the years 1519–24, when both scholars were engaged in polemical controversy, it is immediately apparent that Erasmus' thinking on the subject was far from consistent. He criticised Fisher for the harshness of his attack on Lefèvre, 'a very honest old man and a worthy servant of learning'.[59] At the same time, and apparently unconscious of irony, Erasmus complained bitterly of his own antagonists in controversy. In 1519 he was embroiled in argument with Edward Lee over the annotations to his new testament. Erasmus reported to Fisher that Lee 'is a more fervent sycophant than ever, a trait which seems to be innate in him. And yet he thinks himself a little saint! For myself, should I feel guilty of so much as an iota of such sycophancy, I would not dare approach the Lord's Table'. Just as Erasmus was trying to act as peacemaker in the dispute between Fisher and Lefèvre, so Fisher was attempting to mediate between Erasmus and Lee. 'Transformed by your beguiling letter, I think', Erasmus wrote, Lee had sent a messenger to Antwerp 'to find with me some way of patching up our friendship'. Erasmus was less than wholehearted in his response: 'I know better than to trust straightway a man whose whims I have so bitterly experienced'. At the same time, Erasmus lamented the rifeness of polemical battle.

> The folly of it all! while we are wasting our labours and the peace of others in such wrangling, we count ourselves as saints, as theologians, as Christians! But, meanwhile, where is Christian peacefulness, where simplicity and where our happy blithesome games in the fields of scriptures?

Porter is right to detect more than a hint of strain in the letters of 1519–20. At a time when theological controversy was escalating and old friends quarrelling bitterly, it seems that Fisher fell prey to attempts to arouse his suspicions of Erasmus, who wrote to exculpate himself.

> I do not number you among those whom I must favour, but among the persons that I must hold in reverence and veneration in every respect, and especially your person, as you have ever been my eminent tutor and most constant patron. The reason you are hardly ever mentioned in my [published] letters is, I assure you, none other than the respect I owe to your lordship. To my eyes you are a very great man in so many ways, what with your dignity of bishop, your admirable erudition, and above all your sanctity of life.

Plainly Fisher was not convinced by this fulsome explanation, and Erasmus wrote again the following February.

> Should your grace suspect me of taking offence either because you have answered Lefèvre, or because you did not send me Lee's book, you do not know Erasmus yet. However, in three letters now, you allude to I know not what. Believe me, there is nothing the matter with me. I do not doubt of your feelings towards me any more than of my own feelings. . . . You will not be offending me even if in print you choose to differ from me. If you suspect in me any such resentment, please thrust aside all doubts from your heart.[60]

This temporary misunderstanding apart, it would seem that Erasmus' last letters to Fisher are no cooler in tone than his earlier ones. He sends news of all kinds from the continent, worries about Fisher's ill health, and describes his own in rather gruesome detail. Perhaps most touching is his lament for their common friend Colet: 'of all the losses of these last thirty years, none has affected me more deeply'. He ended this letter with, 'Farewell, Reverend Father, and embrace Erasmus doubly for, with Colet now gone, he is cleft asunder.'[61]

Thus Erasmus' correspondence does not bear out Porter's assertion that he and Fisher were divided by controversy. It is, however, something of a mystery why none of Fisher's later letters to Erasmus have survived; Erasmus' latest to Fisher comes from 1524. Possibly, given Fisher's involvement in the royal divorce, each considered it prudent to destroy any correspondence. What is known is that Erasmus sent Fisher a last letter when he was in the Tower, which was shown to Cromwell by Edward White, Fisher's half-brother, and then given to him. This missive is not extant.[62] That Erasmus should have sent a letter is quite extraordinary, given his fear of offending the king of England and his anxiety about his pension from the archdiocese of Canterbury, which was a financial necessity rather than an addition to his income.[63]

Fisher has been linked closely with Thomas More in Catholic iconography and hagiography, and since they have been perceived as holding similar views and as having died for the same cause it is often assumed that they were close friends. However, it is hard to disagree with Bradshaw that this is an 'incidental association'. Surtz has argued convincingly that Fisher and More were not intimate friends, but that 'Intellectual and scholarly kinship rather than emotional involvement distinguishes their personal intercourse.' Certainly, each expressed admiration for the other on numerous occasions. More praised Fisher as 'a man illustrious not only by the vastness of his erudition, but much more so by the purity of his life'; for More, Fisher was 'distinguished for virtue as well as for learning, qualities in which he has no superior among living men'. For his part, Fisher praised More's work in his 1526 sermon against Lutheranism and his 1527 book against Oecolampadius. In addition, Surtz notes that Fisher's defence of papal authority in his *Confutatio* against Luther was 'a decisive factor in the crystallization of More's personal convictions on the papacy'.[64]

Perhaps a more personal note is struck by a letter of More to

Fisher of about 1517–18. Describing his life at court, he is careful to praise the king while at the same time mocking the courtiers who were hopeful of royal favour: 'everyone . . . finds a ground for imagining that he is in the king's good graces, like the London wives who, as they pray before the image of the Virgin Mother of God which stands near the Tower, gaze upon it so fixedly that they imagine it smiles upon them'.[65] This was surely a somewhat dangerous comment to write to a bishop famous for his piety, unless More were sure that the remark would not be taken amiss.

Respect, admiration, even friendly feeling notwithstanding, More resisted all attempts to trick him into accepting royal supremacy by leading him to believe that Fisher had already done so. Indeed, More protested to Margaret Roper that he would not be influenced in either direction by Fisher.

> For albeit, that of very truth I have him in that reverent estima-
> tion, that I reckon in this realm no man, in wisdom, learning,
> and long approved virtue together, meet to be matched and com-
> pared with him, yet in this matter I was not led by him. . . . Verily,
> Daughter I never intend (God being my good lord) to pin my
> soul at another man's back, not even the best man that I know
> this day living; for I know not whither he may hap to carry it.[66]

While it is impossible to construct a 'Fisher circle', it would seem that Fisher was highly regarded by other humanists. His dealings with Linacre's legacy for the foundation of a medical lecture at Cambridge is discussed elsewhere.[67] Richard Pace, who as the king's secretary had no need to hope for Fisher's patronage, praised him warmly to the pope.[68] Foreign scholars, too, admired his learning as well as his integrity; Etienne Poncher, Johannes Cochlaeus, Johann Eck and Paolo Giovio are but a few names that spring to mind.[69]

It is striking that all tributes to Fisher made at different times in his life coupled his exceptional learning with his unusual holiness of life. However, lest it should seem that Fisher was a friendless, coldly pious intellectual, it is fitting to quote from his own prayer of self-reproach.

> Thy strict commandment is that I should love thee with all my
> heart, with all my soul, with all my mind, with all my power.
> And this, I know, I do not, but am full far short and wide there-
> from; which thing I perceive by the other loves that I have had

of thy creatures heretofore. For such as I sincerely loved, I loved them so that I seldom did forget them. They were ever in my remembrance and almost continually mine heart was occupied with them and my thought ran ever upon them as well absent as present. Specially when they were absent I much desired to have their presence and to be there where they were, or else my heart were never in rightful quiety.[70]

Naturally, allowance must be made here for the humility of the penitent in prayer. However, it appears from a number of sources that Fisher was far from indifferent to the charms of friendship with congenial men of learning.

Fisher's industry as a scholar notwithstanding, Richard Rex has discerned in his thought a rueful realisation that his learning must be limited by his pastoral obligations.[71] It would seem that here Fisher did not do justice to himself. Despite his manifold responsibilities, Fisher's scholarship in terms of his knowledge of biblical tongues and production of literary works in a number of spheres undoubtedly makes him one of the most erudite English bishops of the age.

3 The Bishop

The seed of sin so thick is sown
Among the clergy with pomp and pride,
And the grass of grace may not grow,
So your sheep are hurt on every side.
But the grace of God be you guide,
To cure your conscience that is so cold;
Beware where that ye run or ride,
For your sheep be scabbed in the fold.

Thus ran the complaint of 'The Duty of Prelates', a sixteenth-century poem preserved in the commonplace book of Richard Hill.[1] Early Tudor bishops, with their manifold secular duties, might well find it hard to follow the model of the ideal prelate as famously delineated by St Paul. This may be summarised as follows.

The good bishop should be the husband of one wife; whatever Paul's original meaning, this was long interpreted by the Church as meaning that he should only have charge of one see. He should be sober, discreet and courteous. Hospitality was a duty for him, and he should be a good teacher. He should be a lover neither of wine nor of money, and he should be peaceable, not quarrelsome. He should rule his own family and household well. Finally, he should be of good reputation, and able to expound the word of God.[2]

How far does John Fisher's career as bishop correspond to the Pauline ideal? Could the criticisms of the author of 'The Duty of Prelates' be applied to him in any measure? Is his reputation for holiness and conscientious performance of duty confirmed or undermined by a consideration of his episcopal ministry? Finally, how does Fisher compare with his contemporaries on the early Tudor episcopal bench?

Fisher was promoted to the episcopate in November 1504, at the age of 34 or 35. Remarkably, he had already acquired a reputation for personal virtue as well as for learning, and it was this renown which decided Henry VII to appoint him to the see of Rochester. Henry, though not conspicuous as an ecclesiastical reformer, was at least pious. The king's letter to his mother shows both Fisher's reputation and Henry's reasons for promoting him.

I assure you, Madam, for none other cause, but for the great and singular virtue that I know and see in him, as well [as] in cunning and natural wisdom, and specially for his good and virtuous living and conversation. And by the promotion of such a man, I know well it should [en]courage many others to live virtuously. . . . I have in my days promoted many a man unadvisedly, and I would now make some recompense to promote some good and virtuous man, which I doubt not should best please God.[3]

Fisher's elevation to the bench of bishops was often ascribed by contemporaries to the patronage of Margaret Beaufort, but it was actually Richard Fox who recommended him. In dedicating his book against Oecolampadius to Fox, Fisher acknowledged the mediation of that prelate while at the same time paying tribute to Margaret.

by the esteem he [Henry] had for me from your frequent commendations, and of his own mere motion, without any obsequiousness on my part, without the intercession of any (as he more than once declared to myself), he gave me the bishopric of Rochester, of which I am now the unworthy occupant. There are, perhaps, many who believe that his mother, the countess of Richmond and Derby, that noble and incomparable lady, dear to me by so many titles, obtained the bishopric for me by her prayers to her son. But the facts are entirely different, as your lordship knows well, who was the king's most intimate counsellor.[4]

It is obvious that Fisher was the 'husband of one wife', in the sense that he remained bishop of Rochester for the whole of his episcopal career. It is pertinent to ask whether he had any choice in the matter. Rochester was a small, poor diocese with an income of about £300. For most of its bishops it was merely the first step on the ladder of episcopal promotion, and most of Fisher's predecessors had moved on to richer and more prestigious sees. Some commentators have wondered whether Fisher remained at Rochester because he never had the favour of Henry VIII and so had no hope of promotion. However, several sources speak of both Fisher's reluctance to become a bishop and of offers made to him of more lucrative and important sees. The *Early Life* speaks of Fisher's lack of ambition for a see and of the persuasion of his friends, especially Bishop Fox, 'that declared unto him the great necessity of the Church at that time'. It also mentions the offer to him of the dioceses of Ely and Lincoln. Ely, which had an income of £2,134, was vacant from August 1505 to November 1508; Lincoln, worth £3,300, was vacant in 1514 and 1521.[5]

Fisher's own statements on the matter are interesting. In his private statute of foundation for St John's, Cambridge he alluded to Margaret Beaufort's plans for him without, however, revealing his own views on the subject of promotion.

> The noble princess Lady Margaret, countess of Richmond, the foundress of this college, in her great condescension had a great desire to procure me a richer bishopric. But when she saw that her approaching death would frustrate this desire, she left me a no small sum of money to use according to my own will and for my own purposes.[6]

In 1527 he told Fox that he was perfectly satisfied with the see of Rochester: 'though others may have greater revenues, yet I have the care of fewer souls, so that as I must before long give an account of both, I would not wish them one whit increased'.[7] Possibly this statement was not without irony, addressed as it was to an episcopal careerist who had ended at Winchester, the richest see in the kingdom, and who had rarely seen his diocese until old age, ill health and the rivalry of Wolsey had made his retirement from court desirable.

A frequent complaint against bishops of Fisher's time (and indeed, against their successors) was that they were either frequently absent or else entirely non-resident. Linked to this was the criticism that bishops were too much occupied with secular affairs, with attendance at court and involvement in government and diplomacy. Stephen Thompson has shown that the residence record of Fisher's contemporaries is extremely varied. William Warham spent only 33 per cent of his time in his archdiocese of Canterbury, while Cardinal Bainbridge, largely resident in Rome, never saw his archdiocese of York at all. However, out of Thompson's sample of ten bishops, eight managed to spend at least 75 per cent of their time in their dioceses.[8]

Thompson shows that Fisher resided in Rochester diocese for a creditable 90 per cent of his time. The cynic might suggest that, as the diocese reached as far as Lambeth Marsh where the bishop's London house was located, it would have been difficult for him to spend less time in his see. None the less, Thompson's itinerary for Fisher shows him moving through the diocese, living at Rochester, Bromley or Halling and visiting Strood, Higham, Gravesend and other places. His commitment to residence in the diocese is borne out by the fact of his keeping his houses in good repair.[9]

All this notwithstanding, Fisher was obliged to be absent from his bishopric on occasion, or at least, to be occupied in non-diocesan business. As a spiritual lord of the realm he was bound to attend parliament, as well as convocation and the provincial synod. At least in the earlier years of his episcopate he was close to the ruling dynasty, and this entailed some attendance at court or elsewhere. For example, he was present with the king in council at Knole in December 1504, and is recorded as having attended Henry VIII's whole council twice, in November 1509 and January 1512.[10]

In addition, he was chaplain and confessor to Margaret Beaufort. Though Henry VII had asked and presumably received her permission to promote Fisher to the episcopate she was evidently unwilling to forgo his attendance and ministrations entirely. In January 1506 she received a papal brief dispensing Fisher from continual residence in his diocese so that she might have the benefit of his services.[11] His great cycle of sermons on the penitential psalms was preached in her presence, probably in summer and autumn 1508. It is evident from his memorial sermon for her that he attended Margaret on her deathbed and heard her last confession; Lord Morley claimed that she actually died during a mass he was celebrating.[12] The two royal deaths of 1509 gave Fisher considerable employment outside his diocese. In May he was at Richmond to sing one of the masses for the repose of the king's soul, and he preached Henry's funeral sermon at Westminster.[13] Doubtless he was present at Margaret's funeral, and near the end of July it was Fisher who gave her month-mind sermon, probably at Westminster.

Aside from his attendance at parliament and convocation, Fisher made sporadic appearances in London and at court. In February 1506 he was at Windsor for the unexpected and hurriedly arranged meeting between Henry VII and King Philip of Castile. In August 1509 he was at Hanworth to witness the renewal of the treaty with Scotland. In 1513 he seems to have been one of the councillors assigned to attend the queen regent while Henry VIII invaded France. Certainly he was with Katherine at Richmond on 8 September, and he preached a sermon after the victory of Flodden, presumably at court. In March 1516 he performed the christening of the king's nephew Henry, earl of Lincoln.[14] In 1520 he was present at the Field of Cloth of Gold in Queen Katherine's train, an event which furnished material for one of his most effective sermons. The royal divorce would necessitate Fisher's more frequent residence in London, or rather at Lambeth Marsh.

There were two occasions when it seemed as if Fisher might be absent abroad for a prolonged time. In 1512 and 1514 he was among the ambassadors appointed by the king to represent England at the fifth Lateran council. For reasons which remain unclear the appointment was cancelled on both occasions. Whether Fisher welcomed or resented the commission to go to Rome is equally unknown. What is certain is that he delegated his episcopal powers to the priors of Rochester and Leeds, thus providing for his diocese in his absence.[15]

Ecclesiastical business sometimes took Fisher out of his see. In November 1515 Wolsey's cardinal's hat was received into England with incredible pomp and ceremony. Not only did Fisher meet the papal notary at Rochester, he was also present at St Paul's in London for the ceremonial reception of the hat. On this occasion, as custom dictated and as he had done during mass at Windsor in 1506, he acted as crossbearer to the archbishop of Canterbury.[16]

In July 1518 Fisher was among the prelates at Canterbury to welcome Lorenzo Campeggio, the cardinal-protector of England. In September 1524 he was again at Canterbury, this time to meet Thomas Hannibal, the pope's ambassador, who was bringing the papal rose to Henry VIII.[17] He was in London to preach two important sermons refuting heresy in 1521 and 1526. As will be seen, he was sometimes in the neighbouring see of Canterbury to assist the archbishop with heresy cases.

The corollary of Fisher's appearances at court and on public occasions was that he was obliged to entertain important visitors who passed through the diocese. Hospitality was a duty enjoined on bishops by St Paul himself, and the geographical position of Rochester meant that Fisher had to receive a number of eminent guests. In 1514 the pope sent an ambassador to England with a sword and cap of maintenance for the king; Fisher, together with the master of the rolls and Sir Thomas Boleyn, was ordered to meet him at 'some place convenient between Sittingbourne and Rochester', entertain him, and conduct him to London. In 1518 Cardinal Campeggio passed through Kent on his way to the capital. At Rochester 'a magnificent dinner' was provided for him, presumably by the bishop. In 1521 Fisher gave hospitality to Lord Morley and Edward Lee, going on embassy to the Habsburgs; Morley mentioned to Wolsey the 'gentle behaviour and cheer' that Fisher had shown them.[18]

The following year, on Sunday, 1 June, Fisher entertained Henry VIII and Charles V, who stayed one night at Rochester before going on to Gravesend. At this stage relations between Henry and Fisher were quite cordial. John Wylbor, master of Strood hospital, told Nicholas Metcalfe that the king had called for the bishop 'as soon as he was come to his lodging, and he talked lovingly with my lord all the way between the palace and his chamber in the abbey'. Finally, in 1527 Fisher had to entertain Wolsey and his formidably large train. The cardinal was going to France on embassy, and broke his journey partly to break to Fisher the news of the king's doubts about his marriage. Once more, and despite his wariness of his guest and his errand, Fisher was courteously hospitable: 'I was right lovingly and kindly by him entertained', Wolsey wrote to Henry.[19]

Matters had not always been so smooth between the cardinal and the bishop of Rochester. In 1519 Fisher had made an astounding speech in synod attacking the worldliness of the clergy and the way they were burdened with secular business. The speech carried more than an oblique rebuke to Wolsey; but it also expressed Fisher's frustration at sometimes having to put his pastoral duties in second place to more mundane occupations.

> For sundry times when I have settled and fully bent myself to the care of my flock committed unto me, to visit my diocese, to govern my church and to answer the enemies of Christ, straightways hath come a messenger for one cause or other sent from higher authority by whom I have been called to other business and so left off my former purpose. And thus by tossing and going this way and that way, time hath passed and in the meanwhile nothing done but attending after triumphs, receiving of ambassadors, haunting of princes' courts and such like; whereby great expenses rise that might better be spent many other ways.[20]

Despite vexatious interruptions from the world Fisher managed to carry out both his pastoral and administrative duties. Bishops were required to perform the *visitatio ad limina apostolorum*, that is, a periodic visit to Rome (usually by proxy) to pray at the tombs of the apostles, have audience with the pope, and report on the state of the diocese. The records of such visits are fragmentary, but Fisher certainly paid his by proxy in 1506, 1508 and 1514; on the last occasion his representative was Polydore Vergil.[21]

Fisher's duty towards the curia might be done by proxy; the diocese had his personal attention. Though elected *in absentia* in November 1504 he wasted comparatively little time in going to Rochester and he commenced his first visitation of the cathedral in May 1505. There he addressed the cathedral monks, promising to fulfil his episcopal duties to the best of his ability.[22] He was more scrupulous than most early Tudor bishops in carrying out a diocesan visitation every three years, usually in person. He was also quite unusual in that he conducted parochial visitations in person. Bishop Longland of Lincoln, by contrast, delegated the visitation of parish churches. It is only fair, though, to remember that Fisher had a smaller and more manageable diocese than most. Fisher was the only bishop personally to consecrate and reconsecrate churches and churchyards. In 1510, for instance, he was in Gravesend to reconsecrate the parish church of St Mary, rebuilt after a fire, and to consecrate the existing chapel of ease as a permanent place of worship.[23]

Fisher was also conscientious about ordinations, personally performing 39 of the 42 ceremonies in the diocese. Tunstal, in a comparable period as bishop of London, personally performed only two out of 42 ordinations. Longland, bishop of Lincoln from 1521 to 1546, performed only three out of 103 ceremonies. Moreover, it was rare that he personally admitted a candidate to a benefice. Cardinals Bainbridge and Wolsey ordained no clergy in person. Fisher's record in this respect is only surpassed by that of Bishops Alcock and West of Ely who personally carried out all their ordination ceremonies, that is, 14 each.[24]

Fisher was more like his brother bishops in relation to his consistory court. Bishops rarely presided in person though Fisher, like Fox and Longland, would be present for the more serious cases, especially those concerning heresy. Fisher's conscientiousness made him ensure that both the act books and the episcopal register were written up regularly and in detail.[25]

Fisher paid great attention to the regular clergy in the see of Rochester, and his relations with the monks of his own cathedral seem to have been particularly close. Rochester cathedral was a Benedictine abbey; with just 20 monks in 1534, it ranked as the smallest cathedral chapter in the country. Fisher was the titular abbot of the house. Thompson notes that Fisher was unique in his supervision of the cathedral monks. As an explanation he suggests the fact that Fisher was often in residence at Rochester, while most bishops whose cathedrals were monastic tended to reside at manors some little way off. It is significant that Fisher reserved one of his four private fellowships at St John's College for a monk of Rochester diocese.[26]

Naturally it was important that bishop and cathedral prior should be able to work together. In November 1508 Fisher chose William Frisell, a monk of St Albans, for the office, as the chapter was unable to agree on a candidate. The two apparently co-operated very well on such matters as ordination examinations, elections and institutions, and examinations for heresy. Robert Wakefield named Frisell as one of the handful of Englishmen who knew Hebrew; it is tempting to speculate that he and Fisher learned the language together. When Frisell died in 1532 he was succeeded as prior by Laurence Merworth of the Rochester chapter, Fisher preaching the sermon before the election.[27]

Fisher's concern for the regular clergy was not confined to his own cathedral chapter. He was one of only four Tudor bishops to be present at monastic elections. Routinely he took the professions of monks, nuns and hermits. When Wolsey dissolved Lesnes abbey in 1524 (without consulting Fisher, as the bishop noted in his register), its prior William Tisehurst became Fisher's chaplain and received ecclesiastical patronage from him.[28]

Fisher's pastoral care for the religious in his diocese is no more clearly shown than in his dealings with the Benedictine nuns of Higham or Lillechurch. In 1522 Higham priory was suppressed at Fisher's request; conveniently, it may seem, for the endowment of St John's, Cambridge. However, Fisher had taken great pains in trying to reform this extremely corrupt and derelict house. Higham was a royal foundation, and subject to the bishop's visitation. On his promotion to Rochester, Fisher discovered that Higham contained only a prioress and two or three nuns. He endeavoured to increase their number, but enlarging the community did not improve its quality. Two of the nuns bore children to the vicar of Higham, and a man named Bardefelde was absolved by Fisher in 1513 of the sin of communicating secretly with them. Fisher seems to have imposed penance on them more than once. In July 1513 they petitioned him to have a stone wall built around the convent because 'they wished to enclose themselves for the increase of virtue and the perfect observance of their rule', 'And on account of the necessity of extinguishing the ill repute spread about concerning them'.[29]

The stone wall – if, indeed, it was ever built – does not seem to have improved matters, and an inquiry by Fisher in 1520 revealed that immorality and financial irregularity were rife. Fisher decided that the nuns were beyond reformation, and that it was better to dissolve the house and use its revenues more fruitfully elsewhere. The priory was dissolved in October 1522 and its possessions granted to St John's in May 1523. The college gained the site of the priory, the rectory of the parish and the advowson of the vicarage. In return St John's had to provide a priest to say mass daily in the priory chapel and four requiem masses a year for the founders and benefactors of the convent, as well as alms of 12d a year for the poor of Higham.[30]

Despite their misdeeds the three remaining nuns were treated with some consideration. Agnes Swayne was allowed to leave with a fair amount of bedclothes and clothing, as well as an alabaster image of St Dorothy, 'a psalter or hymnal' and 'an English book'. The other two nuns seem to have tried to make off with substantial amounts of the priory's moveable property. They were sent to different nunneries. Elizabeth Penny went to St Sepulchre's, Canterbury with a pension. Godlive Lawrence was sent at her own request to St Helen's, Bishopsgate in London; on her admission there Metcalfe as Fisher's proxy handed over £40 in gold.[31]

It is possible that Fisher found the Dominican nuns of Dartford priory more congenial; certainly they gave him no cause of scandal, rather they had a good reputation for the upbringing of children.[32] The convent was a royal foundation, and rich; among the nuns was Bridget, daughter of Edward IV, who died in 1517. More interesting in relation to Fisher is the fact that his half-sister Elizabeth White was a nun at Dartford. That the two were close is attested by two devotional treatises Fisher composed for her while in prison. On the dissolution of the priory in 1539 there were allegedly 24 nuns. While the prioress received the princely pension of £66 13 6d Elizabeth White was among those nuns who received £5 a year.[33]

The nuns of Dartford would seem to have been more committed to the religious life than their sisters of Higham. One of the informants for the Elizabethan biography of Fisher stated that he had a half-sister, 'a nun, who was so like the said bishop of Rochester in person, that Queen Mary knew her'. Mary I permitted the nuns to return to Dartford, and a reduced community was established; nine of its ten members were survivors from the Henrician priory, and among them was Elizabeth White. After Queen Elizabeth's accession the aged nuns chose exile and, in a state of penury, fled abroad. Among them, remarked the Dominican prior of Smithfield, 'is a sister of the martyred bishop of Rochester, of no less constancy, could she but put it to the test, than was her brother'.[34]

If Bishop Fisher is to be assessed for reforming qualities, it is pertinent to ask how he disposed of his episcopal income. Canon law was not explicit as to how bishops should spend their money, and opinion in early Tudor England differed. Edmund Dudley thought that episcopal incomes should be divided in three and assigned to hospitality, almsgiving and the upkeep of churches and mansions. John Colet believed that the income should be divided four ways, a quarter being reserved for the support of the bishop's family.[35] The *Early Life* states that Fisher divided his income into three: 'he took such order in his revenues, that one part was bestowed upon reparation and maintenance of the church, the second upon relief of poverty and maintenance of scholars and the third upon his household expenses and buying of books, whereof he had great plenty'.[36] Fisher himself alluded to his episcopal income in his private statute for St John's when he announced that he would use Margaret Beaufort's gift of money to him to endow the college.

> Now, as I receive from the annual revenue of the bishopric of Rochester quite enough for the decent maintenance of a prelate, and since the college has sustained certain losses, I have considered that it was better that both that legacy of hers, and also a considerable addition of my own, should be spent for the good of my own soul, in the education of theologians, than squandered on my relatives, or wickedly and uselessly consumed for other vain purposes.[37]

Fisher was scrupulous in the expenditure of his diocesan income: 'He would tell his brother that was steward of his house that he would have his revenues fully spent every year, so that [provided that] he were not brought in debt'. Most wisely, in 1534 he gave away much of his money as soon as he received the summons to go to London to be offered the oath of succession.

> calling his officers to him to consult for the disposition of his goods, he first allotted to Michaelhouse in Cambridge (where he was brought up) a hundred pounds, which was after paid to the college in gold. Another portion he caused to be divided among his servants, allowing to every one of them a rate, according to

his place and worthiness. Likewise to poor people in Rochester he assigned another sum to be distributed. The rest he reserved for himself, to defend his necessity in prison, whereof he accounted himself sure, as soon as he was come before the commissioners.

Thus the *Early Life*. One of the informants for that work added a further detail.

I have heard Master Trusley [Truslowe] (who was his [last] steward) say that at his apprehension he had no money in all the world, but thirty or forty pounds at the most, which remained in his hand, being steward. Which money was taken from him.[38]

Fisher seems to have kept up the custom, instituted by a previous bishop of Rochester, of keeping the sum of £300 in hand for emergencies; this was roughly the annual income of the diocese. To this he added a further sum of £100.[39] Altogether, he was conscientious in spending his episcopal revenues; but he made no personal endowment in the diocese, preferring to reserve his bounty for the colleges in Cambridge.

Turning to the issue of Fisher's clerical patronage as bishop, a number of questions must be asked. What sort of men was he appointing to benefices within the diocese – especially those with cure of souls – and what was the level of their education? Did Fisher attempt to deal with the age-old, related ecclesiastical abuses of pluralism and non-residence? In short, and in view of contemporary criticism of the Church, did he show any concern with the quality of his diocesan clergy and of the spiritual service they rendered their flocks?

In the first place, it must be noted that bishops had relatively small scope in the matter of parochial patronage.[40] They could do little against nominees armed with papal dispensations for pluralism or letters of recommendation from the king or some other great patron. Sometimes they were obliged to accept undesirable candidates. The case of Christopher Nelson illustrates this well. In 1528 Bishop Fox told Wolsey that Nelson had made indecent advances to a young wife, the daughter of a widow, in his diocese, for which behaviour Fox had first imprisoned and then expelled him. Some years later Fisher refused to institute him to the vicarage of Deptford Strand, but was forced to change his mind after Nelson was 'recommended' by Henry VIII. Obviously it was impossible to override the king's will in such cases. However, there are instances of bishops rejecting candidates who were unsuitable through lack of education or who were under canonical age. Both Fisher and Fox refused candidates who were not considered learned enough, telling them to reapply after a year spent at grammar school.[41]

Fisher seems to have been concerned to appoint educated clergy in his see. Out of all the clergy instituted in the diocese and recorded in Fisher's register only a handful are not shown as having a degree. Peter Heath has suggested that graduates made up a 'statistically significant' proportion of parish clergy in the country as a whole. He found that of the 52 incumbents in the city of London in 1522, six were doctors and 33 were masters. Roughly one-third of the candidates admitted to livings in the diocese of London by Bishop Tunstal were graduates, as were just over one-sixth of those presented to livings in Norwich diocese in the years 1503–28.[42] By contrast, Stanford Lehmberg has shown that other dioceses had fewer graduate clergy. In the city of York in the sixteenth century only two or three parish priests were graduates. In Lincoln diocese under Bishop Longland only about 25 per cent of resident parish clergy were graduates, as were only nine out of 76 clergy surveyed for literacy in the same diocese in the years 1520–44.[43]

Thus Rochester under Fisher had a higher proportion of parish clergy who were graduates than other dioceses. Whether or not they were resident on their livings, however, is another matter. The scope of the present study, which focuses on Fisher's work as bishop rather than on the diocese of Rochester itself, precludes a detailed examination of the diocesan clergy as this would form a disproportionately lengthy digression. Rather, it is pertinent to consider the appointments Fisher made to the livings in his own gift, and to address the related questions of education or learning, non-residence and pluralism.

There were 122 parishes in Rochester diocese; 21 of these were in the bishop's gift, and he had the right to appoint to nine livings elsewhere. Altogether, the bishop's parochial livings constituted 20 per cent of the patronage in Rochester diocese.[44] A pattern emerges from the analysis of Fisher's exercise of patronage; he used his livings to reward scholars, chaplains and – in just one instance – a relative.

John Addison, Doctor of Divinity and Fisher's chaplain, held a number of the bishop's Rochester livings: St Nicholas in the city of Rochester from 1522 to 1525; Woldeham from 1524 to 1533;

Snodland from 1525 to 1530; and Bromley from 1531 to 1534. Thus he was usually in possession of two benefices. In 1534 he was attainted of misprision of treason [that is, concealment of another's treason] in connection with the Nun of Kent and lost all his spiritual promotions.[45]

Richard Sharpe was also Fisher's chaplain and a Doctor of Divinity. All his benefices were in Rochester diocese and in Fisher's gift. Sharpe had connections with both Margaret Beaufort's Cambridge colleges, being fellow of Christ's in 1513, fellow of St John's by 1515, and president of St John's in 1515–16. He had ceased to hold a position in Cambridge by the time he started receiving patronage in Rochester. He was vicar of Kemsing from 1517 to February 1525; rector of Chislehurst from March 1521 to 1522; rector of Stone from October 1521 to April 1525; and rector of Bromley from 1524 to his death in 1530. He also held the free chapel of Halling from 1517 to 1530. He seems to have been resident frequently in the diocese, though not necessarily on one of his current livings. Usually he was in attendance on Fisher, often involved in managing the bishop's Cambridge affairs.[46]

Robert Truslowe, MA, was another chaplain of Fisher's. In 1530 he received the rectory of Snodland on Addison's resignation and the free chapel of Halling on the death of Sharpe. He survived the bishop's fall, and was rector of Halstow from 1533 to 1544. Much later he was one of the sources of information for the Elizabethan biography of Fisher.[47] Robert Doket, MA, a Cambridge scholar possibly of Queens', received some preferment in Fisher's gift. He was rector of Lamberhurst from April to October 1510. In 1522 he became vicar of St Nicholas', Rochester city, and received a prebend in Malling Abbey. He was also rector of Chevening, Canterbury diocese, from 1493 to 1522. Robert Shorton, DD, was master of St John's College from 1511 to 1516, and somewhat later was Queen Katherine's chaplain and almoner. From 1510 to 1517 he was vicar of St Werburgh's, Hoo (in Rochester diocese, though not directly in Fisher's gift), during which time he held two benefices elsewhere.[48]

As far as they can be traced, it would seem that all the men promoted by Fisher to the livings in his own gift held one or more degrees. The one instance of Fisher's bestowing clerical patronage on a relative concerns his nephew Henry White, who received the free chapel of Feckenham in 1510, when he was already BA. In 1514 he became incumbent of Frekenham, Norwich diocese, which was in the gift of the bishop of Rochester. Compared with the lavish amount of preferment lavished on their nephews by even such enlightened prelates as Longland and Warham, these are slim pickings indeed.[49]

It is obvious that the clergy described above were pluralists in a modest way, holding a maximum of two parochial livings at a time. How conscientious they were about cure of souls in their benefices cannot be known. It is worth noting, however, that in 1534 several of the livings in Fisher's gift are recorded as having curates as well as vicars or rectors; Bromley, Southfleet, Kemsing, Trottiscliffe, Milton and Gravesend, Snodland, and Stone.[50]

There was one outstanding pluralist in Rochester diocese in Fisher's time; Nicholas Metcalfe, who was also the bishop's chaplain. Metcalfe was undoubtedly learned, being BD and DD and master of St John's College from 1518 to 1537. He was also undoubtedly acquisitive, and the amount of preferment he received is fairly staggering; he took the precaution of procuring a papal dispensation for pluralism. He was rector of Stourmouth, Canterbury diocese from 1509 to 1510 and vicar of Kemsing, Rochester diocese from 1509 to 1517. He was vicar of St Werburgh's, Hoo from 1517 to 1534, and apparently resided there for a year or two. He was rector of Henley-on-Thames from 1510 to 1521 and rector of Southfleet from 1531 to 1537 (both of these being in Fisher's gift), as well as being archdeacon of Rochester from 1515. He held three other benefices at different times, and was a canon of Lincoln from 1526 until his death in 1539.[51]

In complete contrast to Metcalfe, one chaplain of Fisher's who received no parochial patronage from him was George Bowker, who was later notorious as the 'Calais heretic' Adam Damplip. It cannot be known whether this was on account of his youth (in 1538 Lord Lisle would describe him as 'a young priest') or because Fisher thought him unsuitable for a cure of souls.[52]

Metcalfe's is the only case of flagrant pluralism in Rochester diocese; but the three appointments Fisher made in Lincoln diocese went to scholars or courtiers who were non-resident.[53] Altogether, 22 per cent of the incumbents in Rochester diocese were non-resident; for comparison, London diocese had roughly 35 per cent and Canterbury 15 per cent of clergy non-resident. As a matter of interest Thomas More presented three priests to livings in the diocese of Lincoln of whom only one was resident. It has been estimated that before 1526 Longland gave half the livings in his gift to men he knew would be unable to reside.[54]

Certainly Fisher, like his humanist contemporaries, connived at the absenteeism of university scholars and administrators. It would have been remarkable if he had not done so; church preferment was seen as a legitimate source of income for such men, and the system of patronage was well-entrenched. Neither Fisher before the reformation nor Cranmer later was able to put an end to pluralism and non-residence. Indeed, in 1530 Cranmer himself, as non-resident rector of Bredon, Worcester diocese, obtained a papal dispensation which licensed him to hold up to four benefices, with or without cure of souls, up to the value of 3,000 florins. Cuthbert Tunstal, another noted humanist bishop, had obtained in his youth a papal licence to hold a benefice despite being under the canonical age for priest's orders and thus unable to care for his flock.[55]

The extirpation of heresy was meant to be the concern of all bishops and an important part of their pastoral work. The importation of Lutheran and other continental ideas in the 1520s and 1530s caused increased difficulties for the English bishops. Fisher is well known as an opponent of heresy in print and in the pulpit. He was also assiduous in confronting personally the problem of heresy in his diocese, and sometimes even beyond its borders.

Fisher's episcopal register records ten cases of the abjuration of heretics in 30 years. No obdurate heretic was burned in Rochester diocese during Fisher's tenure of office. There is no reason to think that Fisher would have shrunk from relaxing recalcitrant offenders to the secular arm. Rather, it seems likely that the absence of burnings testifies to his energy and thoroughness in persuading heretics to recant.

The first heretic to abjure his errors before Bishop Fisher, on 17 May 1505, was John Mores alias Wever of St Nicholas' parish, Rochester city. Mores had gone about the city interpreting scripture according to his own ideas and putting forward two heresies in particular. The first was that Christ did not die in perfect charity, since he redeemed Adam and Eve but not Lucifer. The second was the ancient heresy which held that Christ was wholly divine, having only the semblance of a human body. Accordingly the Virgin 'is but a sack, and the Son of God desired the Father to come to middle-earth to take a sack upon his back'. In 1516 occurred the abjuration of William Moress, a weaver of the parish of Snodland whose offence was that, on being asked why he had not received communion at Easter, Moress had replied that he could buy 24 loaves as good as that one was for a penny. Thus he was a sacramentary. A similar case was that of Paul Lomley, a 'wedded man' of Gravesend who abjured in 1526. He had declared 'that priests maketh us to believe that the singing bread they hold over their heads is God, and it is but a cake'.[56]

A 'heretic' of a different metal was Richard Gavell of the parish of Westerham, who abjured before Fisher in 1507. Gavell does not seem to have been guilty of any significant doctrinal deviation. Rather, he was an anticlerical swaggerer who had repeatedly tormented his curate and caused scandal.

Gavell said that it was not necessary to take holy water at the priest's hand and that oblations and offering days were equally unnecessary because they were only invented by the clergy 'by their own covetous minds and singular avails'. One Sunday he persuaded another parishioner to withdraw her offering. He was in the habit of refusing to hear the word of God and of leaving the church for the alehouses during different services and at sermon time. He had often spoken against both the curate of Westerham and the word of God, saying, 'Now the priest doth stand in the pulpit, but he doth nothing but chide and bawl; for I look more on his deeds than of his words.'

Such behaviour was counted as outrageous and led to Gavell's being 'accursed' or excommunicated by the archbishop of Canterbury and openly denounced by his victim the curate in Westerham church. Far from being sobered by this, Gavell declared that the curse of the Church was of no effect: 'only the curse of God is to be dreaded, which the priests and bishops have not in their power'. This, presumably, was where his heresy lay.[57] Gavell was clearly a formidable character, and it says much for Fisher's own adamantine will that he was able to bring him to heel so early in his episcopate.

Two of the Rochester heretics expressed unorthodox views about life after death. Henry Petter alias Heythorn of West Malling recanted after saying, 'I will not believe that a man that departeth this world shall arise again at the day of doom till I see it.' John Pylchar, 'wedded man' of the parish of Cuxton, recanted the belief that 'my soul shall arise at the day of judgment but so shall not my body and bones'.[58]

Two features of the heresy cases recorded in the episcopal register are surprising. The first is that Rochester was not involved in the great drive against heresy of 1511 which affected so many other dioceses. The second is that there were so few cases of Lutheranism and its derivatives. True, in 1528 Fisher prosecuted William

Mafelde, precentor of Rochester cathedral and teacher of grammar there, for not surrendering his copy of the English new testament in obedience to Wolsey's command.[59] However, the episcopal register records only three cases of overt Lutheranism.

In 1524 Thomas Batman, hermit of the parish of St Margaret near Rochester, recanted of a number of errors, 'Specially that I have to many and divers persons preached, defended and said the heresies of Luthers, a great heretic'. Some of his statements relate to the cult of the saints. These should not be worshipped or prayed to, and in church offerings should only be made to the sacrament, not to the statues of saints. Offerings should not be made to the Rood of Grace near the shrine of Our Lady of Walsingham, or indeed to any image, 'for they be but stocks and posts'. Rather, money should be given to the poor, and Batman had complained that 'priests do make so many offering days and holy days that the poor convenient[ly] cannot get their living'. He had counselled different people not to go to confession nor to fast on Fridays or other fast days, and had foretold that holy bread and holy water would cease to be used.

Much of this might as easily have been said by a lollard as by a Lutheran, but Batman revealed that he had heard and accepted Luther's teaching. He had spoken against clerical celibacy, and in favour of communion in both kinds.

> I have said that priests and religious persons take wives beyond the sea and leave their religion; and that I think best to avoid further incontinencies. . . . I have said that priests beyond the sea use to consecrate both wine and bread and minister both to the lay people, and therefore it is far amiss and a great error in this country not so to do.[60]

The second case of Lutheranism occurred some eight years later. John Bechyng, parson of Ditton, recanted of heresy against the sacrament of penance. He had not believed in the sacraments of the Church, and in the past six months or so had been to confession only two or three times, though he had celebrated mass. He had told a layman 'that the layman might as well hear my confession as I being a priest might hear his', and had said in front of several witnesses that he was not bound by scripture to go to confession.[61]

The final case of Lutheran belief occurred in 1532. Peter Duer or Dure, priest of Gravesend, had denied that Luther was a heretic and affirmed that popes and prelates had no authority to make laws. He also said that his prayer was as good with the omission of the Virgin's name as if he mentioned her, and that St Augustine's soul was not in heaven. An even more confused and illogical case (one wonders why Duer picked on St Augustine) had occurred the previous month, when a group of men from Rochester city recanted of a number of errors. These ranged from a demand that the gospel should be preached in the mother tongue to the statement 'That Christ Almighty was a wroth and an angry fellow, and did naught in casting down the poor men's goods in the temple': and from admitting to having heard in London that God alone should be worshipped, not his saints or their images, to the idea that 'a man should not show his confessor all his sins'.[62]

The relative scarcity of heresy cases in Rochester diocese may indicate that those with unorthodox views, knowing their bishop's vigour and uncompromising nature, spoke and acted with discretion. On the other hand, many of Fisher's flock may have shared the views of Elizabeth George of Dartford. Her son was a friar at Cambridge, where doubtless he had heard new doctrines discussed, and she was highly displeased to hear 'that you are now of the new fashion, that is to say, a heretic. Never none of your kindred were so named, and it grieves me to hear that you are the first'. She warned him thus.

> you send me word that you will come over to me this summer, but come not unless you change your conditions, or you shall be as welcome as water into the ship. You shall have God's curse and mine, and never a penny. I had rather give my goods to a poor creature that goeth from door to door, being a good Christian man, than to you, to maintain you in lewdness and heresy.[63]

Two heresy cases took Fisher into the neighbouring diocese of Canterbury; that of John Browne, burned at Ashford in 1517; and that of Thomas Hitton, burned at Maidstone in 1530. The offenders came under Archbishop Warham's jurisdiction, but the offences had been committed in Rochester diocese. Browne attracted interest after an altercation with a mass-priest at Gravesend, whence two of the abjured Rochester heretics came. Gravesend may well have been a centre of religious disaffection. In 1522 Fisher cited the churchwardens there for negligence in failing to ring the church bells when he visited the parish – an omission that may have been a deliberate slight. Browne had previously been found guilty of heresy in the reign of Henry VII; it is possible that his business at Gravesend was not entirely innocent.[64]

While Fisher was an assiduous administrator he saw the bishop's role as primarily that of pastor and teacher rather than judge or ruler.[65] His fatherly care extended to all in his see. Cardinal Pole later recalled that Fisher used to say that he had a special responsibility for Henry VIII because the king was born in his diocese; Henry for his part used to boast that no other prince had in his realm a bishop so endowed with virtue and learning.[66]

Fisher considered preaching to be an important aspect of the bishop's ministry. The *Early Life* states that he was a devoted preacher in the diocese; when he grew too frail to stand in the pulpit, he would preach sitting down.[67] There is some contemporary evidence of his preaching in his see. At the diocesan synod of 1527, for example, he celebrated the mass of the Holy Spirit and gave the sermon, after which the constitutions against the keeping of concubines were read. It is quite likely that Fisher's sermon was on the same theme.[68] The episcopal register records just one instance of his granting a preaching licence to a cleric from outside the diocese. This was issued to Laurence Godfraye, a learned Observant Franciscan of Canterbury, in April 1530.[69] Fisher probably shared the general episcopal reluctance to license outsiders, as they would be less easy to control than diocesan clergy and might, too, spread heretical ideas.

The record affords occasional glimpses of Fisher at work among his flock. In April 1510 he witnessed the vow of chastity taken by Elizabeth Fitzwarren, a widow. He also witnessed the vows of two hermits of Dartford, in December 1509 in Bromley church after an ordination ceremony, and in December 1518 during mass in his palace at Rochester.[70] In April 1521 he witnessed the will of Sir John Peche of Lullingstone. He and Warham were appointed supervisors of the will and each received a gift of plate (Warham's being the more ornate and, presumably, more valuable). Peche made provision for a chantry priest in his chapel at Lullingstone, who was to be chosen by his wife and, after her death, by Fisher.[71] Once Fisher asked Metcalfe to take a child sent by the prior of Leeds into St John's College, though whether as scholar or servant is not known.[72] He was said to have spent money on repairing the bridge at Rochester, and to have punished an 'incontinent nun, which by W[illiam] Warham of Canterbury was borne out; for the which [he] reproved him sharply by writing'.[73]

Fisher maintained a household befitting his episcopal rank though avoiding ostentation: 'His servants used not to wear their apparel after any courtly or wanton manner, but went in garments of a sad and seemly colour, some in gowns and some in coats as the fashion then was, whom he always exhorted to frugality and thrift, and in any wise to beware of prodigality.'[74] Despite his distaste for worldly splendour, however, Fisher sometimes had to pay some attention to outward show. When preparing for the Field of Cloth of Gold he had to take some care over his wardrobe. Sharpe asked Metcalfe to buy some satin for a 'chymmet' or riding habit for Fisher for which he would also receive more than four yards of tawny sarcenet. Fisher's hat was two inches too small; either it must be altered, or a new one made 'without fringe'. Metcalfe should 'inquire whether other bishops have hats or not and send my lord word of these things as shortly as ye can'. Fisher was also anxious to know whether the king, queen and cardinal would pass through Rochester on their journey to France; doubtless dreading the arrangements for their entertainment which would have to be made if they were.[75]

The *Early Life* credits Fisher with the virtue of hospitality, as enjoined on bishops by St Paul: 'If any strangers came to him, he would entertain them according to their vocations with such mirth as stood with the gravity of his person, whose talk was always rather of learning or contemplation than of worldly matters.'[76] An extension of hospitality was to send gifts of food, which Fisher did to Lord Bergavenny, one of the magnates of Kent, on at least one occasion. Bergavenny had sent Fisher some venison; Fisher responded with a salmon, which Bergavenny found 'good and right dainty in this heath country'. He offered the bishop the chance to indulge his love of hunting.

> If such game as I have in these parts may do you pleasure, it may please you to send to the keeper, and he shall hunt for you at such time as ye shall give him in commandment. Or else if it shall please you to see your greyhounds run at any time either within or without, I have commanded my keeper to give you attendance and make you such disport as if I were there present, which I beseech you to take when it shall best like you.[77]

Fisher's fondness for the chase appears in his devotional tract *The Ways to Perfect Religion*, which contains a comparison of the life of the nun with that of the hunter.

Within the household Fisher's steward was his brother Robert, an unmarried layman. Robert Fisher was MP for Rochester in the Reformation Parliament from 1529; he may have sat in earlier parliaments, but this cannot be known as the names of the Rochester MPs have been lost.[78] Robert provided food and other necessities for his brother in the Tower until his own death early in 1535. His presence in the household, taken together with Elizabeth White's residence at Dartford, might seem to indicate a degree of familial closeness.

Fisher's chaplains played an important part in the life of the household. When the bishop had no visitors,

> his order was now and then to sit with his chaplains, which were commonly grave and learned men, among whom he would put some great question of learning, not only to provoke them to better consideration and deep search of the hid mysteries of our religion, but also to spend the time of repast in such talk that might be (as it was indeed) pleasant, profitable and comfortable to the waiters- and standers-by.[79]

Though hospitable to others, Fisher was frugal with himself: 'His diet at table was for all such as thither resorted plentiful and good, but for himself very mean.' Nor would he linger at table: 'he was so dainty and spare of time that he would never bestow fully one hour at any meal'.[80] At the same time, and like his brother bishops Fox, West and Ruthal, he regularly had the poor fed at his gates.

> he gave at his gate to divers poor people (which were commonly no small number) a dealy alms of money, to some two pence, to some four pence, to some eight pence, and some more after the rate of their necessity. That being done, every of them was re-warded likewise with meat, which was daily brought to the gate. And lest any fraud, partiality, or other disorder might rise in distribution of the same, he provided himself a place, whereunto immediately after dinner he would resort and there stand to see the division with his own eyes.[81]

The *Early Life* also describes Fisher visiting the indigent sick, and personally preaching to the dying in order to comfort them.

> Many times it was his chance to come to such poor houses as for want of chimneys were very smoky, and thereby so noisome, that scant any man could abide in them. Nevertheless himself would there sit by the sick patient many times the space of three

or four hours together in the smoke, when none of his servants were able to abide in the house, but were fain to tarry without till his coming abroad. And in some poor houses, where stairs were wanting, he would never disdain to climb up by a ladder for such a good purpose. And when he had given them such a ghostly comfort as he thought expedient for their souls, he would at his departure leave behind him his charitable alms, giving charge to his steward or other officers daily to prepare meat convenient for them (if they were poor) and send it unto them.[82]

The *Early Life* is, of course, a hagiography, and conventional descriptions of episcopal saints often show them visiting the sick and relieving the poor. None the less the individual detail of the smoky and ladderless houses makes this picture seem veracious.

Fisher's personal austerity is attested by inventories of his possessions in the palace at Rochester and the manor of Halling. Both were taken on 27 April 1534, after Fisher's refusal to swear to the succession, and together they form a detailed document of ten pages.[83] The bishop had disposed of most of his money before his departure from Rochester, and it is possible that the more valuable of his moveable property was treated similarly.[84] Even so, it does not seem that Fisher's style of living was opulent; his furniture, hangings and other goods are described in the inventories as 'old', 'trash' and 'nothing worth'.

In the great chapel at Rochester there were hangings of yellow Bruges satin, blue damask and red and white sarcenet, eight gilt images on the altar, and a cloth to cover the pyx which was garnished with gold. But on the ground before the altar there was an 'old carpet', and the chapel in the crypt, hung with 'old dornexe' and a painted cloth depicting the Three Kings of Cologne, only had timber images. In the sacristy the hangings were of old painted cloth, and there was a broken looking-glass and an old folding bed.

In summarising Fisher's episcopal career, it has to be said that he was not an administrative reformer, nor was he able to abate clerical abuses such as pluralism. His record as regards heresy is open to interpretation; either he was superbly efficient in persuading his flock to avoid or renounce its enticements, or his intransigence merely drove the unorthodox to silence and passivity for a season.[85] Perhaps study of the diocese after Fisher's time would indicate how effective or otherwise he had been.

He was not a great founder or builder in the diocese; indeed, he made it plain that his priorities lay with the Cambridge colleges. On the other hand, he did not plunder the episcopal revenues and patronage to enrich his relatives, and he liked to appoint learned clergy. As bishop he was resident, a preacher, conscientious in the performance of all his obligations, and vividly aware of his pastoral duties.[86] It is surely significant that Fisher inspired Carlo Borromeo, the great reforming archbishop of Milan, who kept a portrait of him in his study.[87]

The *Early Life* depicts the sorrow of Fisher's flock when he left Rochester for the last time.

> there were by that time assembled a great number of people of that city and country about to see him depart, to whom he gave his blessing on all sides as he rode through the city bareheaded. There might you have heard great wailing and lamenting, some crying that they should never see him again, some others said: *woe worth they that are the cause of his trouble,* others cried out upon the wickedness of the time to see such a sight, everyone uttering his grief to others as their minds served them.[88]

For his first biographer, 'in all things belonging to the care and charge of a true bishop, he was to all the bishops of England, living in his days, the very mirror and lantern of light'.[89] In 1536 Cardinal Pole turned back on Henry VIII his own boast that he was the prince with the best bishop in Christendom.

> For what other man . . . have ye presently, or of many years past have ye had, comparable with him in sanctity, learning, wisdom and careful diligence in the office and duty of a bishop, of whom ye may justly above all other nations glory and rejoice? That if all the corners of Christendom were narrowly sought, there could not be found out any one man that in all things did accomplish the parts and degrees of a bishop equal with him.[90]

Fisher's assiduity in fulfilling his episcopal duties as well as many others shows that Henry VII was not mistaken in promoting him on the basis of his reputation. His polemical and devotional writings show that Fisher regarded himself as a pastor to the whole of Christendom. It is to his credit that he did not forget his smaller flock of Rochester.

4 The Preacher

unto all nations the gospel must first be preached (Mark 13:10)

It would be hard to exaggerate the value John Fisher placed on the preaching ministry. In his estimation, Christ's 'fishers of men' were those who preached the gospel to the people. He would have agreed with the medieval writer of homilies who said, 'By these fishers be understood doctors, the which . . . . should let out into the world holy teaching of God's love, for to catch souls from sin in to the way of salvation.'[1] In this respect, as in others, he took seriously Paul's injunctions to Titus: the bishop should be 'embracing that faithful word which is according to doctrine, that he may be able to exhort in sound doctrine and to convince the gainsayers' (Titus 1:9). Fisher's own spirituality was based on the concepts of sincere and humble repentance, trust in the divine mercy, and grateful love of God. This could be most effectively conveyed to the people through the medium of preaching.

Bishops were not formally required by canon law to preach, though the general expectation seems to have been that they should do so. Indeed, the reforming Archbishop Peckam had declared that 'the episcopal order is called by the holy fathers the order of preachers'. However, in 1215 a decree of the fourth Lateran council had recognised that bishops were often unable to preach themselves for a variety of reasons, and had authorised them to delegate the task of preaching to suitable clergy. It seems probable that bishops gave few sermons themselves, and John Fisher was one of only three Henrician bishops who considered preaching to be as important as a bishop's sacrificial and supervisory duties.[2]

There is abundant evidence of his furtherance of the preaching ministry, and of his own practice of preaching. A considerable number of his sermons are extant, composed for a variety of occasions and with different objects in view, though all share an overriding purpose. Thus it is possible to study this aspect of his pastoral career in some detail.

Before considering Fisher's own sermons it is instructive to see how he sought to stimulate the preaching ministry, not just in England, but throughout Christendom. To this end he tried to engage the talents of Erasmus by commissioning from him a handbook on the method of preaching. A number of scholars and churchmen suggested a project of the kind to Erasmus, the first being Jan Becker of Borsselen, in 1519; but Erasmus himself said repeatedly that it was Fisher who most strongly urged him to it.[3] In September 1524 he apologised to Fisher for not having finished the book.

> I had just set myself to the work you require of me – you are not the only one – when the ever-present serious illness and several other circumstances compelled me to break it off. I shall devote the winter to this task, God willing ... in *Ratio Concionandi*, I am led to denounce the faults of certain preachers and hence to touch upon the dogmas of some theologians; but I shall put on the armour of your auspices.[4]

Fisher meant this work to be of benefit to the Church universal, but he did not live to see its appearance. In the preface Erasmus was lavish in praise of Fisher and Margaret Beaufort for their work of foundation at Cambridge, whose aim was the education of good priests and preachers. Margaret, he said, had given Fisher a large sum of money, and he had devoted this to training preachers and to poor relief. Both Margaret and Fisher believed 'that to reform the morals of the people nothing was so valuable as preachers capable of sowing the seeds of evangelical teaching'.[5] Erasmus' treatise echoes Fisher's own ideas on the subject: the ideal preacher should have a thorough knowledge of scripture and theology; training in philosophy and rhetoric; sound judgement; and eloquence.[6]

Above all, said Erasmus, the preacher must be open to the influence of the Holy Spirit. Fisher in his 1526 sermon said that the word of God is the seed cast by Christ the sower, and 'The preachers of this word be but nothing else but as the coffins and the hoppers [baskets] wherein this seed is couched.' But eloquence is empty unless the preacher is moved by the Spirit of God: 'The preacher may well rehearse the words of scripture; but they be not his words, they be the words of Christ. And if our saviour Christ speak not within the preacher the seed shall be but cast in vain.'[7]

Fisher expended considerable time and labour to ensure both that preachers would be well-educated and that academic learning would be put to a pastoral use. In May 1503, when he was university vice-chancellor, Cambridge obtained a papal licence to appoint 12 preachers annually from among the doctors, masters and graduates. They were not merely to deliver erudite sermons in the university, but to preach throughout England, Scotland and Ireland to both clergy and people. The papal bull states explicitly that the licence was granted at the request of Dr John Fisher.[8]

Margaret Beaufort – doubtless prompted by Fisher – sponsored both preaching at Cambridge and preaching to the people by Cambridge scholars. The Lady Margaret divinity reader was permitted to preach rather than lecture during Lent. The Lady Margaret preacher had duties outside the university as well as in it. He was to be a Doctor or at least a Bachelor of Divinity; was to reside at Cambridge and hold no benefice, being a perpetual fellow of some college; and would receive an additional stipend of £10 a year. This financial provision and lack of a cure of souls meant that he was free to preach his obligatory six sermons a year at specified places in London, Westminster, Cambridgeshire, Hertfordshire and Lincolnshire.[9]

Fisher saw all this as a logical extension of Margaret's educational benefactions. As he later told the university, her general aim was 'the education of a multitude of youths who, when they had grown into men of learning and virtue, would spread the gospel of Christ throughout the land of Britain with superabundant fruit'. Erasmus, too, praised Margaret for her patronage of learned men who would preach the gospel to the people.[10]

Fisher intended that St John's College should be a source of good preaching as well as a learned academy, and his first code of statutes, drawn up in 1516, made provision for this. One quarter of the fellows was to be occupied in preaching to the people in English. These preachers earned a nominal salary of one mark a year but were allowed to hold a benefice of any value whatsoever. They also received a week's commons for every sermon delivered. Moreover, they were exempt from disputations and from holding college offices. In exchange for these privileges they were to give eight sermons a year to the people and one in the college chapel.[11]

The regulations for preachers were amplified in Fisher's new code of statutes of 1524; experience had doubtless shown that some fellows would abuse the office to escape other duties. Preachers were not to hold two benefices with cure of souls or have any preferment worth more than £20 a year. Those who were vicars were not to reside in college away from their cures. Preachers who failed to give sermons would lose their fellowships, and obstinate idleness would result in deprivation. Fisher was clearly concerned with the quality of preaching, since he allowed that other members of the university might become preachers and thus fellows of St John's; it would seem that fewer of the existing fellows than he had hoped were suitable to be preachers. At the same time, the preacher-fellows were to make a greater contribution to instruction in the college. Those who were not absent taking the gospel to the people were to expound the scripture lessons read in hall. Divinity students were ordered to attend these expositions (to learn the art of preaching by example, no doubt), and were warned not to mock the preacher.

The regulations of 1524 show that Fisher was not an unrealistic idealist but a practical reformer and practising pastor who was aware of the difficulties involved in the furtherance of preaching. The fact that this formal provision of preachers seems to be unique among medieval and early Tudor academic statutes reveals his realisation of the importance of making educated preachers available to the populace.[12]

The Elizabethan biography of Fisher observes that an extraordinary number of effective preachers came from both St John's and Christ's College.[13] To take but one example, Henry Gold was a foundation fellow of St John's, and the first incumbent of Ospringe to be nominated by the college. He was one of the university preachers in 1522, and one of his extant sermons displays both his learning and his awareness of the needs and limitations of his auditors. In this sermon, delivered at the visitation of a monastery, he was careful to translate the scriptural quotations from Latin into English for the benefit of 'you that be here unlearned', while at the same time using his knowledge of Greek and Hebrew for the edification of the more erudite monks.[14] In 1529–30 fellows of St John's, along with other colleagues, friends and protégés of Fisher, were active in making sermons against the preaching of the evangelical Hugh Latimer. Erasmus praised Fisher's work at Cambridge to Alfonso Fonseca, archbishop of Toledo, who had himself contributed to the development of universities in Spain. At Fisher's colleges, Erasmus said, young men were so instructed that they emerged ready 'to proclaim the word of God with gravity and in the spirit of the gospel, and by an effective eloquence to make it of value in the eyes of men of learning'.[15]

How far was Fisher able to sponsor the preaching ministry within his diocese of Rochester? Stephen Thompson's work has shown that bishops had relatively little influence on patronage at the parochial level, but Fisher did what he could respecting preaching.[16] He would not license preachers from outside the diocese unless they had good qualifications or sound references; such as one

Laurence Godfraye, *'lectore sacrae theologiae'* of Canterbury, whom Fisher licensed to preach on 21 April 1530.[17]

By all accounts Fisher himself was an assiduous preacher. The Elizabethan biography alludes frequently to his activities in his own diocese.

> We have hitherto declared unto you his great and painful diligence in preaching the word of God: which custom he used not only in his younger days when health served, but also even to his extreme age, when many times his weary and feeble legs were not able to sustain his weak body standing, but forced him to have a chair and so to teach sitting.

When visiting the dying he would preach to them personally. In 1531 he left London after an unsuccessful attempt to poison him; returning to Rochester, he 'then fell to his old trade of preaching to his flock and visiting of sick persons, beside an infinite number of other deeds of mercy'.[18]

Both passing references in the records and his own extant sermons indicate that Fisher did indeed preach frequently. His notable and popular cycle of ten sermons on the penitential psalms was preached before Margaret Beaufort and her household, probably on Sundays in August and September 1508.[19] The following year he preached both the funeral sermon for Henry VII and the 'month-mind' or memorial sermon for Lady Margaret. In September 1513 he preached on the death of James IV at the battle of Flodden, probably at court before Katherine of Aragon. He is recorded as preaching at the Rochester diocesan synod of 1527, and doubtless preached in his see on other occasions. His sermon on the Passion, delivered on Good Friday in an unknown year, may have been given in his diocese. He is said to have preached at the Field of Cloth of Gold in 1520. No such sermon is extant, though he did preach a sermon in 1520 which described and criticised that splendid meeting of kings in some detail.

Just as Fisher played a leading role in the literary battle with Luther and his followers, so his oratorical skills were enlisted in the fight against heresy. In 1521 he was the preacher at the solemn ceremony in St Paul's churchyard when the papal sentence of excommunication against Luther was read and the works of the reformer burned. In 1526 Henry VIII chose him to preach at the formal abjuration of Robert Barnes and other heretics, when more books were burned. Bishop Longland told Wolsey that the king 'thinks my lord of Rochester to be most meet to make that sermon afore you, both *propter authoritatem, gravitatem et doctrinam personae*'. In addition, the Elizabethan biography notes,

> Many other sermons and homilies to the same effect he made besides at London . . .taking thereby great occasion to tax as well the negligence of curates as the rashness and levity of the people, exhorting all sorts in their vocations to play the valiant soldiers in stoutly resisting these devilish assaults of heresy.[20]

The sermon of 1526 in St Paul's was the last official occasion on which Fisher preached, as his support for Katherine of Aragon put him out of Henry's favour; when a third ceremony of burning heretical books took place some time before 1528 it was Tunstal who was chosen to preach. Fisher, meanwhile, was putting his learning and his rhetorical skills at the service of the queen. In June 1532 the emperor's ambassador Chapuys reported that Fisher had preached boldly in Katherine's favour and that his sermon had sealed the mouths of those who had spoken for the king.[21] Needless to say, this particular sermon has not survived.

What was the focus of Fisher's preaching? His constant theme, regardless of the circumstances or immediate occasion of a particular sermon, is the urgent need for repentance. True, heartfelt penitence is required, not mere lip-service: 'Contrition is none other but an inward sorrow of the mind set in the privy place of the heart, which needs must go before confession made by mouth; for truly, confession without contrition had before profiteth very little or nothing.'[22] To induce repentance and amendment of life, Fisher harps on four strings: the loathsome nature of sin; the pains of purgatory and hell; the inferiority of earthly pleasures, however splendid; and the love and mercy of God.

Fisher is struck by the horror of sin, and he uses different types of vivid imagery to convey and evoke revulsion. Sin is frequently compared with infection, disease and physical pain. Fisher speaks of 'the grievous sickness which is sin', and says that 'It is the property of sin to infect any creature.' Confession is likened to the lancing of 'a filthy wound'.[23]

Fisher held strongly to the Pauline and Augustinian view that virginity is a higher state than either matrimony or widowhood, and that sexual desire, even if not itself a sin, is at least the occasion of it. When pursuing this theme he often compares sin and sinners with the attributes and habits of unattractive animals. Pigs in particular symbolise sensuality. In one sermon Fisher speaks of 'the filthy voluptuousness of the body, wherein the sinner waltereth and wrappeth himself as a sow walloweth in the stinking gore pit or in the puddle'. In another place he exclaims, 'What may better be understood by the uncleanness of hogs or swine than the filthy appetite of the flesh?' Similarly, the sinner luxuriating in his offences is like a horse wallowing in the mire.[24]

Dogs as well as pigs are used to arouse disgust for sin. In a passage of striking imagery Fisher describes the fatal burden of sin.

> Peradventure some sinner will say, 'I perceive not nor feel any weight in myself, do I never so many sins.' To whom we answer, that if a dog having a great stone bound about his neck be cast down from an high tower he feeleth no weight of that stone as long as he is falling down, but when he is once fallen to the ground he is brasten all to pieces by reason of that weight. So the sinner going down toward the pit of hell feeleth not the great burden of sin, but when he shall come into the deepness of hell he shall feel more pain than he would.[25]

Sinners are warned that any creature which is defiled with sin, however beautiful, 'is abominable in the sight of God, and far more abominable than is the stinking carrion of a dog or any other venomous worm in the sight of men', and are adjured never 'to fall and turn again to sin like a dog that turneth again to his vomit or a sow once waltred in the clay will return to that filthy place'.[26]

Fisher uses unsavoury images from everyday life as well as from nature to arouse revulsion for sin. Sin in the soul is like 'urine or stinking liquor put in a vessel, the longer it be kept in the same, so much more it maketh foul the vessel and corrupteth it'.[27] Confession and penance are not enough; the source of sin must be destroyed: 'For if it be so that the stinking filthy water continually flow out of a pond or pit into a goodly and delectable garden, if remedy be not found to stop the same, it shall make foul and corrupt that garden within a while, be it never so fair.'[28] In another garden image Fisher speaks of 'the weeds of carnality', and heresy is described in similar terms.

> These heresies be like the stinking weeds, the which in every earth spring by themself; for these evil weeds need no setting, no sowing, no watering, no weeding, nor such other diligence as the good herbs require, but spring anon withouten all that busyness:

and where they have entered once in any ground, it is very hard to deliver that ground from them: even so it is of these heresies. They need no planting, they need no watering, they need no looking nor weeding, but rankly spring by themself of a full light occasion.[29]

Sin is also likened to dust, and to cold: 'O hearts so sore congealed in the frosty cold of sin, that cannot warm nor delight in the remembrance of these most comfortable joys!'[30] In the sermon on the Passion he criticises women for caring more about outward neatness than inward cleanness.

Ye women, when there is any black spot in your faces, or any moole in your kerchiefs, or any mire upon your clothes, be you not ashamed? Yes forsooth, sir. But I shall tell you whereof you ought to be ashamed; surely, if your souls have any spots of deadly sin in them. For when our saviour so dearly with his most precious blood, and with all these grievous pains, did wash and wipe and cleanse our souls from every spot of deadly sin, ye should be much ashamed to defile them again. If you be ashamed for a foul, miry shoe, and not of a foul, stinking soul, ye make more dearer your shoes than your souls.[31]

If sin is disgusting, then even the innocent pleasures of this world are vastly inferior to the joys of heaven, and so they must not be overvalued. Fisher is far too dexterous a preacher to denigrate earthly delights altogether; rather, he depicts them in all their desirability in order to emphasise the higher, purer and more lasting joys of heaven.

Fisher's most sustained treatment of this theme occurs in his sermon preached on All Saints Day, 1520. Here he alludes to the recent spectacle of the Field of Cloth of Gold to show that the splendours of earthly pageantry, however rich and gorgeous, are far beneath the delights of the heavenly kingdom. The festivities of 1520, graced by kings and queens, had been wondrous and designed for pleasure: 'such dancings, such harmonies, such dalliance, and so many pleasant pastimes, so curious houses and buildings so preciously apparelled, such costly welfare of dinners, suppers and banquets, so delicate wines, so precious meats, such and so noble men of arms, so rich and goodly tents, such joustings, such tourneys, and such feats of war'.[32] Yet all these splendours were as nothing compared with the joys of heaven, as Fisher demonstrates by five points of comparison.

In the first place, earthly delights eventually become wearisome, inducing boredom and disgust, but the joys of heaven never grow stale. Secondly, worldly pleasure is always tempered by the fear of loss through poverty, sickness or death; but in heaven there is no envy, greed, fear of death or sickness but 'charity, concord, peace, tranquillity and perfect rest'.[33]

In addition, earthly pleasures are prone to interruption, as occurred at the Field of Cloth of Gold.

> Sometime there were such dust, and therewithal so great winds, that all the air was full of dust. The gowns of velvet and cloth of gold were full of dust; the rich trappers of horses were full of dust; the hair and faces of men were full of dust; and briefly to speak, horse and man were so encumbered with dust that scantly one might see another.... Sometime again we had rains and thunders so unmeasurably that no man might stir forth to see no pleasures.[34]

In comparison, heaven is free of such annoying disturbances: 'There is no night nor darkness, but a continual day, a continual temperance, a clear air without mists or clouds'.

Earthly joys are ephemeral while those of heaven are eternal, and finally the magnificence of man, consisting as it does of borrowed plumage, is merely counterfeit compared with the celestial glory. An emperor without his clothes is no better than a poor man; a fine lady without her gowns and jewels is no different from a humble woman: 'Kings and emperors, all be but men, all be but mortal. All the gold and all the precious stones of this world cannot make them but mortal men.... They be in themself but earth and ashes, and to earth they must return, and all their glory well considered and beholden with right eyen is but very miserable.' The opposite obtains in heaven, where the blessed are robed in immortal light and possessed of imperishable glory: 'O what marvellous joy shall it be to see that glorious sight of that court, where the least groom is clad so richly above all the kings and princes of this world!'[35] All in all, the splendid sights of earth are wearisome, ephemeral, subject to interruption, accompanied by fear and envy, and ultimately illusory; but the sights of heaven – the angels, saints, Virgin, and above all the Trinity – are unimaginably beautiful, dazzling and eternal.

In other sermons, too, Fisher pursues the theme of the transience of earthly joy and the end of all physical matter in decay. He speaks of 'The vain pleasures of this world and the false joys of the flesh ... like as a man in his dream many times thinketh to have great pleasures when no cause is so to be thought, then waking he perceiveth himself deceived by his dream.'[36] Even the splendour of kings does not endure, as Fisher shows in the sermon on Psalm 102. 'Where is now the innumerable company and puissance of Xerxes and Caesar? Where are the great victories of Alexander and Pompey? ... But what shall we say of them which some time were kings and governors of this realm? ... where be they now? Be they not gone, and wafted like unto smoke?'[37]

This threnody was an apt reminder of mutability for Fisher's chief listener, that veteran of the Wars of the Roses, Margaret Beaufort. It was echoed in his funeral oration for her son, which depicted Henry's virtues and achievements in order to stress their ephemeral nature.

His politic wisdom in governance it was singular, his wit always quick and ready, his reason pithy and substantial, his memory fresh and holding, his counsels fortunate and taken by wise deliberation ... His treasure and richesse incomparable, his buildings most goodly and after the newest cast of all pleasure. But what is all this now as unto him? All be but *fumus et umbra*, a smoke that soon vanisheth and a shadow soon passing.[38]

Margaret Beaufort would seem to have shared Fisher's awareness of the transience of glory and good fortune. In his memorial sermon for her Fisher mentioned this lack of complacency as a virtue to edify his audience.

She never yet was in that prosperity but the greater it was the more always she dreaded the adversity. For when the king her son was crowned in all that great triumph and glory she wept marvellously, and likewise at the great triumph of the marriage of Prince Arthur. And at the last coronation, wherein she had full great joy, she let not to say that some adversity would follow; so that either she was in sorrow by reason of the present adversities, or else when she was in prosperity she was in dread of the adversity to come.[39]

Bodily wellbeing, too, is ephemeral, and men would be foolish to trust in it.

How many be deprived from their beauty which some time were well favoured of face and well-proportioned in every part of their bodies? How many lie in streets or highways full of carbuncles and other innumerable botches? ... how many be crucified in manner by intolerable aches of bones and joints with many other infirmities? And how many, I pray you, be blind, deaf and dumb?[40]

Others suffered the ravages of the pox, still others had mental afflictions: 'We may see innumerable creatures that want reason, memory, and liberty of will, which three be parts of the image of God, wherewith the soul of man is made noble.' No trust should be put in youth and strength: 'We be daily taught by experience how feeble and frail man's body is; also beholding daily the goodly and strong bodies of young people, how soon they die by a short sickness.'[41]

Old age, on the other hand, is sordid and weak. Thus if Margaret Beaufort had lived longer her sufferings would only have increased: 'Her body daily would have waxen more unwieldy, her sight should have be darked, and her hearing should have dulled more and more, her legs should have failed her by and by, and all the other parts of her body wax more crazed every day.'[42] The transience of earthly things was at no time more poignant than on the deathbed. Thus Henry VII found his torment increased because his material joys were turned to sorrow.

All his goodly houses so richly decked and apparelled, his walls, and galleries of great pleasure, his gardens large and wide with knots curiously wrought, his orchards set with vines and trees most delicate, his marvellous richesse and treasure, his meats and drinks were they never so delicately prepared might not then help him, but rather were painful to him.[43]

For Fisher, then, mortal life was sweet and splendid, though prone to change and pain, and it was not to be compared with celestial bliss.

Like many preachers of his time Fisher harps on the torments of purgatory and hell in order to intimidate his flock into repentance and amendment of life. He is, however, more subtle than the average indulgence preacher. With Fisher there are no graphic descriptions of hideous devils and their fiendish instruments of torture. Rather, and more practically, he tries to stir the imagination of his audience by comparing earthly pains and terrors with those which the sinner shall suffer after death.

Be there not some grievous pains in this life? Those that be vexed with the stone, strangury and the flux, feel they not marvellous great pains, when they cannot keep themself from wailing and crying for sorrow? What shall I say of they which suffer pain in the head, toothache and aching of bones, do they not suffer great pains? . . . Notwithstanding, to be punished in the fire of purgatory is far more grievous pain than all these we have rehearsed.[44]

Purgatory is a debtors' prison, despair of God's mercy is a dungeon, hell is like a pit full of wild beasts.

In his sermon on the Passion Fisher makes an extended comparison of the sufferings of Christ on the cross with the torments of the sinner cast into hell. Christ was stripped, thrown on the cross and pierced with nails: 'this he suffered for thy sake, O sinful creature, and if thou wilt not amend thy life betimes thou shalt be spoiled of all thy clothes and so cast down into hell, upon a more painful couch than was the cross'. Christ hung on the cross for a time, but the unrepentant sinner shall hang on the gibbet of hell for all eternity. Christ endured heat, but the sinner shall burn everlastingly: 'If thou shouldst be compelled to lie but one sennight upon a soft featherbed, I suppose thou wouldst be weary thereof. But how weary shalt thou be, ever to lie stewing and burning without end?' Christ suffered cold on the cross, and so shall the sinner in hell: 'O Jesus, a tender hand wherein the frost and snow it hath been made extreme cold and suddenly is brought into the heat of the fire, it feeleth a great pain; but nothing comparable unto that shifting from that cold into that heat which is in hell.'

Christ endured the insults of the Jews, but far worse will be the taunts of the devils in hell. Christ wept on the cross, but far more bitter shall be the tears of the damned: 'such tears as shall scald their bodies, and yet they shall be never the better'. The thirst of the crucified Christ, his sorrow and heaviness, and the infamy and shame he suffered will be magnified horribly for the sinner in hell.[45]

Purgatory differs from hell in two vital respects. Firstly, though the pains are quite as bad they are temporary, unlike those of hell: 'O Jesu, in what misery shall they be in, that ever shall covet death and never may fully die!' Secondly the souls in purgatory, like Christ on the cross, lack the Father's presence for a time; but the true horror of hell lies in the fact that its denizens shall never see God.

The damned sinners which shall be punished for their own sins in hell shall ever be forsaken and fully be deprived, not only from all joy and comfort, but from that most glorious sight of the face of almighty God, wherein standeth all blessedness and comfort. And this shall more pinch the damned souls than all the other torments of hell besides.[46]

Thus Fisher, following Chrysostom, shows the appalling consequence of unrepented sin in the loss of the presence of God. Pain and suffering as the price of sin are emphasised in his sermons; but even stronger than the description of purgatory and hell is the stress on the love and mercy of God towards those who repent.

Against the horrid darkness of sin and hell Fisher sets the image of God's mercy as light, particularly sunlight. In the sermon on Psalm 38 there is an extended and quite beautiful metaphor of Christ as the sun of righteousness after the night which is sin, and of the Virgin as the morning which gave him birth. Thus, for example: 'The angel at her salutation said, *Ave plena gratia,* Hail full of grace. This blessed Virgin full of the beams of grace was ordained by God as a light of the morning, and afterward brought forth the bright shining sun with his manifold beams, our saviour Christ.'[47] Elsewhere, the grace of God is likened to the generative powers of the sun.

> From the eyen of almighty God, which may be called his grace, shineth forth a marvellous brightness like as the beam that cometh from the sun. And that light of grace stirreth and setteth forth the fruit of good works, even as the light of the sun causeth herbs to grow and trees to bring forth fruit.[48]

At the same time the light of God, like that of the sun, is fierce to those who are unprepared or too weak to face it.

> God is without mutability or change, he is alway one. For as we see the beam that cometh from the sun, alway one in itself, hurteth and grieveth the eye that is not clean and perfect, and comforteth the eye which is pure, without any change in his operation; so almighty God is called grievous unto a sinner infect with the malice of sin, and meek and gentle unto the righteous man that is purged from sin.[49]

God's mercy is irresistibly drawn to the penitent.

> Almighty God may not deny his own self, he cannot but have mercy on wretched sinners that trust in him. He may no more withdraw from them the beams of his grace, if their souls be made open by steadfast hope to receive it, than the sun may withstand his beams out of windows when they be open.[50]

Indeed, God is a master craftsman who would not willingly destroy the work of his hands, though the co-operation of the sinner is essential.

In his stress on the role of free will in repentance Fisher stands in stark contrast to Luther, who sees man as helpless to avoid sin and reliant on faith alone to save him. Yet Fisher is like Luther in his characterisation of God as a mighty fortress: 'Almighty God is a strong tower for our defence against all adversaries. . . . Whosoever may come within the circuit of this tower [by penitence], none enemies shall at any time have power to hurt him in body nor soul.' The Father is not a vengeful tyrant, but is always ready to temper justice with mercy: 'Almighty God withdraweth the rigour of his righteousness and is alway so ready to forgive that he coveteth more his mercy to be magnified than the power of his justice.' God's promise of forgiveness to the penitent is made repeatedly in scripture: 'O sweet words, more sweeter than honey or sugar! Blessed Lord, give me grace to make recognition and have it in experience. Thou never despised creature that asked mercy because thou art meek and merciful, ready to forgive them that be sorry for their offences.'[51]

The final and finest proof of God's loving forgiveness is the sacrifice of Calvary: in the sermon on the Passion the crucifixion is not only pain and suffering, but tenderness and generosity; not the appeasement of a tyrant, but the reconciliation of God with man through love.[52]

Fisher's sermons are original and effective compositions. Preachers were not always so scrupulous about making sermons of their own. In 1334 Richard de Bury had complained:

> O idle fishermen, using only the nets of others, which when torn it is all ye can do to repair clumsily, but can net no new ones of your own! Ye enter on the labours of others, ye repeat the lessons of others, ye mouth with theatrical effort the superficially-repeated wisdom of other men![53]

John Fisher's evangelical contemporary Thomas Becon denounced Catholic preachers for using 'False things, fables, lies, errors, saints' lives out of the Festival, examples out of the *Vitas Patrum*, authorities out of sermons *Dormi Secure*'.[54]

Fisher is guilty of none of these sins. As far as his style and eloquence are concerned, his preaching encompasses both medieval and renaissance practice and learning. In the medieval tradition he makes use of spiritual allegory, notably in the sermon for Margaret

Beaufort and in the 1526 sermon against Lutheranism. However, he also explains the literal sense of scripture. Certainly he never falls into the excesses of the preachers derided by Erasmus in the *Praise of Folly*, who use word-play and numerology as the tools of exegesis.[55]

Fisher took pains to ensure that his sermons, though erudite, would be understood by a lay audience. He quotes the Latin of his text and sources in short though complete phrases, and always supplies an English translation. In this he compares favourably with some medieval preachers, who dissected every word for hidden meaning, and with his contemporary John Longland, whose heavy chunks of Latin quotation must have been indigestible to the majority of his hearers.[56]

Fisher's use of sources is indisputably humanistic. His teaching is firmly based on scripture, though as a Catholic theologian he buttresses the truth of the bible with later Christian authorities inspired by the Holy Spirit. His text (apart from the commissioned series of sermons on the penitential psalms, and a digression in the 1526 sermon to discuss the parable of the sower) is usually from one of the liturgical readings for the day. The vast majority of his references comes from the new testament, and he is especially fond of Paul. Augustine is the Church father most frequently cited, and plainly Fisher followed his dictum that the aims of preaching were to instruct, to divert and to move.[57] Other patristic writers quoted by Fisher are Chrysostom, Origen, Jerome, Ignatius, Ambrose, Gregory, Cyprian and Eusebius.

Medieval saints and schoolmen appear only rarely in those of Fisher's sermons that survive. There is one quotation from Aquinas, one allusion to Francis of Assisi, four references to Bernard and one to St Christian. Petrarch is quoted once. Among the classical authors cited are Plato, Aristotle, Cicero, Ovid and Seneca. Fisher's preference for humanistic authorities appears most strikingly in his sermons against Lutheranism. Not only does he eschew the schoolmen as supporters for his argument, he also makes some use of Erasmus' Greek new testament rather than the vulgate, on the grounds that the Greek text was a more effective weapon against heresy.[58]

While Fisher makes use of the medieval devices of division and recapitulation, his sermons are singularly free from *exempla*, that is, fables, 'merry tales', or improbable lives of legendary saints. Those saints he does mention are either solidly historical or biblical. His favourites among the latter are Peter, Paul and Mary Magdalen, doubtless because they are examples of penitent and reconciled sinners. Nor are there irrelevant jokes to humour the audience. C.S. Lewis observes that Fisher is rarely scurrilous, though it must be said that occasionally he resorts to heavy sarcasm for effect. Thus, referring to a Catholic slander against Luther he remarks: 'within six weeks after the marriage his woman had a child. This was speedy work, a woman to have a child within six weeks after her marriage. This must either be a great miracle – or else they had met together before'.[59]

How effective a preacher was Fisher? A couple of passing references might be taken to show that he did not exactly captivate his audiences. During the funeral sermon for Henry VII some of the mourners went out 'to refresh themselves'; while Fisher himself said in the preface to his 1526 sermon that he had caused it to be printed, 'which for the great noise of the people within the church of Paul's, when it was said, might not be heard'.[60]

It must be said that both disruptive behaviour and sleeping during sermons was quite usual; so much so, that they are mentioned in almost every extant English medieval sermon collection.[61] A heretical member of Fisher's own diocesan flock, Richard Gavell of Westerham, made a point of leaving the church for the alehouses during sermon-time.[62] Perhaps Fisher's effectiveness and popularity as a preacher may be better gauged by the number of printed copies of his sermons which have survived, despite the royal condemnation of his works, and by the strong reactions of his enemies to his preaching.

As might be expected, the two royal funeral sermons have survived in some numbers, that for Henry VII in two editions and more than nine copies, that for Margaret Beaufort in ten copies of one edition. Fisher's two sermons against Lutheranism and for papal supremacy survived Henry VIII's displeasure, that of 1521 in four contemporary editions and 18 copies, that of 1526 in three editions and six copies. The 1521 sermon also exists in one edition of a Latin translation by Richard Pace.[63] The sermons on the penitential psalms had an enduring popularity; eight early editions survive, and more than 67 copies.

By contrast, the sermon on the Passion is extant in only one posthumous edition, while the *Two Fruitful Sermons* preached in 1520 only exist in four copies of the reprint of 1532. As the subject-matter would hardly be pleasing to Henry VIII it is tempting to view their reappearance in 1532 as an opposition publication. It is even possible that the text was altered for the new edition, though this cannot be known; besides an unflattering if implicit comparison of Henry with Herod, Katherine of Aragon is mentioned as 'the noble queen our mistress, the very exampler of virtue and nobleness to all women'.[64] These features probably also account for the rarity of the sermons. Only one manuscript fragment of a sermon survives, the conclusion of a sermon on a text of Psalm 128, 'And peace upon Israel'.[65]

The effectiveness of Fisher's oratory provoked his opponents to refute, denigrate and even attempt to suppress his sermons. William Tyndale felt obliged to answer the 1521 sermon against Luther at length and with savagery in his *Obedience of a Christian Man* of 1529. Tyndale called Fisher 'both abominable and shameless, yea, and stark mad with pure malice, and so adazed in the brains with spite that he cannot overcome the truth that he seeth not, or rather careth not what he saith'.[66]

The chronicler Edward Hall, though somewhat more moderate in his language than Tyndale, also imputed sycophancy to Fisher, though with reference to the sermon of 1526: 'he spoke so much in honour of the pope and his cardinals, and of their dignity and pre-eminence, that he forgot to speak any thing of the gospel, which he took in hand to declare, which sermon was much praised by the cardinal [Wolsey] and the bishops'.[67] Hall's oustanding loyalty to Henry VIII is well known; even a cursory glance at the sermon in question reveals the falsity of his accusation.

After Fisher's death the king found it necessary to take action against his works. A royal proclamation of December 1535 ordered the surrender of a number of books, among them Fisher's sermon of 1521; its defence of orthodoxy and papal authority was interpreted retrospectively as an attack on the royal supremacy of the Defender of the Faith. The court of London aldermen resolved that

> the proclamation last made concerning a sermon made by John Fisher late bishop of Rochester, in derogation and diminution of the royal estate of the king's majesty, shall be put in print so that every parish may have one of them to be openly published by the curate in the pulpit upon Sunday next, and the same after to be fixed to tables, and set upon their several churches at the costs of the churchwardens of their several parishes.[68]

The authorities were vigilant in tracing and calling in copies of Fisher's work. Sir Thomas Elyot, still convalescent after an illness, wrote to excuse himself to Cromwell.

> As for the works of John Fisher, I never had any of them to my knowledge, except one little sermon, which about eight or nine years past was translated into Latin by Master Pace. And for that cause I bought it, more than for the author or matter. And where it is, I am not sure. For in good faith, I never read it but once since I bought it.[69]

Even after his death, Fisher's sermons were judged to be dangerous to King Henry and his subjects.

As a preacher Fisher is uncompromisingly stern in his condemnation of heretics and obdurate sinners. Yet he shows compassion to all repentant offenders, living and dead. The people of God are bound to perform the corporate works of mercy, and to relieve the suffering souls in purgatory by active prayer. In the royal funeral sermons time is allotted for prayers for Henry VII and Margaret, and the sermon on Psalm 130 – *De Profundis*, the traditional prayer for the dead – has a pause during which the entire psalm is recited for those in purgatory.

The Christian should show pity and mercy to his neighbour; he must also repent of his own sins. For John Fisher the preaching ministry was an essential instrument to bring sinners to penitence. True repentance, generated by the Holy Spirit, must come from within. In a strongly autobiographical passage in his devotional work *A Spiritual Consolation* Fisher warned that 'Neither building of colleges, nor making of sermons, nor giving of alms, neither yet any manner of business shall help you without this.'[70] As Fisher declared in his sermon of 1526: 'Now to us the laws of [our] saviour Christ be made easy by the abundance of grace, and by the dulceness of love, which the Holy Ghost hath put in our hearts'. Repentance and obedience to God and his Church would bring the highest reward: 'And doubt not, but this way shall finally bring you unto the glorious country of heaven, where ye shall have the presence of almighty God, with endless joy and bliss: to which he bring us all'.[71]

5 Heresy

> For heresy is a perilous weed; it is the seed of the devil; the
> inspiration of the wicked spirits; the corruption of our hearts;
> the blinding of our sight; the quenching of our faith; the destruction
> of all good fruit; and finally the murder of our souls.[1]

In such forceful and eloquent language did John Fisher express his
revulsion for heresy. The early sixteenth century was not an age of
toleration, and deviation from the teachings of the Church was
viewed with as much fear and repugnance as was infectious physical
disease. Though a man of many duties, Fisher devoted much time
and energy to preaching against heresy in England, writing Latin
polemical works for a learned European audience, and attempting
to root out heresy from his diocese of Rochester and his university
of Cambridge.

Fisher was among the first of the humanists to identify the doctrinal challenge to Christendom posed by the German reformation.
He perceived that Luther was not simply a critic of abuses such as
the sale of indulgences, but a rebel theologian whose doctrines
threatened the authority and unity of the Church. He was also, to
Fisher, an assassin and the bishop mourned 'the souls that by his
false doctrine he slayeth and murdereth'.[2]

Soul-murder is the very worst effect of heresy, but heresy can
also lead to civil disorder, war and physical death. In 1526 Fisher
excoriated Luther for bringing conflict to Germany, 'to the subversion of that country ... and such a murder of men as in our days
hath not been heard of. ... Doubtless it is the hand and stroke of
God upon them, for the favouring and supporting of his most
mischievous doctrines. ... This is the fruit which is sprung of this
most wicked seed'.[3]

In 1529 Fisher feared that the anticlerical legislation of the reformation parliament would lead to both spiritual death and political upheaval and destruction. Accordingly he made a provocative
and controversial speech in the house of lords: 'you see daily what
bills come hither from the common house, and all is to the destruction of the Church. For God's sake see what a realm the kingdom of Bohemia was; and when the Church went down, then fell
the glory of the kingdom. Now with the commons is nothing but

'Down with the Church!'; and all this me seemeth is for lack of faith only'.[4]

Christian pastors would be called to account if they did not fight heresy vigorously. Fisher wrote in emotional terms about this terrible responsibility.

> My duty is to endeavour me after my poor power to resist these heretics, which cease not to subvert the Church of Christ. If we shall sit still and let them in every place sow their ungracious heresies, and everywhere destroy the souls which were so dearly bought with that most precious blood of our saviour Christ Jesu, how terribly shall he lay this until our charge, when we shall be called until a reckoning for this matter![5]

He advocated compulsion, by the authority and discipline of the Church, to reduce heretics to conformity.

> The heretics contend that it shall not be lawful thus to do; but they would have every man left unto their liberty. But doubtless it may not be so; for the nature of man is more prone to all naughtiness rather than to any goodness. . . . If every man should have liberty to say what he would, we should have a marvellous world. No man should stir anywhere for heresies.[6]

At the same time the heretic's abjuration must be sincere and wholehearted: 'He may be compelled to come bodily; but if he come not also with the feet of his soul and be fully assent unto the Church, he cannot have this true faith.'[7] In writing against Luther, Fisher justified the use of the harshest penalties against heretics. It would be preferable, he said, to remove those wolves whose doctrine poisons the flock without exterminating them. But the experience of 15 centuries has shown that this is not possible; they must be surrendered to the secular arm like the worst malefactors because they threaten the spiritual life of all Christians. If public order demands the punishment of thieves who take money, the public good demands that heretics, killers of souls, be sent to the stake.[8]

Given the strength of Fisher's feeling against heresy and his sense of duty in repressing it, the fact that no heretic was burned in Rochester diocese during his episcopate seems extraordinary. Indeed, the ten cases of heresy brought before him all resulted in abjuration. This paradox may be explained by Fisher's desire to save heretics from themselves. The prefatory epistle to the printed version of his 1526 sermon is most revealing in this respect. Clearly thinking of Christ's discussions with Nicodemus, he makes a surprising offer. If any disciple of Luther should wish

> to come unto me secretly, and break his mind at more length, I bind me by these presents both to keep his secrecy, and also to spare a leisure for him to hear the bottom of his mind, and he shall hear mine again, if it so please him: and I trust in Our Lord, that finally we shall so agree, that either he shall make me a Lutheran, or else I induce him to be a Catholic, and to follow the doctrine of Christ's Church.[9]

It is noteworthy that Fisher postponed publication of his first great polemical work against Luther for two years because of a rumour that Luther would recant his errors.[10]

Fisher's pity for the souls of heretics did not prevent Protestant writers from charging him with gratuitous and sadistic cruelty to their bodies. John Foxe accuses him of causing the deaths of John Frith, John Tewkesbury and James Bayfield; but they were within the jurisdiction of the Bishop of London, and Fisher was not among the assessors at their examinations.[11] (Indeed, Foxe seems not to have noticed that Cranmer was among Frith's 'tormentors' at his trial.) Fisher certainly knew about the notorious Tewkesbury, and had the sentence against him copied into his episcopal register; but he had nothing to do with the case.

Foxe also charges Fisher and Archbishop Warham with first torturing and then killing John Browne and the more famous Thomas Hitton. Fisher was certainly involved in the two cases; though Hitton and Browne came under the jurisdiction of Canterbury, their offences had been committed in Rochester diocese and it was natural that he should be involved.

John Browne got into trouble in 1517 as the result of an altercation with a 'soul-priest' or chantry priest at Gravesend. The two were sharing a barge; the priest objected to Browne's sitting on his clothes; Browne made some heavyhanded jokes about the soul for whom the priest sang mass; the priest called him a heretic, and swore to be even with him. The upshot was that Browne was arrested some days later, taken to Canterbury, examined, and sentenced to be burned at Ashford, where he lived.

> his wife then hearing of him, came and sat by him all the night before he should be burned: ... and told, how he could not set his feet to the ground, for they were burned to the bones; and

told her, how by the two bishops, Warham and Fisher, his feet were heated upon the hot coals and burned to the bones.[12]

Without wishing to whitewash either Fisher or Warham, a number of points must be made here. In the first place, Browne was a relapsed heretic, having 'borne a faggot' in the reign of Henry VII. Such people were deemed irredeemable, and so were automatically liable for the death penalty. Thus there would have been no point in torturing him so as to convert him. Secondly, Foxe's informant was Browne's daughter Alice. The Brownes seem to have become something of a heretical dynasty; Alice's brother Richard had been condemned to the stake in the reign of Mary and had only been saved by the death of that queen. It is possible, then, that filial piety combined with the wish to establish the family's Protestant credentials caused Alice to embellish her father's sufferings. (Certainly, there is something rather pat about Foxe's statement that an official at Browne's burning 'bade cast in Browne's children also, for they would spring, said he, of his ashes'.) Finally, the episode endows Fisher with a sadism which appears nowhere else in his career except, it is alleged, in the controversial case of Thomas Hitton.

The evidence about Hitton's case furnished by Tyndale, More and Foxe is inconsistent and at times misleading. In his *Practice of Prelates* Tyndale says that Hitton was 'dieted and tormented' by Warham and Fisher who then secretly murdered him, though in other works he states correctly that Hitton was burned at Maidstone. More says that Hitton was arrested at Gravesend, and only condemned 'after much favour showed him, and much labour charitably taken for the saving of him'. Foxe's story is that Hitton was arrested on his way to Rochester. During his examination by Fisher, Warham and others he was assailed by 'both threats and fair promises'. Fisher and Warham, 'after they had long kept him in prison, and tormented him with sundry torments', had him burned.[13]

What is certain is that Hitton was a somewhat eclectic sacramentary, having espoused both Lutheran and Zwinglian tenets. He was also involved in the illicit book trade. Thus if captured, and obdurate after examination, he would be subject to the full rigour of the law. Again, the use of torture seems redundant.

Fisher was vigilant against heresy in his diocese from the very start of his episcopate; the first offender to abjure before him did so on 17 May 1505.[14] He only had to deal with three heretical cases before 1521, and it is noteworthy that Rochester diocese was not involved in the great episcopal campaign against heresy of 1511. As this can hardly be attributed to laxity or tolerance on Fisher's part, it must be assumed that there were no real problems there.

Something must be said of Fisher's view of the Church, and of what, for him, constituted orthodox theology.[15] The central problem of the reformation was that of authority; how did Christians know what to believe, how were they saved, and how should they live and worship? Fisher's ecclesiology rested upon the two promises of Christ recorded in scripture: that he himself would remain with the Church for ever (Matthew 28:20); and that he would send the comforter, or Holy Spirit (John 15:26).

Thus the Church could never be in serious error; otherwise Christ would have lied, and the Spirit would have deceived the Christian people. Therefore, while scripture was the chief and most important source of the revelation of God's truth to man, it must be interpreted and supplemented by Christian tradition; that is, the teachings of holy fathers and doctors throughout the Christian era, and the decrees of popes and councils. True, individual theologians, popes or councils might fall into error, because they were only human; but over all, the Spirit would not permit the Church to languish in error.

Fisher's view of the presence of Christ and the Spirit within the Church is neatly summarised in his defence of the priesthood against Luther.

> For if so long the truth had remained imprisoned in darkness, waiting during so many centuries for Luther, and him only, to set it free, then Christ's solicitude for our fathers in the faith, was in vain; in vain, too, the coming of the Holy Ghost to teach them all truth; in vain their prayers and devout search for the truth, if all along they were unanimously teaching to the churches so dangerous a lie.[16]

Besides scripture and other written sources the Church was to be guided by the 'unwritten verities' or apostolic tradition. The new testament itself states in several places that not all the acts and sayings of Christ had been written down; therefore oral tradition, analogous to the Hebrew cabbala, would also inform the Church.

For Fisher, papal supremacy over the Church was proved by Christ's injunctions to Peter, the fact that Peter was the undisputed chief of the apostles, and that the lineage of popes, descending directly from Peter, had continued, while churches founded by the other apostles had died out. In addition, the Church was distinguished by four 'notes' or characteristics as declared in the creed; she was one, holy, catholic and apostolic. Obedience to the papacy was only right in view of its apostolic continuity from Peter, and it was a guarantee of that Christian unity and universality which distinguished the true Church from spurious ones. Therefore schism was on a par with heresy as a crime, and the one would lead inevitably to the other. Salvation – eternal life – was only to be found within the Church Catholic.

Thus Fisher would accept and defend doctrine and devotional practice as it had evolved since the time of the apostles. It was only natural that he should consider Luther and other exponents of bible-based religion to be arrogant in flying in the face of the Christian consensus and interpreting scripture for themselves. Fisher thus reproached Luther himself for intellectual and spiritual presumption.

> we know that the Holy Spirit resides ever in the Church. Are we then, because you propose some novelties, to set aside the consent of ages and fly to you, as if some new spirit had descended on you? And even if the doctrine of the fathers had to be proved from scripture, does that entitle you to pass sentence on them, you who twist scripture as you like, and bend it like a nose of wax?[17]

Similarly he rebuked Oecolampadius for thinking that he alone knew the true nature and meaning of the Eucharist. The fathers Chrysostom, Basil, Cyril, Cyprian, Jerome, Ambrose and Augustine had all laboured long in study; were Christians to think that the Holy Spirit had hidden the truth about the sacrament from them so that Oecolampadius might have the glory of discovering it?[18]

A sort of prelude to Fisher's polemical engagement with heterodoxy is formed by his controversy with another humanist, Jacques Lefèvre d'Etaples. Though not concerned with heresy, this prolonged argument does show Fisher's preoccupation with authority for Christian belief and the sin of giving scandal to little ones, the unlearned people.

The controversy formed part of a wider discussion about the identity of Mary Magdalen which was unwittingly generated by Louise of Savoy. Inspired by a pilgrimage to the Magdalen's shrine near Marseilles, Louise asked for a new life of the saint from the humanist François du Moulin. Somewhat perplexed, he consulted his colleague Lefèvre. After examining the scriptures and the Greek fathers Lefèvre concluded that the bible spoke of, not one, but three Magdalens: the penitent sinner who anointed Christ's feet; the woman out of whom Christ cast seven devils; and the contemplative sister of Martha and Lazarus. He published his findings in late 1517 or early 1518, and thereby instituted a controversy which involved both humanists and schoolmen.

Initially Lefèvre was answered by Marc de Grandval, whose reply drew from him a second, enlarged edition of his work which also discussed and dismissed the legend that St Anne had three husbands. Fisher published a reply to this in Paris in February 1519. The next step was a defence of Lefèvre's work by Josse Clichthove which was refuted by both Grandval and Fisher. Lefèvre then published a new work on the Magdalen provoked by Fisher's criticisms. Fisher replied in a third work, and the controversy was concluded by a treatise against Lefèvre by the notorious anti-humanist Noël Beda.[19]

The details of the discussion need not be of concern here; but how did Fisher come to be drawn into it? Certainly the identity of Mary Magdalen has nothing to do with the Church's teaching on salvation. Fisher himself said that an initial reading of Lefèvre's work had not worried him; he had found it distasteful, but not dangerous. However, he was induced to enter the controversy by Etienne Poncher, archbishop of Paris, who was on embassy to England late in 1518.

It was pastoral concern which made Fisher take up his pen. Not only did Lefèvre impugn the judgement of the Latin fathers and misinterpret the Greeks to suit his own fancy; not only did he give the lie to many authors and preachers; the division of the Magdalen into three figures severely undercut her value as an eminent example of a repentant sinner. Therefore Fisher undertook to refute Lefèvre for the sake of the faithful, for preachers and modern authors, and for the Church herself.[20]

That Fisher continued to be devoted to the 'one' Magdalen is shown by his dealings with Elizabeth Barton, the 'Nun of Kent', in the early 1530s. Elizabeth claimed to have spoken with the Magdalen, who had written a hortatory letter to a London widow in her own and Elizabeth's name and had herself delivered it disguised as Elizabeth's maid. Fisher sent one of his chaplains to question the Nun as to whether there were three Maries or just one, and Whatmore in the *English Historical Review* concludes that her reply made Fisher give credence to Elizabeth's revelations.[21]

The significance of the Magdalen controversy in relation to Fisher's polemical work against the reformers is threefold. Firstly, it shows his reliance on tradition, written and unwritten, for the interpretation of the bible. Secondly, his methods in arguing from scripture and the fathers and in answering his opponents point by point first appear in his work on the Magdalen. Finally, this first controversy shows well the pastoral concern with the avoidance of giving scandal to little ones which was to animate Fisher's work against heresy.

Fisher's activity as a polemical theologian and preacher formed part of the English humanist campaign against Luther and other reformers which was spearheaded by the king himself. While Henry composed his book in defence of the seven sacraments Fisher wrote a number of important works against Luther, Velenus and Oecolampadius. He also preached two significant public sermons which are useful points of entry to his polemical thought and tactics.

The first of these was preached on 12 May 1521, at a solemn ceremony in St Paul's churchyard when the papal sentence against Luther was read out and the reformer's works burned. The ceremony took place in the presence of Wolsey, Henry VIII being unable to attend due to a bad cold. The second sermon was preached on Quinquagesima Sunday 1526, this time in St Paul's cathedral because of rain. The occasion was the abjuration of Robert Barnes and some German merchants of the Steelyard (the area near London Bridge granted to the Hanse by Henry III) who had been caught in possession of Lutheran books. The two sermons were important in that they underlined publicly the Henrician regime's rejection of Lutheranism. They are also significant for their clear understanding of Luther's doctrine and exposition of Fisher's own attitudes. The sermons come at the beginning and almost at the end of Fisher's polemical career; they show an overall consistency in his opinions and arguments as well as his response to new developments in the reformation. They are particularly useful as guides to Fisher's theology in that they attempt to explain doctrine and refute error in terms that the laity could understand.

The text for the 1521 sermon is the gospel of the day, John 15:26. This is most apposite, concerning as it does the relation of Christ and the Holy Spirit to the Church: 'When the comforter is come, he shall bear witness of me.' The sermon opens with the dramatic image of heresy as a thunderstorm.

Full often when the day is clear and the sun shineth bright, riseth in some quarter of the heaven a thick black cloud, that darketh all the face of the heaven and shadoweth from us the clear light of the sun; and stirreth an hideous tempest, and maketh a great lightning, and thundereth terribly; so that the weak souls and feeble hearts be put in a great fear, and made almost desperate for lack of comfort. In like manner it is in the Church of Christ, when the light of faith that shineth from the spiritual sun, almighty God, hath been clear and bright a good season, hath risen many a time some black cloud of heresy.[22]

Fisher rehearses the infamous line of heretics from Arius to Wyclif which now has a new scion, 'one Martin Luther, a friar'. Fisher goes straight to the crux of the matter by denouncing Luther's erroneous reading of scripture; erroneous because he is not inspired by the Holy Spirit. Luther

hath stirred a mighty storm and tempest in the Church, and hath shadowed the clear light of many scriptures of God. And he maketh issue from him a perilous lightning, that is to say a false light of wrong understanding of scriptures, which passeth not from the Spirit of truth but from the spirit of error, and from the spirit of this tempest, of this most perilous heresy.

Such heresies were foreseen by Christ, who promised to send the Holy Spirit to safeguard the Church from error. Fisher's premise, then, is that Luther is wrong because he lacks the guidance of the Holy Spirit, and after a pause for prayer to that same Spirit he launches into the attack.

The sermon is divided into four 'instructions' to refute Luther. The first concerns the issue of papal authority, which Luther denied. But, says Fisher, as Luther himself admits in his *Babylonian Captivity*, Christ's promise to send the Spirit was made to the Church universal. Fisher demonstrates that the pope is the head of that Church as Peter's successor by an extended comparison of Moses and Aaron with Christ and Peter. He draws on both Greek and Latin fathers to show the common conviction that Peter was the chief of the apostles, and is contemptuous of Luther's arrogance in face of this patristic consensus: 'If all these so many testimonies both of Greeks and Latins shall not counterpoise against one friar, what reason is?' Luther lacks spiritual truth because he has divided himself from the head of the universal Church, 'with such pride, arrogancy and presumption, which is most odious unto this Holy Spirit'.[23]

The second instruction attacks Luther's doctrine of justification by faith alone, showing from scripture that hope and charity are also necessary in the process of salvation. Most percipiently (indeed, more percipiently than most), Fisher sees that Luther's doctrine subverts the sacramental system; if faith alone justifies, then the sacraments are superfluous. Fisher chooses to fight Luther on his own ground of the new testament, basing his argument not only on the epistle of James, which Luther was to reject as uncanonical, but also on Paul and other apostolic writers.

Fisher cites Paul in the famous passage from I Corinthians 13 to support his argument that hope and charity are necessary for salvation as well as faith. Equally, the epistle of James states plainly that faith without works is dead, and that though the devils tremble and believe they are still damned. Fisher goes to Augustine to reconcile the apparently contradictory statements in James and Romans, which Luther uses to say that faith alone justifies. As Augustine explains, Paul meant that we are initially justified by faith, and that works done before we believe cannot help us; while James refers to works which follow faith.[24] Neither James nor Peter in his second epistle contradict Paul; rather, they explain his doctrines which had been misunderstood by some readers and hearers 'as now doth Martin Luther to his own peril and damnation'. Finally, Fisher cites Luke and Matthew as well as Paul and James to show the necessity of works.

The third instruction demonstrates that God has always been with his people. The Father taught the Jews, the Son taught the Apostles, and the Spirit teaches the Church. Much of this divine teaching was not written down. The old testament prophets, 'whose prophecies albeit they be written in scripture, yet was there many more things which they spoke unwritten that was of as great authority, as that that was written which the master of Jews calleth cabbala, which is derived from man to man by mouth only and not by writing'. Equally, Paul adjured the Thessalonians to be 'constant, and keep those instructions and eruditions that ye have learned of us, other by mouth or else by writing'. Origen and other fathers are also cited to show the existence and authority of 'unwritten verities'.[25]

Fisher asserts that the Spirit speaks through fathers and doctors of the Church, especially when they are gathered together in council. He is sarcastic about Luther's response to this: 'Here Martin

Luther for his shrewd brain will some thing wrestle against us. He will say that the councils sometime err, and that the doctors full often disagree.'[26] This, Fisher more than implies, is mere folly. God permitted prophets, fathers, doctors and councils to err so that we could see they were men, not divine beings. In any case, Luther is in no position to judge, as he is bound to err because he lacks the Spirit of truth.

> For he cutteth away the traditions of the apostles, and refuseth the general councils, and contemneth the doctrine of the holy fathers and doctors of the Church, and laboureth to subvert all the ordinance of the Church, and namely the seven sacraments, and taketh away the freedom of man's will, and affirmeth that all thing faileth by necessity, contrary to all the doctrine of Christ's Church.[27]

This is probably one of the most concise and comprehensive catalogues of Luther's teaching at so early a date.

The final instruction is a response to the defence of Luther by his followers. In style it is both rhetorically sarcastic and sincerely angry. Most striking is Fisher's use of the concept of persecution, which he turns against the heretics themselves. Christ prophesied that his people would be persecuted. Some have thought the persecutors were the Jewish and Roman tyrants; but if this were so, Christ's warning would not apply to the universal Church, since these persecutions were long ago and of short duration. The persecutors meant by Christ, then, were the heretics who 'hath persecuted the Church from the ascension of Christ, and shall do unto the coming of antichrist'. They are much worse than the Jewish and pagan tormentors because 'these heretics pretend a special favour unto Christ, and colour all their heresies with his scriptures'. Finally comes the most devastating effect of the heretical persecution of the Church.

> The Jews and the tyrants when they had slain the bodies of Christian men, yet they sent their souls to everlasting glory. But the heretics, misconstruing the scriptures of God by their false doctrine and erroneous opinions, and pestilent heresies, doth slay the souls of Christian people, and send them to their everlasting damnation.[28]

The sermon of 1521 is both an ordered refutation of Luther's doctrine and a passionate denunciation of him as a killer of souls.

The sermon of 1526, while quite as virulent in its hatred of heresy, is slightly different in focus. The men who stood before Fisher in St Paul's were abjured heretics. While he may have doubted the sincerity of their recantation, he exerted himself to stir them to true repentance.

John Foxe gives a full if prejudiced account of the ceremony which reveals not only the importance attached to it by Wolsey and the hierarchy as an anti-Lutheran statement but also its essentially penitential character.[29] The cathedral was 'so full no man could get in'. A platform had been erected on the stairs to accommodate Wolsey, 36 lesser prelates, his chaplains and his theological advisers. To give splendour to the occasion these last wore gowns of damask and satin while Wolsey was robed in purple, the liturgical colour of penitence, 'even like a bloody antichrist'. A new pulpit had been placed at the top of the stairs, and great baskets of Lutheran books stood ready for the bonfire. After the sermon and the cardinal's departure the heretics were marched round the bonfire.

> And so were they brought to the bishops, and there, for absolution, kneeled down; where Rochester stood up and declared unto the people how many days of pardon and forgiveness of sins they had for being at that sermon; and there did he assoil Dr Barnes with the others, and showed the people that they were received into the Church again.

Once more the gospel of the day furnished Fisher with his text: 'Open thine eyes, thy faith hath made thee safe' (Luke 18:35–43). These are the words spoken to the blind man who asked Christ to heal him. The story was most apt for a recantation sermon, and Fisher does not lose the chance to identify the abjured men with the blind man of the gospel.

Firstly, as the man was 'singular and by himself', so the heretics had been singular in their opinion: 'Singularity and pride is the ground of all heresy'. Secondly, the man was physically blind, while the heretics 'be blinded in their hearts, and have not the clear light of faith'. Thirdly, the man sat off the path, 'so likewise these heretics sit out of the right way, and walk not in the journey toward heaven'. Finally, 'this man was divided from this people, among whom Christ Jesu was, and so be the heretics likewise: they be divided from the Church of Christ, with whom our saviour Christ continueth unto the world's end.'[30]

As with the earlier sermon, Fisher stresses that faith without love is insufficient for salvation. Expounding I Corinthians 13 he comments: 'Wherefore if a man have all manner of faith and wanteth charity, he is never the more justified ... who that hath charity hath also good works.' As Paul teaches in Galatians, true faith is 'faith which worketh by love, and that is by love pregnant with good works'. Naturally it was the Holy Spirit who inculcated charity: 'now to us the laws of our saviour Christ be made easy by the abundance of grace and by the dulceness of love, which the Holy Ghost hath put in our hearts'.[31]

The blind man is the recurring motif of the sermon, but the bulk of it is concerned with the parable of the sower (Luke 8:5–15). From this text Fisher took four 'collections' to consider; the sower, the seed, the good earth and the increase of fruit.

The sower, of course, is Christ himself, who ever remains with his Church together with the Holy Spirit. Not to believe Christ's promise that he and the Spirit would abide with the Church is to call him a liar.

> Who is so devilish, that may think that our saviour Christ, the which so dearly loved his Church, that for the weal of it would suffer so bitter, so villainous, so horrible a death, and shed his most precious blood in the cross, to prepare the hearts of his people for the receiving of this seed: I say who may think that ever he that did so much for us, would break his promise unto us?[32]

In Fisher's view this is precisely what Luther has done, and his fury breaks out in strong language.

> O cursed Luther! O mischievous apostata! O most execrable heretic, that denyest and despisest all the fathers that ever were before us ... and that our saviour Christ Jesu nothing regarded his promise all this long time, either as concerning his own presence to be continually with the Church, or as concerning the presence of his Holy Spirit.[33]

The second collection concerns the seed which is the word of God, whole and complete. The true gospel, unlike Luther's false doctrine, forms a unity: and the teaching of the Church is so much in harmony with it as to be one with it.

> It is like ... a song, where be many singers that diversely descant upon the plainsong: but for as much as they all agree without any jarring, without any mistuning, they make but one song and

one harmony. In like manner it is of the scriptures of God and of the doctrine of the Church: there be many singers, and some sing the plainsong and some sing the descant.[34]

The apostles and evangelists sing the plainsong, while later doctors of the Church sing the descant, and all is a melodious whole with no disagreement on any point of faith. For Luther such consistency is impossible, as he even disagrees with himself.

Fisher exploits the differences of opinion among reformers, and does so with biting sarcasm.

> this is a very truth that I say unto you: twain of them, that is to say Luther and Oecolampadius, fully disagree and make plain contradictory expositions of these same words. And the third, which is called Carlstadius, holdeth clean contrary to them both! Here be worthy masters for a good Christian man to put his soul in their hands, that so repugnantly vary in expounding the scriptures.[35]

The third collection concerns the good earth of the parable, which is the Catholic Church descended directly from Peter. Christ told his disciples in Matthew's gospel, 'this generation shall not pass unto than all these things that I have spoken of shall be performed'. Christ cannot have meant the generation to whom he was speaking, for they were long since dead; therefore he must have meant his Church. Fisher follows Augustine in arguing for the Petrine supremacy. Augustine perceived the uninterrupted succession of popes, while the churches founded by apostles other than Peter had died out. The Roman Church, surrounded by heresies, had alone kept herself pristine and earned the name of Catholic. Luther, then, is guilty of schism: 'We came not out of him and of his sect, but all they came out of us, and so have divided themself from us.'

In the fourth collection concerning the increase of good fruit, Fisher gives full vent to his fury and disgust at Luther's teachings and doings. He follows the traditional interpretation of the parable. The crop of thirtyfold represents virtuous matrimony; the sixtyfold crop means chaste widowhood; and the increase of a hundredfold represents virginity. Thus Fisher is unremarkably in the Pauline tradition, seeing sexual activity as inherently unclean and virginity as the most proper state for a Christian.

Evidently the Lutherans cannot bring forth fruit a hundredfold, since they despise virginity. Worse still, they break their vows of chastity and live carnally, and thus it is unlikely that they will respect chaste widowhood. As for marriage, which as a sacrament takes away the sin of the carnal act, the Lutherans cannot benefit from it. Luther's own marriage to a nun is adulterous and sacrilegious. Moreover, he has said that marriage is no sacrament: 'A very madman, he to marry and yet to affirm that this sacrament hath no virtue in it.' In Fisher's eyes the Lutherans cannot even attain to the fruit of thirtyfold, and he urges the abjured men to turn from so scabrous and blasphemous a sect.

Fisher's two sermons against Lutheranism were published in English; possibly it was hoped that they would be useful as summaries of orthodox teaching for the laity, or even as model sermons for the parish clergy.[36] Fisher himself in the preface to the second sermon addressed the reader thus: 'My dear brother or sister in our saviour Christ Jesu, whosoever ye be that shall fortune to read this quire, Our Lord for his great mercy grant you his grace, that the reading thereof somewhat may profit your soul.' As has been mentioned, he added that he had been persuaded to print the sermon 'by the motion of divers persons', since the great noise in the cathedral when he preached meant that many of the people could not hear it.[37]

The sermon of 1521 was also translated into Latin for the benefit of a wider, European audience; Fisher's belief in the unity and universality of the Church thus extended his pastoral care beyond England. The translator was the king's secretary, the humanist Richard Pace. The Latin version was made after the sermon was preached but before the English text was published, and a letter from Richard Sharpe to Nicholas Metcalfe shows that there were some difficulties. Sharpe said that Fisher wanted Metcalfe 'to send his sermon as shortly as can be that Master Secretary hath. My lord is very sorry that the last part of his sermon is lost; it will cost him some labour, for I think he have not the copy'. Fisher's feelings on the subject may easily be imagined. Sharpe added: 'My lord taketh great labour against Luther, I think verily that his work shall pass all other men's. Our Lord send him strength and health, and I doubt not but he shall do that thing that shall be both profitable to the faith of Christ and also for his honour and fame'.[38]

The matter of the sermon ended well, and the translation was quickly finished. It was printed in Cambridge by Siberch in 1522, but on 1 June 1521 Pace sent a copy to the pope with a covering letter which praised Fisher, who was not more learned (though his learning was singular) than he was holy and virtuous in life. Fisher had one special quality, Pace said; as much as he fled from glory, so much did glory pursue him.[39]

The pope sent a letter of thanks to Fisher, as appears from a summary of a letter Fisher wrote to Pace which is contained in a letter to Metcalfe from his official. 'First there is thanks for his last letters, then he signifies to him the pope's great thanks for the sermon: which thanks my lord reckoneth Master Secretary most worthy of all, because he hath taken such pains in turning it into Latin.' At the same time Fisher was sending Metcalfe the English text of his sermon, 'which he prayeth you to put to Wynkyn [de Worde] to print; and he prayeth you to speak to John Gough, to see it diligently done and truly printed'.[40]

Fisher distinguished himself in the reformation debate by composing a series of weighty and significant polemical works against Luther and other reformers; these were written in Latin and published abroad, for the edification of the Church universal. His first polemical work was the *Confutation of Luther's Defence*, written in 1521 and published at Antwerp in 1523. This was an answer to Luther's *Defence of all the Articles*, which justified the 41 'errors' condemned in the papal bull. A massive tome, it was in Rex's words 'the nearest thing to a complete critique of Luther's doctrine then available'.[41]

In a few months in 1522 Fisher dealt briefly and decisively with Ulrich Velenus' argument that papal supremacy was invalid because Peter was never in Rome. Drawing on scripture and tradition, and turning Velenus' argument from silence against its author, he asserted that it was more likely that Peter had died in Rome than in Jerusalem, and employed a battery of ancient and modern authorities to demolish his opponent. So effective was this riposte that Rex postulates that Fisher's work was the reason why Velenus' line of argument was not taken up by other reformers.[42]

Fisher returned to the attack on Luther in 1523, answering the reformer's reply to Henry VIII's defence of the seven sacraments; in particular, he defended the sacrifice of the mass. This work was published in 1525, as was his defence of the priesthood in opposition to Luther's doctrine of the priesthood of all believers. His final polemical work, published in 1527, was a defence of the real presence of Christ in the sacrament of the altar against the Swiss reformer Oecolampadius. Fisher seems to have been the first among English theologians – conservative or evangelical – to perceive that the Swiss or Reformed movement constituted a much more radical attack on Catholic theology than did Luther and his followers.

The importance of Fisher's polemical work is attested by the frequency of its publication. The *Confutation* ran to more than 20 editions in the course of the century, the *Defence of the Priesthood* to seven, the work on the Eucharist to six, and the defence of the king's book to four.[43] Through these works Fisher was able to exert a posthumous influence on the formulation of doctrine at the Council of Trent.[44]

There is evidence of some demand for vernacular translations of Fisher's work on the continent. Most interesting is the case of Nicolaus Roll, a curate of Utrecht found guilty of heresy in 1557. His penance included (besides a diet of bread and water three times a week) the task of translating Fisher's *Confutation* into Dutch.[45]

It is clear from many sources that Fisher's work was treated with respect. In June 1524 Clement VII informed Wolsey of his intention of calling a meeting of prelates in Rome to discuss the removal of abuses in the Church. (Needless to say, this conference never materialised.) He wanted Wolsey to send two or three bishops or abbots, and expressed a preference for Fisher and Tunstal. In 1526 the archbishop of Capua was demanding with some urgency that Fisher's work, together with the king's, should be sent to Rome.[46]

German Catholic polemicists showed appreciation of Fisher and his work. Johann Eck seems to have had access to the manuscript of Fisher's defence of the king's book before it was published. Eck went to England in 1525 specifically to consult Fisher and other notables. His visit lasted so long that Fisher had to write to the Duke of Bavaria to apologise for keeping him in England.[47]

Eck drew heavily on Fisher's polemical writings for his own great work against Luther, *Enchiridion Locorum Communum*. He also sent his nephew Severinus to study in England with Fisher. Thomas Murner was entertained at Rochester by the bishop in 1523. Fisher may also have met Johann Fabri, bishop of Constance, when the latter was on embassy to England in 1527. Certainly Fabri praised Fisher's pastoral fervour in one of his own publications.[48]

Fisher's greatest German admirer was probably Johannes Cochlaeus, with whom he corresponded. Cochlaeus translated parts of the *Confutation* and of the work against Oecolampadius into German, and dedicated some of his own books to Fisher. After Fisher's execution he would write two works defending Fisher and More and denouncing Henry VIII.[49]

Fisher consulted Cochlaeus when writing his book on the Eucharist against Oecolampadius. For his part, Cochlaeus frequently urged Fisher to continue to write against heresy even when Fisher had told him plainly that he had retired from the arena. In 1528 he asked Fisher to write against the Anabaptists. In 1529 he wrote that he approved of Fisher's decision to write no more against Luther because Luther would not listen to any warning, especially one from the English. At the same time, Cochlaeus wanted him to write to warn the German nobility and imperial officials about the danger to their lands; Fisher was so well-known in Germany that they would heed him. Even in 1531, when Fisher was deeply embroiled in the 'king's great matter', Cochlaeus hoped that he would write against Melanchthon.[50]

Fisher's theological expertise was greatly respected by his colleague in anti-Lutheran polemic, Thomas More. One example, from the book More wrote as 'Gulielmus Rosseus', will suffice. 'The reverend father John, bishop of Rochester, a man illustrious not only by the vastness of his erudition, but much more so by the purity of his life, has so opened and overthrown the assertions of Luther, that if he has any shame he would give a great deal to have burnt his assertions.'[51]

Important though Fisher's individual contribution was to the reformation debate, he did not work in isolation. English humanist opponents of heresy read each others' works and exchanged opinions. Fisher himself acknowledged the collaboration of other scholars in the preparation of his polemical works. His greatest debt was to Cuthbert Tunstal. He contributed greatly to the composition of the *Confutation*; helped with the *Defence of the Priesthood*, which was dedicated to him; brought the anti-papal work of Velenus to Fisher's attention; and lent Fisher copies of the Greek liturgies of Basil and Chrysostom when he was preparing his work on the Eucharist. Fisher also had help from Nicholas West, bishop of Ely, with the defence of the king's book; in gratitude Fisher gave him the dedication of the work.[52]

It has often been doubted that Henry VIII actually wrote the *Defence of the Seven Sacraments*. Indeed, the collected edition of Fisher's works published at Würzburg in 1597 included that book and attributed it to Fisher. Quite possibly Fisher, along with other scholars, helped Henry with his book in one way or another. But Henry was certainly capable of producing such a work, and it is surely significant that he never disclaimed its authorship even after he had rejected papal supremacy.[53]

On the practical as opposed to the literary level, Fisher was extremely active in the attempt to extirpate heresy in England. He was effective in controlling heresy within his diocese and vigilant against itinerant outsiders who caused trouble there. Cambridge University also kept him busy. In the 1520s and early 1530s Fisher was involved in some famous heresy cases. It is notable that all the offenders either were or had been scholars at Cambridge.

Fisher took part in the trial of Thomas Bilney and Thomas Arthur as a member of the commission of bishops appointed by Wolsey in 1527 to investigate heresy in London.[54] Both the defendants were Cambridge scholars. Indeed, Arthur had been a fellow of St John's, and as late as Easter term 1525 had received his commons and wages as well as the sum of 13s 4d for preaching during the last year.[55] The two were particularly questioned as to whether they believed sincerely that Luther's assertions were justly condemned by Fisher, and that Luther and his followers were heretics. Great pains were taken to argue with the accused, especially by Tunstal. Eventually they recanted, and carried the faggot at Paul's Cross.[56] Bilney later repented of his recantation, was condemned by Bishop Nix and burned at Norwich.

Fisher was closely involved with the case of Robert Barnes, prior of the Augustinian house at Cambridge, whose abjuration was the occasion of his 1526 sermon. On Christmas Eve 1525 Barnes preached on Luther's postil for the day in St Edward's church. A recent writer has remarked that this does not necessarily mean that he had embraced Lutheran doctrine.[57] However, the authorities were bound to view the matter differently. The vice-chancellor immediately prohibited Barnes from preaching. He was arrested early in 1526; questioned by the vice-chancellor and others (including Fisher's associate John Watson, master of Christ's College); and sent to London to be examined by a committee of bishops which included Fisher.

Barnes' own account of his troubles, given in at least three different editions of his *Supplication to Henry VIII*, is both disingenuous and informative. Barnes argued that man was not bound to serve God on Christmas Day or Easter Day more than on any other day; this was superstition, and all days should be held holy. Fisher agreed, saying that he would not condemn this as heresy for a hundred pounds: 'but it was foolishly said, quod he, to preach this afore the butchers of Cambridge'.[58] Sarcasm apart, this remark demonstrates Fisher's concern with not giving scandal to the unlearned.

Barnes was then asked whether it was lawful to labour on holy days. Barnes said it was; if not, then the king and cardinal acted unlawfully in making men 'carry their stuff' on holidays. Barnes records Fisher's answer to this, while implying that he was senile and that he condoned immorality: 'at the last my lord of Rochester remembered himself (he is an old man, and his blood is cold about his heart) and objected in this manner: "A goodly reason, I will make you a like reason. The bishop of Winchester suffereth the stews, ergo the stews be lawful." Barnes was amazed, and afraid to answer: 'For I perceived that it was as lawful for our noble prince to carry stuff on the holy day, which is not against the word of God, as it is for an harlot of the stews to live in open whoredom, which is against the word of God.'[59] Given Fisher's disgust at the sins of the flesh, expressed most strongly in the sermon preached at Barnes' recantation, it seems unlikely that he would approve the legality of brothels. Rather, this was an unsubtle criticism of the bishops of Winchester for tolerating such profitable businesses on their doorstep in Southwark, as well as of Wolsey and Henry for making men work on holy days.

Foxe accuses Fisher of having caused the death of John Frith in 1533. The *Early Life* has Fisher trying to convert Frith by argument, but there is no contemporary evidence for this.[60] Certainly Fisher, unlike Cranmer, was not one of Frith's examiners or judges. The sole connection between them seems to be that Frith chose to answer Fisher's arguments in defence of purgatory in the *Confutation*. Frith also wrote against Rastell and More, but while these two entered into controversy with him Fisher did not bother to reply.[61]

One of the most important cases of heresy which concerned Fisher as chancellor of Cambridge was that of Hugh Latimer. Here it is necessary to go back and consider events at Cambridge after the condemnation of Luther.

Fisher himself went to Cambridge in 1521, doubtless to scotch any incipient heresy in the university. An immediate challenge to the chancellor's authority was the defacement of a papal bull on indulgences, copies of which he had caused to be posted at several places. As it came out later one Peter de Valence, probably a pensioner of Gonville Hall, had added the words, 'Happy the man who places his trust in the name of the Lord, and decries these false and mindless vanities.'[62] The culprit failed to come forward, and Fisher began to read the sentence of excommunication: 'but after that he had proceeded a space in the reading thereof, he stayed and began again to consider in his mind the great weight of his grievous sentence, which so much pierced his heart, that even before them all he could not refrain from weeping'. This led to a general outbreak of compassion for the offender, and he was given a final chance to appear. When he failed to materialise Fisher had no choice but to excommunicate him.

> And so ordering himself after a grave and severe manner as well in his countenance as other gesture of his body, he pronounced this terrible sentence from the beginning to the ending, against this desperate wicked person, but not without weeping and lamenting... as a right reverend and worthy prelate once told me, which then was a young man and present at all that business.

Cambridge scholars were employed by the authorities to examine Luther's works. At Wolsey's command four representatives were sent to London for this purpose in 1531, meeting in a commission with theologians from Oxford. It has been shown that the four Cambridge men were associates of Fisher and Erasmus. Henry Bullock, Humphrey Walkden and John Watson had all attended Erasmus' Greek lectures at Queens' and corresponded with him. Robert Ridley, later secretary to Tunstal, was also a friend of Polydore Vergil, who dedicated a book to Fisher. Both Bullock and Ridley owned copies of Fisher's work against Luther. Ridley would be associated with Fisher on the queen's council during the royal divorce and, like Fisher, would speak out courageously in the legatine court at Blackfriars.[63]

All this notwithstanding, it is undeniable that Lutheran and other reformed ideas were circulating at Cambridge in the 1520s. However, the famous White Horse coterie is more aptly described as an informal academic discussion group than a heretical conventicle. A book-raid by Wolsey's agents in 1526 which resulted in the arrest of Barnes uncovered relatively little illicit literature. Such heretical material as there was had to remain covert. It is perhaps noteworthy that the Cambridge men who migrated to Wolsey's college at Oxford were only found to be heterodox once they had reached the other university.

Vigilant though Fisher and the Cambridge authorities were, some institutions and individuals were suspect. Gonville Hall produced a number of evangelical preachers as well as chaplains and other clients of Anne Boleyn. The advent of the royal divorce and the ascendancy of Anne meant that what was dangerous in religion before

1527 could, if discretion were exercised, be the means of advancement after that date for men like Hugh Latimer.

Latimer's provocative preaching in 1529 caused a great commotion at the university, with many sermons for and against him. Prominent among his opponents were fellows of St John's; it may be assumed that Fisher took a personal interest in the matter.

The vice-chancellor of Cambridge, William Buckmaster, received a letter of reprimand from Edward Foxe, provost of King's and a scholar as deeply involved in asserting the king's cause as Fisher was in defending the queen's.[64]

> it hath been greatly complained unto the king's highness of the shameful contentions used now of late in sermons made between Master Latimer and certain of St John's College, in so much as his grace intendeth to set some order therein which should not be greatly to your and other the heads of the university's worship.

Foxe indicates the chief reason for the king's interest in the matter as well as hinting at Fisher's role.

> It is not unlikely but that they of St John's proceedeth of some private malice towards Master Latimer, and that also they be animated so to do by their master, Master Watson, and such other my lord of Rochester's friends. Which malice also peradventure cometh partly for that Master Latimer favoureth the king's cause; and I assure you it is so reported to the king.

On Foxe's advice Buckmaster enjoined both sides to peace under pain of excommunication. Latimer was warned 'that ye be circumspect and discreet in your sermons and that ye speak no such thing which may be occasion of offence unto your audience in any wise'. His opponents Baynes, Rudde, Greenwood and Brickenden of St John's, together with Dr Buckenham, prior of the Blackfriars, were adjured that 'ye touch no such matters as hath been in controversy, ne to invey or cry out in the pulpit as ye have done in times past; for this hath caused the slanderous bruit which runneth of us in every place, to our shame and rebuke'.

In 1529–30 the debate about the royal marriage was carried into the European universities, Cambridge and Oxford among them. Both the English universities ultimately returned verdicts favourable to the king, and a notable part was played in this victory by men like Hugh Latimer and his colleague from Gonville Hall, Nicholas Shaxton.[65] Yet (Anne Boleyn notwithstanding) it was by no means certain that evangelical religion would triumph, as the king himself seemed to remain orthodox while tolerating suspect scholars like Latimer and Cranmer as long as it seemed that they could furnish material and authority for his cause.

Consequently the Cambridge evangelicals or heretics experienced mixed fortunes. Dr Edward Crome, formerly of Gonville Hall and later favoured by Anne Boleyn, preached twice in Lent 1530 before Henry VIII. In May he was on the Cambridge committee appointed by Buckmaster to examine heretical books; this seems to have been a balanced body, including (among others) Crome, Shaxton and Latimer on one side and Baynes and Watson on the other.[66] However in March 1531 Crome was in trouble for preaching against purgatory, the cult of saints, pilgrimage, images, fasting and papal supremacy. He was examined in the presence of the king, and while Henry found some of his beliefs objectionable he approved of Crome's denial of papal authority. It was this as well as the intercession of Anne and Thomas Boleyn that saved Crome, though he was compelled to recant some of his beliefs (not for the last time) at Paul's Cross.[67]

Hugh Latimer fared similarly. After his part in securing the right verdict from Cambridge on the royal marriage he was brought to London by William Butts, a royal physician and former member of Gonville Hall. However in March 1532 he was examined for points of heresy similar to those which Crome had been forced to recant. After excommunication and imprisonment Latimer decided to make a partial recantation, and was absolved. One of the judges in the case was John Fisher.[68]

It is impossible to say how much progress reformed religion would have made at Cambridge without the occurrence of the royal divorce. That heresy and the 'king's great matter' tended to overlap is undeniable, and was perceived by contemporaries. A Cistercian monk of Woburn, for example, said that Fisher, More and the executed Carthusians had been taken away 'so that naughty heretics may have their swing'.[69]

John Fisher devoted great time and energy to his battle with heresy, which for him constituted the gravest peril to Christian souls. His assiduity in preaching and writing against heresy and schism was tremendous. On at least two occasions, in 1529 and 1533, he requested and received papal dispensations from the requirements of fasting and reciting the canonical hours so that he could devote his strength to these tasks. Possibly these licences were in the nature of' 'repeat prescriptions', the original application having been made somewhat earlier.[70] He did not neglect his other duties, however. Rex has estimated that he wrote the greater part of the *Confutation*, a tome of some 200 000 words, during the second part of 1521, while residing at his episcopal manor of Halling and presumably occupied with diocesan and other business.[71]

Yet it would seem that the task was not wholly congenial. According to the *Early Life*; 'talking on a time with a Carthusian monk, who much commended his zeal and diligent pains in compiling his book against Luther, he answered again, saying that he wished that time of writing had been spent in prayer, thinking that prayer would have done more good and was of more merit.'[72] Perhaps this seems like a pious interpolation by the first biographer. Yet Fisher did grow tired of addressing a Luther who would not listen. Certainly, to judge by his devotional writings it seems that Fisher would indeed have preferred to spend the time communing with that Holy Spirit who, for him, inspired the Church and proved the truth of her doctrine.

6 The Devotional Writer

Therefore, seeing he hath taught us the necessity of prayer, and that we ought always to pray, it cannot be doubtful to any ... especially of us Christians, who wander in the miseries of this world, exiled from the face of our heavenly Father.[1]

John Fisher has not been especially noted as a devotional writer; indeed, only a handful of his pietistic works is known.[2] Yet this aspect of his literary output is highly important, both as an expression of his piety and as an extension of his pastoral mission to the whole of Christendom. His devotional writings show that Fisher, like Erasmus, sought to close the gap between the work of the scholarly elite – theologians, philologists, biblical scholars – and the piety of the common man and woman.

The character of Fisher's devotional thought can be summed up in one of his favourite phrases: the fervour of charity. For Fisher the Holy Spirit

is the author of all good love, he is the very furnace of charity, and he is the fountain of all gracious affections and godly desires. He is the spiritual fire that kindles in the heart of them where he enters all gracious love; he fills their souls in whom he is received with the abundance of charity; he makes their minds secretly to burn in all godly desires and gives unto them strength and power courageously to follow all ghostly affections.[3]

Worship in spirit and of the spirit is the key to Fisher's own spirituality, and it is in this charismatic approach that his originality lies. His pietistic writings have four hallmarks. God is a spirit, and must be worshipped in spirit; divine love, rather than divine wrath, is stressed; the soul must love God with all the fervour of charity; and the soul's co-operation, that is, its positive exercise of free will, is necessary for salvation.

There are broad resemblances between Fisher's writings and those of late medieval mystics such as Richard Rolle, Julian of Norwich, Catherine of Siena, Thomas à Kempis and Walter Hilton. It seems likely that Fisher would have read at least some of these authors, and he shares their emphasis on the fire of love and on worship in spirit rather than prayer by mere repetition of words.[4]

While in the Tower awaiting death Fisher composed two short devotional pieces, *A Spiritual Consolation* and *The Ways* to *Perfect Religion*. These are addressed to his half-sister, Elizabeth White, who was a Dominican nun at Dartford in his diocese of Rochester. They are written in English, and since Fisher was deprived of books in prison they lack detailed quotations and references. However, he did not intend to offer learned disquisitions on the art of contemplation, but to stir up his reader's fervour of charity by putting certain considerations to her.

A Spiritual Consolation is somewhat inaptly named (the title was probably bestowed by the Elizabethan editor rather than the author), as it is a minatory piece written in the person of a man on the point of sudden death.[5] Fisher conveys skilfully the horrible apprehension and uncertainty endured by such a one.

> Alas! alas! I am unworthily taken. All suddenly death has assailed me, the pains of his stroke be so sore and grievous that I may not long endure them. My last hour, I perceive well, is come.... But whither I shall go, or where I shall become, or what lodging I shall have this night, or in what company I shall fall, or in what country I shall be received, or in what manner I shall be intreated, God knoweth: for I know not.[6]

The dramatic effect here is perhaps a reminder that Fisher was a writer of plays as well as of polemical works. In contrast to Luther's doctrine of the bondage of the will, Fisher is concerned to stress that free will as well as divine grace is necesssary for repentance; thus the dying man has lost his chance.

> But how may I think that my repentance or mine amendment cometh now of my own free will, since I was before this stroke so cold and dull in the service of my Lord God? Or how may I think that I do this more rather for his love than for fear of his punishment? ... Even as a merchant that is compelled by a great tempest in the sea to cast his merchandise out of the ship, it is not to be supposed that he would cast away his riches of his own free will, not compelled by the storm. And even so likewise do I; if this tempest of death were not now raised upon me, it is full like that I would not have cast from me my sloth and negligence.[7]

The dying man bitterly regrets the time he wasted in pampering his body which, like an earthen wall painted and gilded on the surface, will soon return to its natural colour of soil.

The usual consolations of the Christian are denied to him who repents too late. The sinner is under no illusion as to the motives for his few good works: 'either I did them for the pleasure of men, or to avoid the shame of the world, or else for my own affection, or else for dread of punishment'. The Church teaches that we may benefit from the prayers of others; but his friends must surely forget to pray for him, because he forgot to pray for himself. As for the saints, who should be the sinner's friends, 'Alas, I had special devotion but to a few, and yet them I have so faintly honoured, and to them so coldly sued for favour, that I am ashamed to ask aid or help of them'.[8] The treatise ends with an exhortation to the reader: 'O ye that have time and space to make your provision against the hour of death, defer not from day to day as I have done. . . . If you follow this counsel and do thereafter, you shall be gracious and blessed, and if you do not, you shall doubtless repent your follies – but too late.'[9]

Fisher's meditation on death bears comparison with the works of his humanist contemporaries Erasmus, More and Richard Whitford, the devotional writer of Syon monastery. Erasmus' *Preparation for Death*, published in 1534, is very different in form from Fisher's tract, being a discourse on natural, spiritual and eternal death. He shows the need for repentance and avoidance of despair, and says that in a sense all death is sudden. Unlike Fisher, he shows repentance as being entirely dependant on divine grace, not on the will of the sinner: 'Only the grace of Christ is cause that a man can repent, and come again to his heart. But he freely and at his own liberty giveth it, to whom he willeth, and when he willeth.' Even so, Erasmus shares Fisher's concern with sincere repentance: 'Only hope doth sever the sinner in this life from hell. For as long as the breath is in man, so long he hath hope of pardon and forgiveness. How be it, we had need to take right good heed, lest our hope which cometh not of faith and charity deceive us.'[10]

More's piece, too, is more formal than Fisher's. He began a treatise on the four last things – death, judgment, heaven and hell – though he only worked on the first section. His work is not, as Fisher's is, a sample of prison writing.

More's aim is to show how transitory and futile are the joys bought on earth with the seven deadly sins in face of the inevitability of death. There are general similarities to Fisher's work, notably in the description of food and drink as medicines to keep the body alive, and in the warning that such things can give no pleasure to a dying man. More exhibits the same disgust with the body as Fisher does, harping particularly on the vices of gluttony and lechery and describing their consequences in revolted and revolting terms. In some ways he goes farther than Fisher. For More, life is a mortal sickness, the world a prison. While Fisher's sinner merely regrets that his friends will forget to pray for him, More paints an unsavoury picture of the anticipatory greed of the dying man's family and executors. In short, More's discussion of death is more formal, more harsh in its *contemptu mundi,* and ultimately of less dramatic effect than Fisher's brief and striking treatise.[11]

Whitford's book *A Daily Exercise and Experience of Death* was, like *A Spiritual Consolation,* written for an audience of religious; in this case the abbess and nuns of his own monastery of Syon. It, too, is more formal than Fisher's work, the first part consisting of scriptural, patristic and mystical 'evidence' to show why death need not be feared, since it is both natural and painless. Similarly to Fisher, he asks his nuns to imagine the terror of one condemned to death or mortally ill.[12]

It might be tempting to see *A Spiritual Consolation* as evidence that Fisher suffered from religious depression or lack of spiritual confidence while in prison, an idea that could be reinforced by the personal tone of the treatise. It is true that Fisher, like his protagonist, was a man on the point of death, by chronic sickness if not by the command of Henry VIII. There is also a clearly personal note in his dictum that without repentance and fervour of charity 'Neither building of colleges, nor making of sermons, nor giving of alms, neither yet any other manner of business shall help you'.[13] Yet such an assumption would be facile. In both *A Spiritual Consolation* and *The Ways to Perfect Religion* Fisher is writing as a spiritual director who is aware of the sinfulness of all mankind, including himself. Indeed, *Perfect Religion* is the greatest argument against a crisis of confidence in Fisher, as it is positive, optimistic, at times humorous, and life-loving.

Perfect Religion aims to make the nun's vocation and obligations more fulfilling by stirring in her the fervour of charity: 'For love maketh every work appear easy and pleasant, though it be right displeasant of itself.'[14] Fisher begins by comparing the life of a nun with that of a hunter. Though playful and witty (and, incidentally, expressive of Fisher's own love of the chase) it has the serious purpose of showing that more is undertaken and achieved by love than by mere fulfilment of duty.

Point by point, the two ways of life are compared. The nun rises at midnight, but she had gone to bed early and can go back to it after the first office. The hunter also rises early, but he is up for the day, 'and yet peradventure he was up late the night before, and full often up all the long nights'. The nun must fast till noon, but 'the hunter yet taketh more pain, which fasteth till the very night, forgetting both meat and drink for the pleasure of his game'. The nun sings in the choir all morning; the hunter 'singeth not, but he halloeth and shouteth all the long day, and hath more and greater pains'. The nun spends time and trouble going to and from the choir for the offices, but yet again she is outdone by the hunter 'in running over the fallow and leaping over the hedges and creeping through the bushes'. Naturally Fisher did not mean that nuns should enjoy late nights and days spent running over the countryside. His point is that they should seek as avidly after Christ as hunters pursue the hare.[15]

Rather than present detailed meditational exercises, Fisher provides Elizabeth with ten considerations which should kindle her fervent love. Among these are the facts that God created her when he could have left her unmade and has forborne to strike her dead in the midst of her sins. She is fortunate to be both one of the Christian elect and, as a nun, an elect bride of Christ. Furthermore, God 'hath elected you to bear his image and likeness', when he could have made her anything in the world: 'It is a more goodly being margarite of a precious stone than of a pebble stone, of the fair bright gold than of rusty iron, of a goodly pheasant than of a venomous serpent, of a pretty faun than of a foul toad, of a reasonable soul than of an unreasonable beast.'[16] Thus Elizabeth is the crown of God's creation. By contrast, Whitford reminded his nun that she began as 'a filthy lump of slimey earth', and was conceived 'by sinful generation with full filthy and loathsome matter'.[17]

Fisher stresses that though God is an invisible spirit, his beauty is reflected in created nature: 'Behold the rose, the lily, the violet, behold the peacock, the pheasant, the popinjay; behold all other creatures of this world; all these were of his making, all their beauty and goodliness of him they received it.' But God's beauty 'is not mortal, it cannot fade nor perish as doth the goodliness of other men, which like a flower today is fresh and lusty, and tomorrow with a little sickness is withered and vanished away'.[18] Further, God's wisdom is shown in the way he has adorned and clothed nature: 'the heavens are apparelled with stars, the air with fowls, the water with fishes; how the stars be clad with light, the fowls with feathers, the fish with scales, the beasts with hair, herbs and trees with leaves, and flowers with scent'. God is good and gentle, Elizabeth, made in his image, should love him like a good spouse: 'For likeness is the ground of love, like alway doth covet like; and the nearer in likeness that any person be, the sooner they may be knit together in love.'[19]

Fisher explains that, though Christ died for all sinners, the love he feels for the individual soul is as intense as if no other existed. Imagine, Fisher says, that a number of mirrors was set before an image of Christ. Each one would reflect it. True, the bigger mirrors would hold a larger image and the cleaner ones a clearer, just as pure souls see God more clearly: but 'every one of the souls receives as full and as whole a love of Jesu Christ as though there were no more souls in all the world but that one alone; for the love of Christ Jesus [is] infinite'.[20]

However, confidence in Christ's love should not lead to complacency; Fisher stresses once more that salvation depends in part on the exercise of free will.

> Good sister, without doubt as I have said, our saviour Christ Jesu is in love towards you, and he is mindful and more loving towards you than I can express. And sure you may be, that he will never cast you away, nor forsake you, if you before cast not yourself away, and willingly destroy yourself; that is your deed and not his; for he never forsaketh any creature unless they before have forsaken themselves.[21]

Clearly, Fisher is arguing here against Luther's doctrine of justification by faith alone and its concomitant idea that God accepts man despite his sins. God, declares Fisher, cannot abide sin; this is why Lucifer and his angels fell, why Adam was expelled from paradise. If a mortal sin were found even in the Virgin Mother or Mary Magdalen they would be damned: 'For sin is so odible unto almighty God, that not the dearest friends that ever he had in all the world, but if there were found in their souls any deadly sin after death, they should never be received into the joy of heaven.' Quoting Chrysostom, Fisher shows the worst aspect of damnation: 'if one should rehearse unto me ten thousand hells, yet all should not be so great pains as it is to be excluded from the blessed sight of the face of Christ'.[22]

Fisher concludes by giving Elizabeth short prayers which will arouse her love. But God must be worshipped in spirit, and formal observance is nothing without the fervour of charity: 'that love once established in you, all the other points and ceremonies of your religion shall be easy unto you, and no whit painful; you shall then comfortably do everything that to good religion appertaineth, without any great weariness'.[23]

The devotional emphases of the Tower works – true repentance, humility, worship in spirit and fervour of charity – are found in more amplified form in Fisher's *Treatise of Prayer*. This longer work, written in Latin, must predate his imprisonment, since it gives detailed and accurate citations from scriptural and patristic sources. Passing references to current heresies ('Let no man here object unto me that absurd and ridiculous reason of the foreknowledge of God') indicate a date after reformation controversy had broken out. Most probably it should be dated between 1521, when Fisher began to write and preach against Luther, and 1527, when the commencement of the king's divorce proceedings committed Fisher's literary energies to defence of the marriage. Perhaps it was his preoccupation with the divorce and supremacy which prevented Fisher from publishing the *Treatise of Prayer*.

Certainly, the first edition only appeared in the 1560s, in an English translation by Anthony Browne, Viscount Montague. The translator worked from a manuscript: 'I could not satisfy myself to see such a pearl hidden, and such a jewel thrown out and cast away to oblivion.' It is possible that the Henrician censorship prevented publication of the treatise at an earlier date; even in the 1560s Montague was careful not to name his author, merely describing him as 'an Englishman, a bishop, of great learning and marvellous virtue of life, such one as seemed perfectly to taste and savour how sweet and pleasant the Spirit of God is'.[24]

Fisher's work on prayer was designed for a general or mixed audience; indeed, many of his remarks show that he had lay people specifically in mind. Moreover, it is significant that, unlike the Tower works or the sermons, the *Treatise of Prayer* was composed in Latin. This seems to indicate that Fisher intended it for a European readership, like his *Psalms or Prayers* published at Cologne and like his polemical works. (Presumably he would have translated it into English for the home market.) As it is not a learned theoretical work but a guide for the layman, it would seem that the treatise shows Fisher exercising his pastoral mission to the whole of Christendom. His appreciation of the needs of the entire, universal Church thus governed not just his polemical campaign and political attitudes, but his ministry as well.

Like the sermons and other devotional works, the *Treatise of Prayer* has a beautiful clarity of structure. It treats in turn of the necessity, fruits and manner of prayer. Fisher's chief influences or sources are Augustine, Bernard, and Pico della Mirandola. He draws directly on Augustine's letter to Proba, who was a widow and head of household. There are also close resemblances to a letter from Pico to his nephew, Giovanni Francesco, who was a layman. It is known from other sources that Fisher read and admired Pico. Fisher is particularly similar to Bernard in his emphasis on loving union with God and in his use of the amorous language of the Song of Songs. Indeed, it seems likely that Fisher drew directly on Bernard's great series of sermons on the Song of Songs, and possibly, too, on his treatise *De Diligendo Deo*.

Fisher takes as his text Christ's precept in the gospel of Luke 'that we ought always to pray'. He opens the treatise with a vivid image to show the necessity for prayer: he pictures a man in a basket suspended by a rope over a deep pit, who depends for survival on the one who holds the rope. God is that being, and we must pray constantly in case he lets go the rope and we fall headlong into hell. Once more, the sinner's partial responsibility for his own salvation is stressed.

Constant prayer seems impossible in the context of daily life, so how is Christ's command to be interpreted? For Fisher, constant prayer is 'the continual desire of the mind, which is always flourishing and moving in the heart'; 'by this desire, which in the heart of holy men is never extinguished, God is always and incessantly prayed unto, and by it we knock perpetually at the gates of his divine mercy for the obtaining of his grace and assistance'. Fisher cites Augustine to show that 'without this desire no muttering of words, though never so prolix, can open the ears of his divine majesty'.[25]

Prayer is necessary for four reasons, the first being our total dependence on God. Prayer is 'a certain golden rope or chain let down from heaven, by which we endeavour to draw God to us, whereas indeed we are more truly drawn by him'.

Who would not most willingly be bound with this most soft and silken cord? Or . . . who doth not desire from the bottom of his heart to repose himself in the arms of so loving a prince, so potent a king? Verily, this only cogitation, if it were deeply considered, might suffice to inflame the most frozen heart, and to stir it up to frequent this holy exercise of prayer.

Though God first stoops to us, we should not be terrified by his majesty; rather, we are invited to love him.

So deeply is God almighty in love with our souls that he doth as it were study to entice and allure us, and endeavoureth by all means to draw us to meditate and contemplate the splendour of his glory, to embrace the largeness of his bounty, to taste of his sweetness, and lastly to kiss the unspeakable delights of his mouth.[26]

The second reason for prayer is that, together with good works, it is the means to the end God has designed for man; beatitude in heaven. We can only lead a good life if we petition God by prayer. Thus once more Fisher rejects the Lutheran theory of justification and, quite overtly, its implicit corollary, predestination. The physician does not refuse to give medicine because God has already decided whether the patient shall live or die; the farmer does not leave his fields unsown because God has decided whether they will be barren or fruitful. Thus though man is helplessly dependant on God, he must co-operate in salvation.[27]

The third reason for prayer is Christ's explicit command to pray constantly, and his promise that what was asked would be obtained. Not to pray is therefore a sin, and we must pray for our neighbour's salvation as well as our own. Prayer is especially necessary 'seeing the times be such and so dangerous as they now be, sinners being so multiplied upon the earth, and sin itself so daily increased as we see it is. Nowadays to sin is to do well, and contrary wise to do well is to sin. Woe be unto us, that we are born in these miserable times!'[28]

Fourthly, we must pray not just for forgiveness of past sins, but for grace to sin no more. No living man can be certain that he is in a state of grace: 'And for this cause it is necessary for all men to contain themselves within the limits and bounds of fear, and to be perseverantly knocking at the gates of God's mercy.' Further, there is no guarantee that one in a state of grace will not fall again. With the Lutherans in mind Fisher quotes Romans 2 ('Thou standest by faith, be not overwise, but fear') to warn against arrogant complacency.

For we read of many, who have stood up like pillars a long time in the Church of Christ, and have shined as burning lamps of sanctity: yet because they have not contained themselves within the limits of this humble fear, they have fallen headlong into the bottomless pit of hell, not only to their own ruin and infamy, but to the ruin of many others.[29]

Fisher next describes the three benefits or fruits of prayer; merit, obtaining that which is asked, and spiritual sweetness. All three are not necessarily received at once. Like Pico, Fisher cites the example of Paul, who had to pray three times to lose the sting of the flesh; though his petition went unanswered, he did not lose the merit of prayer. Equally, the publican in the gospel rose from his prayer justified, but did not experience spiritual sweetness.

'Merit' here corresponds to a reward in heaven, and only those whose prayers spring from the root of charity shall obtain this. Once more, Fisher rejects justification by faith alone: 'sins are not thought to be blotted out of the memory of God by any other way than by the gift and infusion of grace and charity'. Indeed, faith depends on charitable prayer.

In discussing the second fruit of prayer, obtaining a request, Fisher answers the most obvious objection to petitionary prayer, that it is not always answered. We must be sure that what we ask for will benefit our souls' health: 'For God, being of his nature most good, most bountiful, cannot grant unto his petitions that which he knows to be pernicious and hurtful unto him. And he knoweth long before we demand it, whether it will damnify or profit us.'[30] This also applies to our prayers for other people. However, even if our petitions are not answered the prayer itself is not wasted, but turns to our good.

The third fruit of prayer, and the one most difficult to obtain, is spiritual sweetness. Here strict attention is necessary as well as humility and charity. Concentration is vital at the beginning of prayer, so that even if the attention wanders later this benefit is not lost. This fruit is the greatest of the three: 'For indeed one only taste of this sweetness incomparably surpasseth all worldly delight whatsoever, for from it there groweth such joy and comfort in the soul that exceeds all joy and contentment that can be imagined.'[31] God, like a good physician, only sends this sweetness when he knows it will do good. When it comes, it is a foretaste of heaven: 'For it is as it were a twinkling or a small glimpse of God's heavenly light, it is a spark of our future happiness, it is a pledge or earnest penny of eternal life.'[32]

As regards the manner of prayer, Fisher is more concerned with the inward desire of man for God than with set formulae, with private prayer rather than with liturgy, though he is careful to recommend that the usages of the Church be followed. Three considerations govern the manner of prayer; attention, length or prolixity, and pronunciation.

Concerning the first, Fisher says that ideally we should attend to the words, the sense, and he to whom we pray. Achievement of all three is hard, so attention to God is the most important aim. We should especially beware of an overfastidious preoccupation with mechnical utterance.

> There be many doubtless who have so weak and so scrupulous consciences, that for fear lest that they should overslip any little word, or pass any syllable in the divine office, they bend all their forces and strength of their mind to the distinct pronunciation of the words. And such, I do verily believe, seldom or never taste the sweetness of prayer.[33]

But hurrying over prayer brings no joy either. Fisher reproves 'those who so hastily huddle over their prayer that they scarcely understand themselves, not considering either the excellency of him to whom they pray, nor the sense of the words'. In similar vein, the Spanish humanist Vives felt that mere pronunciation was useless unless matched by spiritual prayer. In his *Instruction of a Christian Woman* of 1523 he declared:

> let her not ween that prayer standeth in the murmuring and wagging of the lips, but in the heart and mind, when she lifteth up her mind from these vile things on earth to heavenly and divine things.... But Christ saith that true worshippers be those that worship the Father in spirit, and that this worshipping is most pleasant unto him, and this prayer most acceptable.[34]

Pico, too, put little value on prayer merely uttered, telling his nephew:

> When I stir thee to prayer I stir thee not to the prayer which standeth in many words, but to that prayer which in the secret chamber of the mind, in the privy closet of the soul with very affect speaketh to God, and in the most lightsome darkness of contemplation not only presenteth the mind to the Father, but

also uniteth it with him by unspeakable ways which only they know that have assayed.[35]

Fisher says that we must not imagine that repetition of scripture is a suitable substitute for inward desire for God, since scripture is not God himself (a passing swipe at the Lutherans, whom he suspected of bibliolatry) but merely one of his creatures.

> For God's holy writ, though it proceeds from himself, yet it is notwithstanding a creature, and what creature or what created thing so ever passeth our minds, be it never so excellent, that thing is interposed betwixt God and us, so that it is but a let unto our minds, that we cannot so inwardly be united with God, and therefore diminish that admirable sweetness which proceeds from the fountain itself.[36]

This is the scholastic distinction between created and uncreated good. Equally, those who do give their whole attention to God must not try to imagine him in material terms.

> that thought or cogitation which the mind formeth or shapeth to itself of God must not be under any colour or light or figure, or any other corporal likeness: for all these things are created, and so not God, whereas we seek the union and conjunction of ourselves with God only, and not with any other thing distinct from him.[37]

This kind of meditation is difficult, so if God is hard to imagine, Fisher says, we should begin by thinking about Christ; thus we 'shall easily from his most sacred humanity mount to the contemplation of the unspeakable, inscrutable, divine majesty of God'.[38]

On prolixity, Fisher says that prayer should last until ardent charity is stirred in the heart. Here he alludes to God's well-known aversion to the lukewarm, as expressed in the Book of Revelations. If fervour begins to fade through bodily frailty the prayer should be ended, lest that ardour be altogether lost. Thus brief but fervent spiritual prayer is preferable to long hours of meditation or recitation of set prayers. Following Augustine, Fisher especially recommends ejaculatory prayer (that is, short exclamations) because of its brevity and because it arouses fervour.

This kind of prayer would certainly answer the needs of those whose lives 'are so troubled with cares, so perplexed with worldly occasions, and full of business'. Citing Chrysostom and the Book of Proverbs, Fisher shows that time can be stolen for prayer, either by withdrawing briefly from company or by praying silently. Homely and biblical examples are adduced to show that prayer is possible at any time.

> If thou wert mending thy shoes or washing dishes or what else so ever, thou mayest pray: it is lawful for the servant, what business so ever he is about of his master's, to pray. In the court, in the market place, in the midst of never so great a multitude of people a man may pray. Saint Paul prayed in the prison, the prophet Jeremy in the dirt, Ezechiel against the wall, Daniel in the lions' den, Jonah in the whale's belly, the thief on the cross: and all these were heard praying in very few words.[39]

On pronunciation, Fisher is at pains to show that he does not condemn vocal prayer, but that he believes that spiritual prayer is better: 'it is far more profitable ... to pray with his heart only, than with his heart and tongue together':

> Wherefore a poor wretch who casteth himself prostrate on the earth, with great humility and and acknowledging himself to be a sinner, and laying open his miseries, pouring forth the bottom of his heart before God, not uttering words, but pitiful groans: this poor soul without all question shall obtain what he requireth at God's hand.[40]

Similarly, Pico tells his nephew: 'Nor care I how long or short thy prayer be, but how effectual, how ordered, and rather interrupted and broken with sighs than drawn on length with a continual row and number of words.'[41]

For Fisher the Holy Spirit must teach and advise as to the way of prayer, and vocal prayer can be useful up to a point.

> I do not deny but that some devout person may begin his prayer with what words he pleases from his lips. But so soon as ever he shall find himself a little enkindled, and as it were set on fire with that sweet flame of the Holy Ghost, then will it be fit for him to leave of vocal prayer and follow the leading of the divine Spirit, and in silence to permit himself to be wholly governed by it.[42]

Thus for Fisher the highest kind of prayer is that of the heart and spirit, wordless, and aimed at throwing the soul in abject humility at the feet of God. Men profit more 'by this prayer of the heart, than if they had repeated innumerable psalms and prayers, as very many do, overburdening their minds'. Here Fisher goes beyond Augustine, who stresses the necessity for vocal and formal prayer. Indeed, he probably goes beyond most mainstream pre-reformation thinkers in this respect.

Fisher's originality in preferring charismatic prayer to formal or vocal prayer appears quite strikingly when his *Treatise of Prayer* is compared with works on the same subject addressed to the laity by his contemporaries. Richard Whitford produced *A Work for House-holders* or heads of families which was published in 1533. This is markedly different from Fisher's book in that it stresses formality in devotion. There is a lengthy morning prayer which Whitford advises the reader to learn by heart. Moreover, the Our Father, Hail Mary and Creed should be learned by the whole household, including children and servants, and recited at least three times a day. Whitford says nothing about the interior prayer life of the layman; his concern is with ordered private worship in the household.[43]

There are more similarities between Fisher's treatise and Erasmus' discourse on prayer, published in 1524.[44] Erasmus, like Fisher, drew directly on Augustine's letter to Proba. Like Fisher, too, he sees the whole of a good life and constant desire for heavenly bliss as fulfilling the injunction to pray continually, and he says that cold and sluggish prayer, mere lip-service and repetition, are not sufficient. Erasmus' concerns and methods, however, are quite different from Fisher's.

Firstly, Erasmus discusses public worship as much as private prayer, an area which Fisher avoids entirely. Secondly, Erasmus is concerned with what is lawful in prayer, and there are long disquisitions on which person of the Trinity should be addressed and on whether the invocation of saints is obligatory, merely permissible, or unlawful. Again, Fisher concentrates directly on worship in spirit rather than entering into theological discussion about the Godhead, and the cult of the saints finds no place in his treatise. Thirdly, Erasmus is much occupied with the paradox that while Christ commanded the disciples to pray constantly he forbade them to use many words. He does this by a long philological discussion about the difference between prolixity and loquacity, citing many scriptural examples to make his point. This examination is not found in Fisher, who in any case saw little point in using many words.

Finally, though both writers see the usefulness of ejaculatory prayer (Erasmus finding it particularly appropriate for those in the public domain such as kings and judges), Erasmus puts much more emphasis on formal, vocal prayer. For him, formal prayer is good in that it leads the soul from the visible to the invisible, just as boys are first taught to read and then to understand what they have read. In this he is much closer to Augustine than is Fisher, for whom formal and vocal prayer is of minimal use. In short, Erasmus' treatise is more academic in form and intent than Fisher's work, which is more directly pastoral, concerned with firing the devotion of his readers.

His emphasis on spiritual prayer notwithstanding, Fisher composed a number of prayers and meditations. In *Perfect Religion* he provides his sister with seven ejaculatory prayers, one for each day of the week. These, in keeping with his own directives, are short and fervent: 'O blessed Jesu, let me deeply consider the greatness of thy love towards me'; 'O blessed Jesu, give unto me grace heartily to thank thee for thy benefits'; 'O sweet Jesu, possess my heart, hold and keep it only to thee'. They are meant to act as a stimulus to mental prayer and spiritual sweetness: 'These short prayers, if you will often say, and with all the power of your soul and heart, they shall marvellously kindle in you this love, so that it shall be always fervent and quick.'[45]

In the same work Fisher gives Elizabeth a somewhat longer prayer concerning God's love for her and her own unworthiness.

O my blessed saviour Lord Jesu, thou askest my love, thou desirest to have my heart, and for my love thou wilt give me thy love again. O my sweet Lord, what is this for thee to desire, which art so excellent? . . . I freely give it unto thee, and I most humbly beseech thy goodness and mercy to accept it, and so to order me by thy grace, that I may receive into it the love of nothing contrary to thy pleasure, but that I always may keep the fire of thy love, avoiding from it all contrary love that may in any wise displease thee.[46]

This verbosity might seem in total contradiction to what Fisher says elsewhere about brevity and wordlessness. However, this formal prayer is probably meant to serve as a prologue to meditation or spiritual prayer. It is possible, too, that in writing this for his sister Fisher was recognising that a nun's way of prayer must necessarily be affected by a lifetime of formal recitation of the office.

Indeed, in his devotional writings as in other aspects of his ministry, Fisher saw himself as charged with the care of all sorts and conditions of souls. As a pastor, he was concerned to stir up the fervour of charity by whatever means was appropriate to the individual. A similar pattern to the two types of prayer found in *Perfect Religion* may be seen in the short Latin prayers Fisher translated from the new testament, presumably using the Greek text of Erasmus. Some, such as the prayer of the repentant thief, or Christ's petition to the Father to let the cup pass from him, are short enough to fall into the category of ejaculatory prayer. But there are longer pieces, among them the Our Father, Magnificat and Song of Simeon, which might correspond to the longer prayer composed for Elizabeth White; a formal introduction to and preparation for prayer in spirit.[47]

A much different work is a collection of pieces by Fisher first published in Latin at Cologne about 1525. Though entitled *Psalms or Prayers* (*Psalmi seu Precationes*), they are neither translations nor paraphrases of the biblical psalms nor formal prayers for recitation. Rather, they are meditations inspired by the themes of the scriptural psalms, designed to evoke the sinner's sense of his own unworthiness, his repentance, trust in God, and loving gratitude.

The printing history of this collection is highly interesting. The fact that Fisher composed the work in Latin and had it published in Germany indicates once more that he was extending his pastoral care to the whole of Christendom, not confining it to his English flock. The little book proved popular on the continent. There were Dutch and German editions, and one Czech translation made sometime before 1554. In 1572 the Jesuit István Szántó included it in a list of Catholic books he suggested should be translated into Hungarian. At least one Magyar edition did appear. The dedication to the bishop of Zagreb praises the work of the 'pious bishop' 'Roffi János' and asks that the book be published and circulated for the education of the Hungarian people.[48]

Psalms or Prayers was also printed in English and Latin at London later in the sixteenth century. Most ironically, the book was appropriated by the Tudor dynasty. The royal printer issued two Latin editions in 1544 as well as an English version which also contained some prayers by Katherine Parr. The collection continued to be printed down to 1608, usually as 'The King's Psalms and the Queen's Prayers'; a fact which attests to its enduring utility and appeal.[49]

A final piece of writing by Fisher is in the same category as his *Psalms or Prayers*. This is a draft of a prayer in manuscript which, doubtless because of its warmth of tone and reference to human love, was formerly attributed to Thomas More.[50] This work, like Fisher's 'Psalms', should be seen as a preparatory meditation rather than a formal, vocal prayer. With its stress on the fervour of love kindled by the Spirit it expresses many of the devotional and theological points made in the Tower works and in the *Treatise of Prayer*.

The dependence of the sinner on God is acknowledged: 'unless thou wilt of thy infinite goodness relieve me, I am but as a lost creature'. The petitioner accuses himself of neglecting God for the love of men, of enjoying earthly pleasures instead of awaiting the joys of heaven. The sight of God's face is the height of bliss, just as the depth of hell is its absence. The petitioner is aware of his 'abominable forgetfulness' of God, but comforted because God has promised to be his father, and much more loving and forgiving than an earthly father. Emboldened by God's love, he comes to the point of his petition: 'I ask none other thing but thy good and holy Spirit to be given unto me.' Explicitly, then, this meditation is but the prologue to spiritual prayer. Fisher concludes:

> I beseech thee to shed upon my heart thy most holy Spirit, by whose gracious presence I may be warmed, heated and kindled with the spiritual fire of charity and with the sweetly burning love of all godly affections, that I may fastly set my heart, soul and mind upon thee and assuredly trust that thou art my very loving father, and according to the same trust I may love thee with all my heart, with all my soul, with all my mind and all my power.

To conclude, then, what is significant about John Fisher's devotional approach? Firstly, he discards all the mechanistic aspects of pietistic practice to concentrate on inward prayer. There is no overt criticism of liturgical practice or the cult of the saints; rather, the reader is given to understand that the rules and ceremonies of the Church should be followed, but that public and formal prayer are not sufficient. As an orthodox reformer, Fisher is seeking to engender spiritual renewal without challenging or overtly rejecting current usage.

Secondly, the devotional works reveal the intensity and the importance in his own eyes of Fisher's pastoral ministry. His mission is addressed to lay people as well as to religious, and is confined neither to England nor to the intellectual elite. He sees Christendom as a single entity, its members suffering common ills. Thus he exhorts all Christians to seek the greatest of the fruits of prayer, spiritual sweetness. He ends his *Treatise of Prayer* by assuring all who pray in spirit of the highest possible reward.

> why should not they (though lying here upon earth and covered with corruptible flesh) be said to be like angels? Seeing they pray as the blessed angels do, and seeing, lastly, they do here on earth find in themselves a pledge or earnest penny of their future happiness, which these blessed angels do now enjoy? In so much that there is nothing wanting to them but the beatifical vision of God's glory, which so soon as they have shaken off this veil of mortal flesh they shall enjoy in heaven.[51]

7 The Dissident

> Plato sayeth . . . then shall commonwealths be blessed, when either
> those that be philosophers govern, or else those that govern give
> them to philosophy.[1]

In these words Fisher praised Henry VIII as Plato's philosopher-
king in his sermon of 1521 against Luther. It has been asserted
that an innate antagonism existed between Fisher and Henry which
would lead inexorably to a clash between the saintly, austere bishop
and the worldly, sensual king.[2] There is little evidence for this. True,
the two were at odds over Margaret Beaufort's legacy and the endowment of St John's College, an issue which, Fisher said, 'made
the king very heavy lord against me'. It is also true that Fisher
ceased to attend meetings of the king's whole council after 1512.
Yet he did appear at or with the court on various occasions. In
1522 he entertained Henry VIII and Charles V at Rochester, and,
as has already been noted, an eyewitness reported that the king
'talked most lovingly' with Fisher.[3]

Longstanding mutual hostility, then, cannot account for Fisher's
conflict with Henry over the 'king's great matter', his attempt to
annul his marriage to Katherine of Aragon. There is absolutely no
reason to doubt Fisher's loyalty to Henry before the business began; but his differences with the king were to lead him into opposition,
and eventually to outright treason. For Fisher the issues at stake
were papal authority and the unity of Catholic Christendom; the
sanctity of marriage; and the fate of the souls of Henry and his
subjects should they fall into schism.

Why should Henry's annulment suit be a cause of such moment?
Other kings had approached Rome to have their marriages declared invalid, most recently, Louis XII of France; surely this was
a political and dynastic matter? Fisher's objections to the case were
very similar to those of Queen Katherine herself. On 14 April 1532
she wrote to Fernando Ortiz in Rome, pointing out the many dangers
which threatened the Church.

> I know not what to say about his holiness, but certainly when I
> see him holding this cause in suspense, and Christendom swarm-
> ing with heretics, it would seem to me as if he wanted their number

to increase, and that while being, as he is, the supreme head and protector of the Church he yet wishes it to have this tremendous fall.[4]

Katherine, then, identified the cause of her marriage with papal authority, Christian unity and the battle against heresy. So did Fisher. Moreover, the sacrament of matrimony had been decried by Luther and other reformers. As Fisher accepted the validity of Katherine's marriage he was bound to defend her whom God had joined in wedlock from the attempts of her husband to put them asunder.

As a Catholic son of the Church Henry tried to rid himself of his wife by means of the pope. In May 1527 as a prelude to approaching Rome a secret court was convened, and Henry had himself summoned before Wolsey and Warham to answer to the charge of living in an incestuous and illicit union. Henry based his case on Leviticus 20:21: 'He that marrieth his brother's wife doth an unlawful thing; he hath uncovered his brother's nakedness. They shall be without children.' Henry took 'wife' to mean 'widow' and, since he had a daughter living, 'children' to mean sons. Most crucially he claimed that the prohibition sprang from divine law, therefore the pope had no power to dispense from it. The court resolved to seek the opinions of several learned bishops, including Rochester, the most notable theologian in England.[5]

Fisher studied the matter carefully.

Having consulted all those silent masters I have by me, and diligently discussed their opinions and weighed their reasons, I find there is a great disagreement among them, a great many asserting that it is prohibited by the divine law, while others on the contrary affirm that it is by no means repugnant to it; and having truly weighed the reasons on both sides in an even scale I think I see it easy to unravel all the arguments which they produce who deny it to be lawful by the divine law, but not so easy to answer the others.

Therefore, seeing that the defenders of the pope's dispensing power were more convincing, considering Christ's delegation of power to the pope, and knowing that a papal dispensation had been issued for Henry's marriage, Fisher concluded that it was lawful for the pope to dispense from such an impediment.[6]

Fisher's arguments about the marriage and the papal dispensing power were elaborated over time. Two examples of his written work may be summarised here. The first is one of two *libelli* or short treatises he presented to the legatine court in 1529. In it Fisher makes six points. There was no impediment to the marriage of Henry and Katherine, and the prohibition in Leviticus did not apply to them. Besides, the pope had complete power to dispense from an impediment arising from positive law. The law of the Levirate proved that marriage with a brother's widow was not only permitted but sometimes obligatory. Even if the terms of the original bull were technically faulty, the intention of Julius II to clear away any possible impediment to the marriage was quite clear. (Indeed, in a letter to Katherine, Fisher stated that there was no doubt of the pope's dispensing power; she should stand firm on the bull of Julius and, lest it contain any technical flaws, apply secretly for a new bull to remedy this.) Finally, the marriage had been celebrated by all the rites and ceremonies of the Church, was without doubt sanctioned and blessed by God, and thus was indissoluble.[7]

The book by Fisher published at Alcalá in 1530 made five assertions. The law of Deuteronomy on the Levirate (the duty of a man to marry a brother's childless widow) constituted a veritable command. The word 'brother' in both Deuteronomy and Leviticus was to be understood in exactly the same sense. (This was a quibbling-point for Henry's theologians.) The Levitical prohibition was to be understood in a limited sense, not a universal one, and was judicial, not moral; and the pope could dispense from Leviticus in one sense though not in another.[8] Fisher's belief in the validity of the marriage, the nature of the Levitical prohibition, and the papal dispensing power remained consistent, though his arguments and tactics developed in response to changing circumstances and the strategies and policies of the king and his advisers.

Almost from the first Fisher was suspected of collaborating with Katherine; whether this was because of a close relation between them, or because Henry was uneasy about his own 'case', is impossible to tell. In early July 1527 Wolsey broke his journey to France to sound Fisher out. Wolsey asked whether he had heard any news from court or received any message from the queen: 'At which question he somewhat stayed and paused', but eventually admitted that she had asked his advice about 'certain matters' between herself and Henry. Fisher said he had replied that he would be happy to advise her on anything concerning herself alone, 'but in matters concerning your highness and her he would nothing do, without knowledge of your pleasure and express commandment, and herewith dismissed the messenger'.

Fisher admitted that, given Wolsey's earlier question to him about the pope's dispensing power, the mysterious message from the queen, and a tale his brother had brought back from London, he suspected that divorce was in the air. Wolsey explained that Henry was keeping the matter secret because he did not wish it discussed by all and sundry. However, he had ordered Wolsey to tell Fisher all about it, while making him swear to keep it secret. As had been agreed with Henry beforehand, Wolsey told Fisher that the French ambassadors, negotiating for Princess Mary's hand, had cast doubts on her legitimacy. Katherine, having an 'inkling' of this, had stirred up trouble by claiming falsely that Henry meant to divorce her. Fisher blamed her strongly for disturbing the peace, and cunningly offered his own services. He 'doubted not, but that if he might speak with her and disclose unto her all the circumstances of the matter as afore, he should cause her greatly to repent, humble and submit herself unto your highness'. This was the last thing Henry wanted, and Wolsey commanded Fisher not to have any communication with Katherine. He submitted, 'for he sayeth, although she be queen of this realm, yet he knowledgeth you for his high sovereign lord and king, and will not otherwise behave himself in all matters touching or concerning your person than as he shall be by your grace expressly commanded'. None the less Fisher 'would not reason the matter, but noted great difficulty in it'.[9]

It does seem as though Fisher kept his promise not to advise Katherine, since she complained that she had no one to turn to in England and sent frequent appeals to Charles V for advisers to be sent to her from the empire. Still, Fisher was busy on her behalf during 1527. A letter from his former protégé Robert Wakefield reveals that Fisher had written a work in the queen's favour. Wakefield boasted that he could defend Henry's case against all comers from scripture and other authorities. In particular, 'I have and will in such manner answer to the bishop of Rochester's book, that I trust he shall be ashamed to wade or meddle further in the matter'.[10]

Wolsey did not give up hope of persuading Fisher to support the king. While in France he met Giovanni Stafileo, who had written on the impediment to marriage of 'public honesty' (*publica honestas*) back in 1509. As applied to Henry VIII's case, this would mean that as Katherine had been married to Arthur in the presence of witnesses she could not then marry his brother, regardless of whether or not the first marriage had been consummated.

Wolsey was delighted with Stafileo and invited him to England. At the end of his stay, and possibly on Wolsey's orders, Stafileo broke his return journey at Rochester. (By now Fisher must have been regretting that his episcopal seat lay on the road to France.) Stafileo argued with Fisher about the 'king's great matter' and was highly pleased with what he considered his success, being willing to have given a small bishopric for Wolsey and Henry to have been present. His confidence in his own powers of persuasion was, however, misplaced.[11]

Meanwhile, Henry's case was proceeding slowly at the papal court. The opening of annulment proceedings had coincided inconveniently with the sack of Rome by an imperial army. Clement VII, unwilling to antagonise either the emperor or the king of England, took refuge in procrastination, and negotiations were protracted and convoluted. At length it was agreed that the case would be tried in England. The judges were to be Wolsey as *legatus natus* and Lorenzo Campeggio, cardinal-protector of England, as *legatus a latere*. Campeggio, then, aided and tormented by severe gout, took his time about reaching England and convening the legatine court. He reached London in October 1528 and the court only opened in June 1529.

In view of the impending trial Katherine was appointed counsellors in November 1528. The theologians were Fisher, Henry Standish, Bishop of St Asaph, Thomas Abell, Richard Featherstone, Edward Powell and Robert Ridley. The canon and civil lawyers were Bishops Warham, Tunstal, West and Clerk.

Campeggio himself tried unsuccessfully to persuade Katherine to become a nun and so avoid further trouble. He discussed the matter with Fisher on 25 October 1528 and seemed to think that he favoured the plan. On 1 November, however, the French ambassador reported Fisher to be of the queen's opinion.[12]

Fisher showed himself ready to defend Katherine in the legatine court at Blackfriars, though she herself challenged its competence and impartiality and, absenting herself, appealed directly to the pope. Fisher's public stance was that he believed Henry had genuine scruples which he sincerely wanted resolved so that he could live happily and legally with Katherine. A letter he wrote to one of the queen's supporters shows that he cannot be acquitted of irony on that score.[13]

Fisher declared that if Henry's conscience had been made uneasy by the Levitical prohibition he ought, as a true Christian and orthodox prince, to submit himself to the pope's judgement: 'I do not see that anyone should object to such a proceeding, especially since the king seems to have woven together some basis for his scruple from scripture.' This did not mean that Fisher thought that Henry's pang of conscience was justified, nor would he encourage him to put it to the test.

> For kings usually think that they are permitted to do whatever pleases them, because of the magnitude of their power. Therefore it is good for these kings, in my opinion, to submit themselves to the decrees of the Church, and this is beyond a doubt to be praised in them, lest otherwise they kick over the traces and do what they please, as long as they can weave together some appearance and colour of right.

At the same time Fisher understood the perils of opposition. The issue was so important and of vital concern to so many persons, he said, that no one could affirm the marriage without openly putting himself in danger.

This is precisely what Fisher did at the Blackfriars court. Katherine made a dignified speech in which she begged the king to confirm that she had been a virgin when he married her, committed her cause to God, and left the court. Henry made a rather less dignified speech, praising Katherine as the woman to whom he would most like to be married and rehearsing his famous scruples. He had asked the bishops for licence to have the matter discussed: 'to the which ye have all granted by writing under all your seals, the which I have here to be showed'. Warham agreed that this was so, and expected all present to support him.

Fisher, however, denied that he had given his consent: 'indeed you were in hand with me to have both my hand and seal, as other of my lords had already done; but then I said to you, that I would never consent to no such act, for it were much against my conscience; nor my hand and seal should never be seen at any such instrument, God willing'. Warham admitted the truth of this, but claimed that Fisher had allowed him to sign and seal for him. Fisher replied that 'there is no thing more untrue,' and the king was forced to conclude the discussion by saying, 'it shall make no matter; we will not stand with you in argument herein, for you are but one man'.[14]

There is an instrument extant which attests that a number of bishops including Fisher had been consulted by the king about his scruples of conscience. Although it is dated 1 July, rather than 29 June as Cavendish states in his account of the trial, it is probably the document in question. There is a signature similar to Fisher's, but though traces of wax remain, his is the only seal which is missing.[15]

Fisher continued to speak out at Blackfriars. The day following the altercation with Warham, says Cavendish, there were many arguments for and against the consummation of Katherine's first marriage. So complex was the matter 'that it was said that no man could know the truth'. 'Yes', broke in Fisher, inconveniently, 'I know the truth'. 'How know you the truth?' asked Wolsey. Fisher's reply was magisterial.

> *Ego sum professor veritatis*, I know that God is truth itself, nor he never spake but truth; who sayeth, *quos Deus conjunxit, homo non separet*. And forasmuch as this marriage was made and joined by God to a good intent, I say that I know the truth; the which cannot be broken or loosed by the power of man upon no feigned occasion.[16]

On 28 July Fisher spoke again of his concern to ease the king's conscience. According to Campeggio's secretary Fisher said he had heard Henry 'testify before all that his only intention was to get justice done, and to relieve himself of the scruple that he had on his conscience'. If he, Fisher, had not come forward with his opinion after two years' study of the matter he would have been failing in his duty. He had to speak 'both in order not to procure the damnation of his soul and in order not to be unfaithful to the king'.

> for this opinion he declared he would even lay down his life. He added that the Baptist in olden times regarded it as impossible for him to die more gloriously than in the cause of marriage, and that it was not so holy at that time as it has now become by the shedding of Christ's blood, he would encourage himself more ardently, more effectually, and with greater confidence to dare any great or extreme peril whatever.[17]

Naturally Henry could not allow Fisher's arguments to go unchallenged. Stephen Gardiner was assigned the task of replying to them in the king's name. A copy of his answer was plainly sent to Fisher, as it contains marginal comments in his hand.[18] Among other matters Henry and Gardiner claimed that Fisher had admitted that the reasons for considering the marriage incestuous and illegitimate were so serious that the case should be referred to Rome so as to restore Henry's tranquillity of mind. Fisher noted: 'I did not say this; certainly the cardinal wanted me to say this.' Thus once more an attempt was made to secure the appearance of Fisher's approval of the king's proceedings.

The failure of the legatine court to pass judgement led Henry to try a variety of policies and tactics: parliamentary legislation and intimidation of the clergy in convocation; production of literary propaganda; and the referendum of the universities of Europe. As one of Henry's foremost opponents Fisher was involved in dangerous counter-measures in all these spheres.

The story of the reformation parliament and its legislation is well known. Fisher showed his consternation at what he regarded as an attack on the Church in the very first session of 1529. He was motivated, it would seem, by the fear that financial anticlericalism might lead to outright heresy. The issue which goaded him into making a virulently critical speech against the commons was the bill concerning probate of wills. The sources for the incident are partisan, and so should be weighed carefully.[19]

Both the chronicler Hall and Fisher's earliest biographer agree that he attacked the commons and – implicitly at least – compared them with the heretics of Bohemia who had wrecked their own kingdom. According to Hall he said, 'now with the commons is nothing but "Down with the Church!"; and all this me seemeth is for lack of faith only'. Similarly the *Early Life* has him saying, 'ye shall find that all these mischiefs among them riseth only through lack of faith'.

Naturally enough the commons was outraged at this slur on its members' faith, or rather lack of it, and a complaint was made to the king through the speaker, Thomas Audley. As might be expected, the *Early Life* has Fisher giving a noble account of himself before Henry.

> he answered again that (being in counsel) he spake his mind in defence and right of the Church, whom he saw daily injured and oppressed among the common people, whose office was not to deal with her, and therefore said that he thought himself in conscience bound to defend her all that he might.[20]

Hall's chronicle, which is as favourable to Henry VIII as the *Early Life* is to Fisher, has that prelate being rather less candid: 'the bishop answered that he meant the doings of the Bohemians was for lack of faith, and not the doings of them that were in the common house'. Henry accepted Fisher's explanation, 'which blind excuse pleased the commons nothing at all'. Whichever is the more accurate account, it is astounding that Fisher should have been bold enough to make such a critical speech at all. It has been argued that Fisher's charge of lack of faith may have deterred the commons temporarily from pressing on with further anticlerical legislation.[21]

Fisher continued to be a dissident voice in both parliament and convocation. In October 1530 the Milanese and Venetian ambassadors both reported that the bishops of Rochester, Ely and Bath and Wells had been accused of *praemunire*, the Venetian stating that they had been arrested. It was no coincidence that the three were among the queen's most prominent supporters. In the event the trial never took place, and it is possible that Henry merely meant to use the threat of *praemunire* to intimidate the clergy in general.[22]

In 1531 came the demand to convocation to accept some degree of royal authority over the Church. There is some evidence that Fisher argued against this.[23] A conscience-saving clause was adopted which accepted Henry as supreme head of the Church 'as far as the law of Christ allows' (*quantum per legem Christi licet*). Fisher is usually credited with introducing this condition, though no sure documentary evidence of his initiative in the matter survives.

While Fisher was among the bishops who put their signatures to this limited acknowledgement, a number of the lower clergy signed protests to the effect that their assent to royal supremacy did not affect or lessen their obedience to papal authority. Among those who signed these documents were Robert Shorton, the queen's chaplain and sometime master of St John's, Cambridge; Robert Ridley as procurator for the clergy of London diocese; Nicholas Metcalfe as archdeacon of Rochester; and John Wylbor and Robert Johnson on behalf of the clergy of Rochester diocese.[24]

At this point the question should be asked, how far did Fisher encourage or even coordinate the moves of the opposition? Was there an 'Aragonese party', and was Fisher its moving spirit? Some light is thrown on parliamentary activity by the confession of George Throckmorton, made in 1537 when he was implicated in the alleged treason of Reginald Pole. In 1532 he was one of those MPs made uneasy by the king's proceedings who frequented the Queen's Head tavern, and he was urged to be vocal in opposition in the commons by three of the most prominent upholders of Katherine's marriage. Friar William Peto, then in prison in Lambeth palace for a bold sermon preached in Henry's and Anne's presence, 'advised me if I were in the parliament house to stick to that matter as I would have my soul saved'. Shortly afterwards Sir Thomas More sent for him and reinforced Peto's exhortation, saying, 'and ye do continue in the same way that ye began and be not afraid to say your conscience, ye shall deserve great reward of God and thanks of the king's grace at length and much worship to yourself'. Throckmorton had many discussions with Fisher, who advised him to consult Nicholas Wilson. Finally, he visited Richard Reynolds of Syon, who told him that if he said or did anything in parliament against his conscience he would answer for it on the day of judgement: 'which opinion was contrary both to the bishop of Rochester and Master Wilson; for their opinion was that if I did think in my conscience that my speaking could do no good, then I might hold my peace and not offend'.[25] For Fisher, then, opposition to Henry was a matter of individual conscience rather than the following of a party line.

In May 1532 Fisher received a deputation of clergy at Rochester who sought his advice on the imminent submission to Henry VIII; he was too ill himself to attend convocation.[26] His last significant action in that body was to vote against denial of the pope's dispensing power in April 1533.[27]

The despatches of Eustace Chapuys, imperial ambassador to England from 1529, are an illuminating source for Fisher's activity in opposition. They show both his tactics in parliament and convocation, and the interplay between those bodies and the royal court. Chapuys has been criticised as an unreliable witness. Certainly he was devoted to the queen and her cause, and the aim of his reports was to persuade the Habsburgs to intervene actively in the affairs of England. His statements must be balanced against other accounts of events, yet where they can be corroborated by independent evidence, they are usually found to be accurate and truthful.[28]

Chapuys' despatch of 23 January 1531 shows both the increasing pressure Henry was putting on Fisher and the cunning with which the two men dealt with each other.[29] In the first place, Henry tried to mislead Fisher. As Chapuys told the emperor, 'Sire, the bishop of Rochester sent to tell me that once more the king has tried new practices to suborn both him and the others who hold for the queen's part, giving them to understand a thousand follies and lies.' These concerned the alleged enmity between pope and emperor which meant that Rome would favour Henry's cause. Chapuys persuaded the papal nuncio to explain the truth of the matter to Fisher, who was satisfied. Henry learned about the meeting, and questioned Fisher about it the following morning.

> To which the bishop responded that it was no other thing, but that the other had come to tell him of the pope's desire to call the council, and that he had asked him to do all that was possible for this, as well with the king as with the clergy. I advised the nuncio of this immediately, so that if they were questioned their stories would match.

Here Fisher was plainly deceiving his king; but that king had already tried to deceive Fisher.

On 21 February 1531 Chapuys reported that Fisher still opposed the proceedings in parliament as much as he could, despite his sickness; though as he had been threatened with being thrown in the river together with his followers he had been obliged to conform to the will of the king.[30] In fact, Fisher had been refused a writ for the parliament of 1531, but had attended all the same.[31] As well as illness and anxiety he had to endure verbal bullying from Anne Boleyn's father. That unlikely theologian 'dared to say to the bishop of Rochester that he wished to argue and maintain by witness of holy scripture that when God left this world he left no successor or vicar'.

Fisher's enemies soon went beyond mere bluster, as Chapuys' report of 1 March shows. The king had informed the peers in parliament about the strange case of Fisher's cook. On 18 February a broth had been prepared in his household which brought all who tasted it to the point of death. In the event two servants died, as well as some poor people who were fed by Fisher's charity, and the rest were in great pain and extremity of sickness. 'By the grace of God the good bishop (whom he knows to be still useful and most necessary in this world) did not taste of the said drugs and so escaped.' Fisher's brother had ordered that the cook be seized. The cook had confessed that someone had given him a powder to put in the broth, saying that it was to play a joke on the servants and would not hurt them.[32]

The poisoning attempt is well documented from other sources. The cook, Richard Roose, was probably a dupe of the real murderer, since he failed to disclose any information despite being severely racked and put to a cruel death. He was sentenced to be boiled alive in chains, an execution which the *Greyfriars Chronicle* recorded in gruesome detail. Such was the king's horror of poisoning – and possibly, too, fear of being suspected of compassing Fisher's death – that a special act of parliament was passed on Roose's account making any such crime treason.[33]

The *Early Life* contains an accurate account of the poisoning, noting that the two fatalities were Fisher's servant Curwen and an old widow. It adds a further attempt on Fisher's life which is not recited elsewhere. While he was at home in Lambeth, 'suddenly a gun was shot through the top of his house, not far from his study where he accustomably used to sit . . . Which at last was found to come from the other side of the Thames out of the earl of Wiltshire's house, who was father to the Lady Anne'.[34] If Thomas Boleyn was still living at Durham House in the Strand, then the shot was a long one indeed. However, Van Ortroy thinks the early biographer got the story from some servant of Fisher and seems inclined to believe it, as does the present writer.[35]

As a postscript to the poisoning affair Chapuys wrote on 9 October that Anne Boleyn feared no one in England more than Fisher, because he had always defended the queen without respect of persons. She had sent a message to persuade him not to attend parliament in case he caught some sickness as he had done before. Despite the veiled threat Fisher defied her; he was determined to come and speak the truth more boldly than he had ever dared.[36]

Fisher's activities had, not surprisingly, been noted; moreover, he was getting perilously close to intrigue with Chapuys. The ambassador wrote to Charles V on 11 January 1532: 'With regard to the bishop of Rochester, I will let him know what it pleased your majesty to command me in your said letters, and that by writing and through a third person, as there is no other way at present.' Fisher had sent to tell him that if they happened to meet in public Chapuys should not try to speak to him and should not take it amiss if he, Fisher, did the same until the present storm had died down. Chapuys said he had sure and safe means of keeping Fisher informed of everything and of maintaining his goodwill, as the emperor had commanded.[37]

Later that month Fisher was once more as devious as his king. His decision to attend parliament, the threats of Anne Boleyn notwithstanding, had put him in something of a quandary, as Chapuys reported to the emperor on 22 January. The horns of his dilemma were that he felt duty-bound to obey the king, yet his conscience prompted him to speak in defence of the marriage. When Henry heard of Fisher's arrival he sent to tell him that he was very glad and had many things about which to talk to him. Fisher, however, was afraid that the king only wished to forbid him to speak about the divorce. Accordingly he went to pay his respects to Henry just as the king was going to mass. Henry received him far better than before, putting off their talk until after mass; but Fisher was too quick for him, and left before the end of the service. As Fisher had confided all this to Chapuys, the ambassador conveyed to him the relevant part of the emperor's instructions. Fisher thanked him and offered his services to Charles, begging Chapuys to write to him only in cipher.[38]

In March 1533 Fisher was vocal in convocation, though Chapuys was doubtful of the effectiveness of his intervention:

> his opinion being alone, notwithstanding that it is very just and very reasonable, will not be efficacious in preventing the triumph of the voices opposite. So much so that the queen and the said Rochester, too, and others who hold for her party take the case as irremediably lost, considering the docility of the synod and the blind and disordered desire of the said king.[39]

Katherine and Fisher were right to be pessimistic. Anne Boleyn was advanced in pregnancy, and Henry's 'divorce' was rushed through a court at Dunstable, remote enough from the capital to frustrate the chance of protest. Fisher was too outspoken to be left at liberty, and he was arrested on Palm Sunday. According to Chapuys he had been 'made prisoner in the charge of the bishop of Winchester; which is a very strange thing, as this prelate is the most holy and learned in Christendom'. Henry justified the arrest to parliament by claiming that Fisher had been rumour-mongering, but the real reason for Fisher's detention was his virile defence of the cause of pope and queen.[40] Fisher was effectively mewed up so that he could not cause trouble either at Dunstable or at Anne's coronation on 1 June. He was released on 13 June through Cromwell's intercession.

Since the failure of the legatine court in 1529 Fisher had been occupied in opposing the king's two interlinked strategies aimed at securing some sort of authority for the annulment of his marriage; literary propaganda, and the canvassing of the European universities. Oxford and Cambridge were asked for a judgement on the marriage early in 1530. It might be expected that they would hasten to accommodate their sovereign by giving him the unfavourable verdict he desired. In fact, conflict and opposition were evident at both universities. As far as Cambridge is concerned it seems likely that Fisher was orchestrating the resistance from a distance.

A sidelight on the dissension over the university determination is thrown by a letter from Edward Foxe, provost of King's College, chaplain to Henry VIII and propagandist in his master's cause, to William Buckmaster, vice-chancellor of Cambridge. It concerned a controversy conducted in sermons between Hugh Latimer and members of St John's College, but there was an ominous comment about the royal divorce. Foxe showed that it was suspected that Hugh Latimer's opponents had been egged on by friends of Fisher such as John Watson, the reason being that Latimer favoured the king's cause.[41]

Three of the St John's fellows who preached against Latimer did oppose Henry's divorce and breach with Rome. Ralph Baynes openly argued against the divorce, and fled abroad in 1534. So, too, did Dr Buckenham, prior of the Cambridge Blackfriars and another who had preached against Latimer. Thomas Greenwood took his DD at St John's in 1532 and became a Carthusian, being one of those starved to death in prison in 1535 for resistance to royal supremacy. As for Watson, he was among the Cambridge delegates appointed to debate the divorce in 1530 but his name is not among those marked as favourable to the king. In January 1531 he was replaced as master of Christ's College by Henry Lockwood, a client of Cromwell.[42]

Though Cambridge could not but give Henry the desired negative judgement, it was not quite on the terms the king desired. The university voted that marriage with a brother's widow who had been known carnally by her first husband was forbidden by divine and natural law. As Katherine continually asserted her virginity at the time of her second marriage this could not apply to her case. It is quite possible that Fisher advised Cambridge to render an innocuous verdict.[43]

So much for Cambridge. Meanwhile, Fisher was kept busy writing works on the marriage and keeping himself abreast of the debate on the case among European scholars. On 31 December 1529 Chapuys sent Charles V two works respectively by Fisher and Tunstal.[44] On 6 February 1530 he reported that Fisher 'has finished revising and correcting the book which I sent lately to your majesty. And he has written a new one which the queen commanded me to send to your majesty by express courier and with all diligence'. Katherine wanted this book sent to Rome for the information of her imperial defenders there. Fisher himself was willing, 'although he is in great fear of being suspected as the author of this last book, as the said queen writes to your majesty'. Chapuys was convinced of the usefulness of Fisher's work.

> What I send is testimony of the trouble he has taken to make the said books, as also of his learning. Which, together with the great renown of his good and holy life, known and revealed at Rome and elsewhere, will be of no little efficacy to give authority and credence to his opinion, especially as he is a subject of this king.[45]

This was quite possibly the book on the marriage by Fisher which was published at Alcalá in August 1530.[46] In November Chapuys reported Fisher's willingness to have his books printed as long as he himself was not informed beforehand of their publication; thus he could satisfy his conscience by obeying the letter of the king's command while continuing to defend the marriage.[47] Chapuys sent the emperor another book lately finished by Fisher with his despatch of 4 December 1530. The queen wanted him to beg Charles to send it to the pope.[48]

Though he might disclaim knowledge of their publication, Fisher's works were too harmful to the king's case for him to be allowed to continue writing without hindrance. On 21 December 1530 Chapuys wrote that Fisher had been summoned to Lambeth palace by Archbishop Warham. There he found John Stokesley, bishop of London waiting for him, together with Doctors Lee and Foxe. The three tried to persuade Fisher to retract everything he had written in Katherine's favour.

> The bishop replied with much prudence and moderation that the matter was in itself so clear that no arguments upon it were needed, and that besides, the pope being sole judge and arbiter, the case could only properly be argued before him.... Upon which the bishop and the others, seeing that they could neither convince him nor draw him into controversy, accused him of being selfwilled and obstinate, and said that he would, in spite of all he could say, be compelled to argue the question, as the king had determined to appoint six doctors on his side, and six on the queen's, to debate the case.[49]

This debate had been scheduled for 12 January 1531. On 8 January Stokesley wrote to Fisher suggesting that they each lead a team of six doctors to debate the case. The tone of the letter was respectful, amicable and disingenuous, as Stokesley claimed that he was writing without the king's knowledge.[50] Katherine's supporters were quite as wily as Henry's, however. Chapuys wrote to Fisher and other counsellors

> to avoid by all means being drawn into arguing this case, and if they are compelled so to do to protest that they are not therein acting as advocates, servants or counsellors of the queen. All have engaged to do so, and for greater security I will obtain from the queen a public instrument disavowing them, and having their names removed from her council.[51]

Fisher had at least one more interview with Warham as well as some correspondence with him about the marriage. During one of his interrogation sessions in 1535 he admitted that he had written to Warham 'saying that he knew certainly that all the universities of the world could never prove that marriage with a dead brother's wife is against the laws of God and of nature'. When asked whether he had so written in order to persuade Warham against the king's cause Fisher answered, 'I did not so write in order to change his opinion, but that he might refrain from urging me to assent to anything against my conscience.'[52]

Despite the attempts to intimidate him by his brother bishops Fisher continued to write for the queen. On 1 October 1531 Chapuys sent Charles yet another book lately finished by Fisher, a reply to a printed book in Henry's favour. Chapuys wanted it sent to Rome because Fisher was the author and because it was very important for the queen's case.[53] On 25 November Chapuys sent Charles the final part of this book, urging once more that it be sent to Rome immediately. The king had ordered publication of a book favourable to himself in England so as to sway the people in view of the impending meeting of parliament; this was a further reason for sending Fisher's book, which would do marvels for the queen's cause, to Rome.[54]

Meanwhile Fisher kept himself informed about the debate on the marriage on the continent. In October 1531 Chapuys wrote to Charles about a Spanish scholar at Paris named Moscoso who had written a book in Katherine's favour. Fisher had been greatly impressed by it, and wanted it printed. He also wanted Moscoso to write a response to the *Determinations of the Universities* composed for Henry since Moscoso, besides being learned, was able to reveal exactly what had gone on at Paris when the university verdicts were returned.[55]

Less evidence of Fisher's literary activity is found for the year 1532, though he was writing a treatise on clerical independence and in June preached a sermon in Katherine's favour which, as Chapuys said, had sealed the mouths of the king's protagonists. However the queen's treatment had not improved, and Fisher himself was now in danger of prison or some other punishment because of the sermon.[56]

The dangerous summer of 1533 saw Fisher hard at his literary labours. Stephen Vaughan wrote to Cromwell from Antwerp in August to report on the book-running activities of the exiled Franciscan Observants led by Peto. A new book against the Boleyn marriage published in Antwerp was, according to Peto, the work of Fisher: 'and so being drawn and made, should by the said bishop be afterward delivered in England to two Spaniards being secular and laymen. . . . If privy search be made – and shortly – peradventure in the house of the same bishop shall be found his first copy'. Vaughan added that 'Peto laboureth busier than a bee in the setting forth of this book.' Meanwhile, 'The bishop of Rochester delivered his copy to the Spaniards as is aforesaid, and the Spaniards, un-knowing to the bishop, set in all haste writers to take another copy, by mean whereof their book is now framed, and intermingled with Greek and Spanish.'[57]

It is impossible to estimate exactly how many books Fisher wrote on the 'king's great matter' as most of the sources do not give them titles or discuss the contents in detail. In addition, most of them seem to have disappeared. Dr Ortiz reported from Rome in April 1531 that he had seen two books by Fisher which were different from the one published at Alcalà, while another of his letters re-veals that Fisher had written a response to the *Determinations of the Universities*.[58]

Fisher himself was quite vague about the number of his books when under interrogation in 1535.

I am not certain how many, but I can recall seven or eight that I have written. The matter was so serious, both on account of the importance of the persons it concerned, and the expressed command of the king, that I gave more labour and diligence to seeking out the truth lest I should fail him and others than I ever gave to any other matter.[59]

When asked about books or copies sent abroad he was able to answer, 'I never sent or consented to the sending of any of these books over sea, nor did the transcriber or his servant have them with my knowledge'. He was also asked whether he had given books to foreigners to be 'published under a strange style by someone who was not the king's subject and feared not his indignation, though he wrote what was lewd and slanderous?' 'Such an idea never occurred to me', was Fisher's dry reply. Fisher was quite circumspect when questioned about his book against the *Determinations*; 'I feel sure that the book I wrote against the opinion of the universities was not sent to Paris, for at that time when the Lady Katherine asked it of me, scarcely half of it was written.' Equally he denied giving advice to Thomas Abell or consenting to the publication of his book on the marriage, nor had he had anything to do with a book 'printed and born without certain author or father'.[60]

These circuitous replies notwithstanding, it is plain that Fisher did keep in touch with other dissident scholars and supporters of the queen. A former servant of Katherine confessed some years later that 'I was sent divers times to the bishop of Rochester that was beheaded for books, and for his chaplain Dr Addison to come to her to Greenwich at sundry times.' In addition, 'as touching the bishops and doctors of her council Master Griffith did practise with them and also with the emperor's ambassador with sending to her learned men at Rome'.[61] As Fisher was one of the queen's official counsellors, and as Henry was trying to give the appearance of giving his wife a legitimate hearing, this was scarcely treasonable.

In 1535 Fisher was questioned closely about letters to Queen Katherine found in his possession. These were written by the servant of an unknown German prince; evidently it was hoped to distil some smell of treason from them. The extracts from the letters quoted in the record of the examination actually seem quite innocuous. Fisher thought there was nothing in them except Katherine's protestation of her virginity when she married Henry. He supposed the queen had sent them to him 'to let me see she was not despised by the princes of other countries', and he strongly denied that he had given 'advice or consent to the writer to do anything with the German princes against the king'.[62]

Fisher was interrogated about other letters he had received, and he was careful in his answers to avoid charges of sedition or misprision of treason. Implicitly he was accused of trying to set George Day of St John's College against the king's cause. He replied: 'George

Day was at liberty to judge me as he wished. For myself, I certainly desired nothing but the victory of the truth'; 'I never blamed anyone for defending the king's cause or advised anyone to advocate that of the king'.[63] Asked why he had concealed letters sent to him by Peter Ligham and by Ralph Baynes he replied that he had not thought they expressed ill will to the king. Indeed, the extract from Ligham's letter quoted in the interrogation goes out of its way to show loyalty to Henry.[64]

After Fisher's death it was discovered that he had sent the dissident monks of Syon copies of letters between himself and Henry which he had promised to show no one, besides one of his own works on the marriage, Abell's book and a work thought to have been written by Chapuys.[65] This was most definitely a breach of confidence; but it seems safe to say that Fisher was furnishing the brothers with arguments for the validity of the marriage rather than inciting them to rebellion.

September 1533 saw the birth of a daughter to Henry and Anne, and Fisher's passage from loyal opposition to overt treason. On 27 September Chapuys told Charles V that papal censures against England would have to be accompanied by a strong remedy: 'as the good and holy bishop of Rochester sent to tell me, who said that the pope's arms with regard to these people are more frail than lead, and that it is meet that your majesty put your hand to the work; and that would be a work as pleasing to God as to go against the Turk'.[66] Fisher's appeal to the emperor was reiterated in Chapuys' despatch of 10 October. The queen, said the ambassador, out of the love she bore her husband asked for no remedy but law and justice; but the good and holy bishop wanted active intervention by the emperor.[67]

In asking for foreign military intervention Fisher was, unequivocally, guilty of treason, and it is highly ironic that Henry never knew of his appeal to imperial arms. Yet his stance is hardly surprising in view of his ecclesiology. The emperor wielded the temporal sword of Christendom, which in Fisher's view should support the spiritual power of the holy see. As his own prince threatened the unity of Catholic Christendom by his defiance of Rome and precipitate, bigamous marriage, he, Fisher, must call upon a higher authority.

How seriously Fisher expected Charles V to answer his call to arms is highly questionable. Certainly there is no evidence that he was plotting against the king in anticipation of an imperial invasion. None the less he remained a thorn in the royal side because of his silent opposition. Consequently Henry and Cromwell took the chance to involve him in the treason of the Nun of Kent.

Elizabeth Barton first came to notice as an innocent visionary, but in the course of time she and her revelations became blatantly political. She took to prophesying that if the king persisted in his evil courses he would lose his throne, his life and his chance of heaven. Such utterances were, of course, treasonable. Elizabeth had clear links with Observant Franciscans and other dissidents. She was known to have approached Fisher and More, and it was hoped that she would provide the rope to hang them.[68]

It was known that Fisher had learned about Elizabeth's revelations from the Nun herself (who also spoke with his chaplain Addison), from Friar Hugh Riche and from Dr Edmund Bocking. These two had also spoken with a merchant named White, who may have been Fisher's half-brother. One of the Nun's associates testified that Fisher had wept for joy when he heard her prophecies, saying that he gave them the more credence because she had been to the king several times and reproached him for his sins.[69]

In January 1534 Fisher was too ill to attend parliament, and wrote to Cromwell for leave of absence.

> I doubt not but if ye might see me in what plight I am ye would have some pity upon me. For in good faith now almost this six weeks I have had a grievous cough with a fever in the beginning thereof, as divers other here in this country hath had, and divers have died thereof. And now the matter is fallen down into my legs and feet, with such swelling and ache that I may neither ride nor go.[70]

Such patent ill health did not prevent his harassment by Cromwell, and two days later he sent his brother with another letter. This, like the preceding one, was not in his own hand, possibly because he was too weak to write. Certainly his fatigue and frustration are evident: 'I perceive that everything I write is ascribed either to craft, or to willfulness, or to affection, or to unkindness against my sovereign'. As for the 'king's great matter',

> my study and purpose was specially to decline that I should not be straited to offend his grace in that behalf, for then I must needs declare my conscience, the which ... I would be loth to do any more largely than I have done; not that I condemn any men's conscience, their conscience may save them and mine must save me.[71]

That Fisher was subjected to rough psychological treatment at this time is attested by a draft of Cromwell's one surviving letter to him. He berated Fisher 'for where ye labour to excuse yourself of your hearing, believing and concealing of the maiden's false and feigned revelations, and of your manifold sending of your chaplains unto her'. He mocked Fisher's credulity, and argued at length that, even though she had told Henry himself of her revelations, still Fisher was bound to report such treasonable words.[72]

Fisher complied as far as he could in a letter to Henry of 27 February 1534. He admitted that the Nun had visited him at Rochester three times.

> The first time she came unto my house, unsent for of my part, and then she told me that she had been with your grace, and that she had shown unto you a revelation which she had from almighty God. . . . She said that if your grace went forth with the purpose that ye intended, ye should not be king of England seven months after. . . . I conceived not by these words, I take it upon my soul, that any malice or evil was intended or meant unto your highness by any man, but only that they were the threats of God, as she did then affirm.[73]

At about the same time and in roughly the same terms Fisher wrote in his own defence to the peers in parliament, as he was too ill to attend the lords. He claimed it was reasonable that he should believe the Nun, given her life and reputation; denied that he had known her revelations were false, or that he himself had coached her in treason; and asserted that he did not see the need to inform the king as Elizabeth herself had visited Henry. Moreover,

> As I will answer before the throne of Christ, I knew not of any malice or evil that was intended by her or by any other earthly creature unto the king's highness; neither her words did so sound that by any temporal or worldly power such thing was intended, but only by the power of God; of whom as she then said, she had this revelation to show unto the king.[74]

Whether Fisher's eloquence was wasted or whether, as Reynolds conjectured, the lords did not have a chance to hear his letter read, he was found guilty of misprision or concealment of treason, together with his chaplain Addison.[75] The penalty was loss of liberty and goods. Fisher was not imprisoned immediately, as Henry was preparing a more dangerous charge against the opposition.

On 7 March 1534 Chapuys reported, 'The holy bishop of Rochester has been sent for and is in very great danger because he spoke several times with the Nun'. Both Fisher and More were really being harassed because they held to the queen's part.[76] That same day an act was passed depriving Katherine of her title and status of queen. This was followed by the act of succession, which affirmed the legality of the Boleyn marriage and acknowledged its issue as heirs to the throne. As the pope had recently found the Aragon marriage to be valid this act – or rather, the oath of succession which it imposed theoretically on all adult males – would prove a test of loyalty for papalists like Fisher. On 16 April Chapuys noted briefly that Fisher, More and others had been sent to the Tower for refusing the oath of succession, and on 22 April he reported the widespread fear that the king would put them to death.[77]

Roland Lee was sent to visit Fisher, whom he found ready to swear to the succession as a *fait accompli*, and to promise 'never to meddle more' in the case of the Aragon marriage. But, Lee told Cromwell, on one matter he would not move: 'as for the case of the prohibition Levitical, his conscience is so knit that he may not put it from him, whatsoever betide him'. Fisher was sick and weary, prepared to accept the Boleyn marriage *de facto* though not *de jure* but wholly unable to impugn papal authority. Lee described Fisher's state with some compassion: 'Truly the man is nigh gone and doubtless cannot continue unless the king and his council be merciful to him, for the body cannot bear the clothes on his back.'[78]

Cranmer made a sensible if cynical attempt to exploit Fisher's and More's willingness to compromise. They could swear to the body of the act though not to the preamble, either because it impugned papal authority or because it denied the validity of the king's first marriage.[79]

The seeming acquiescence of Fisher and More would have been a tremendous propaganda coup for the regime. Henry, however, was bent on unconditional surrender. Cromwell's letter to Cranmer conveying this message exists in a draft whose handwriting gets wilder as it proceeds.

If they swore only to the act and not to the preamble, it might seem that they still accepted papal supremacy and did not recognise the Boleyn marriage. They would swear to both; for the accomplishment of this 'the king's highness hath special trust and expectation in your grace's approved wisdom and dexterity'; and

Henry was firm 'that ye will in no wise suppose, attempt or move him to the contrary'.[80]

In November 1534 Fisher was attainted of misprision of treason for the second time, charged with having refused the oath of succession, and belatedly condemned to imprisonment and loss of goods. (Fisher's property had been seized by the king's men in April, when he was imprisoned.)[81] The act of supremacy was also passed that November, but Henry was preparing something with rather more teeth for the dissidents.[82] The new act made it high treason maliciously to wish or attempt any harm to Henry and Anne and their heirs, to deprive them of their titles (such as supreme head), or to call the king a heretic, tyrant or usurper.

Henry did not move against the opposition immediately, probably because he still hoped for conformity. A letter of Fisher to Cromwell of 22 December shows that he was still under pressure and that conditions in the Tower were a good inducement to submission.

Despite the attainder Cromwell still demanded that Fisher should write his opinion of the succession to the king. Fisher was loth to do so as he knew this would only anger and displease Henry. He reminded Cromwell that he had been willing to swear to the succession as he accepted that any prince could, with the assent of his parliament, bequeath the crown as he wished: 'Albeit I refused to swear to some other parcels, because that my conscience would not serve me so to do.'

While technically not under torture, Fisher's conditions amounted to such. He implored Cromwell's help, 'for I have neither shirt nor sheet nor yet other clothes that are necessary for me to wear but that be ragged and rent-to shamefully. Notwithstanding I might easily suffer that, if they would keep my body warm'. Ill health and old age meant that he could only eat a little and a few kinds of food. He had no resources 'but as my brother of his own purse layeth out for me, to his great hindrance'. In desperation Fisher begged Cromwell 'to move the king's highness to take me unto his gracious favour again, and to restore me unto my liberty out of this cold and painful imprisonment'. Finally, he asked that he might be allowed some spiritual consolation,

> that I may take some priest within the Tower by the assignment of Master Lieutenant, to hear my confession against this holy time; [and] that I may borrow some books to stir my devotion

more effectually these holy days for the comfort of my soul. This I beseech you to grant me of your charity, and thus Our Lord send you a merry Christmas and a comfortable, to your heart's desire.[83]

This letter hardly shows Fisher to be the dangerous conspirator Henry later claimed him to be. Yet when it was plain that neither he nor More would accommodate their consciences to suit the king, strenuous attempts were made to prove collusion between them in the plotting of treason. The king's anger was particularly provoked by the news that Fisher had been made a cardinal, and this undoubtedly accelerated both his own and More's trial and condemnation.[84]

There began detailed examinations of Fisher, More and any witnesses who might incriminate them. Fisher's servant Richard Wilson was first interrogated on 7 June 1535.[85] He testified that at midsummer 1534 Robert Fisher, John Wylbor and Robert Johnson had tried to persuade Fisher to take the oath of succession; he had replied that he hoped some great misfortune would befall him if he did so. Round about Candlemas 1535 Robert Fisher had informed his brother that the act of supremacy had been passed, whereupon the bishop 'took up his hands and blessed him saying, "Is it so?"' About the same time Robert told him about the treasons act; Wilson could not remember whether Fisher had said anything about it. Wilson deposed further that Fisher had received a visit from his half-brother Edward White, but that their sole topic of conversation had been the anabaptists.

Wilson was questioned about letters or other communication between Fisher and More or anyone else. All that he could remember was that Addison had brought two letters. Wilson had persuaded Fisher to send for the statute book, which he read and then burned. Because he made much of the word 'maliciously' it was suspected that he had been in contact with More. Wilson admitted only to sending More's servant half a custard recently and some green sauce a while back. More's servant had sent an image of St John and apples and oranges 'shortly after the snow that fell in winter'. On new year's day More's servant had sent a paper on which was written the sum of £2,000 in gold – presumably one of More's jokes – and an image of the Epiphany. Wilson suspected that letters had been carried between Fisher and More by George Golde, the lieutenant's servant.

Wilson said that Fisher had burned papers 'that I might not see them', and had asked him to burn other papers in his presence;

'but I was never so bold to look in any paper that he bade me burn'. Wilson had carried one letter from Fisher to More which he had not read, and said that 'we were agreed to deny any letters to be sent between my lord and Master More'. He had heard Fisher tell Golde that he had never carried any letter which concerned the king's business.

On one occasion Golde brought Fisher some scrolls of paper which he had cut out of books belonging to the Carthusian monks who were executed for denying royal supremacy. Wilson managed to glimpse one text, '*Pasce oves meas*', and some discussion about the supremacy. When the Carthusians were under examination Fisher had said, 'I pray God that no vanity subvert them'.

Golde admitted to cutting the pages out of the monks' books and to carrying about a dozen letters between Fisher and More, some written in ink and some with a coal. He confessed that Fisher, Wilson and he had agreed to deny that letters had been exchanged, though if Golde were 'sworn on a book' he should tell the truth. Golde was particularly questioned about when and where he had heard the news of Fisher's creation as cardinal, as were other witnesses.

Another piece of relevant testimony came from More's servant John à Wood. Fisher had asked More through Golde what answer he had made to the king's council. More said he had replied that he would not think about the king's title but give himself to his beads and think on his passage hence. He advised Fisher not to give the same answer lest the council should think they were agreed; for himself, he would meddle with no man's conscience but his own.

Fisher was interrogated on 12 June about his knowledge of the statutes and communication with More.[86] He admitted exchanging letters with More but was fairly evasive about their contents; the ones he had received he had burned once read. He had sent letters to Robert Fisher, Edward White and others chiefly about his diet and expenses, as well as a letter to Lady Oxford 'for her comfort'. He had received no letters from outside the Tower except for 'one that Erasmus did send unto him, which this respondent's brother Robert Fisher showed first to Master Secretary or it came to him'. He admitted that he had agreed with Wilson and Golde to keep secret the exchange of letters with More.

All his caution was of no avail. Fisher was specifically condemned for denying royal supremacy at the Tower on 7 May by saying 'The king our sovereign lord is not supreme head in earth of the Church of England.'[87] The truth of this is confirmed by Wilson, who deposed that on 7 May ('the Friday after Ascension') Cromwell and others had examined Fisher at the Tower; Wilson was in the room behind a partition, and had managed to hear part of what was said. The act of supremacy was read to Fisher, who said 'that he could not consent nor find in his heart to take the king to be supreme head of the Church of England according to the said statute'. The treasons act was then read to him. Thus as early as 7 May Fisher was technically guity of uttering treason; the continued interrogations can only mean that Henry was still hopeful of securing his submission.

Both Rastell and the earliest biographer say that Fisher was tricked into speaking treason by a secret messenger sent by the king, who told him that Henry only wanted to satisfy his conscience and that Fisher's opinion would not put him in danger of the law.[88] The *Early Life* casts Richard Riche, More's betrayer, in the role of Judas.

As Fisher had already told Cromwell and others that he could not accept royal supremacy this might seem a superfluous measure and the story suspect. Perhaps, though, Henry used such a device either to make sure of his prey or to change Fisher's opinion. Most extraordinary is the account of Chapuys, very likely a witness of Fisher's execution, of the authorities' eleventh-hour attempt to change Fisher's mind: 'He was marvellously solicited once he was on the scaffold to consent to the king's desire, mercy being offered him. But he did not comply, and died most virtuously.'[89] Chapuys' report is credible; the last-minute conversion of one of the most obdurate opponents of royal supremacy who was also a cardinal of the Roman Church would have made magnificent theatre indeed.

The issue of Fisher's trial on 17 June was scarcely in doubt, and on 22 June 1535 he was beheaded on Tower Hill for the crime of treason. So weak was he that he had to rest several times on the short walk from the Tower; one account has it that he was carried part of the way in a chair. He had hardly courted martyrdom, but his opposition to Henry VIII, principled and consistent, could only lead to his death. While willing to accommodate his king by accepting the succession as a matter of dynastic politics, his conscience refused to be moved on two points: the validity of the Aragon marriage, for which the pope had power to dispense; and the supremacy of the pope as Christ's deputy on earth.

Fisher's pastoral concern for Henry is shown in his last words as recorded by the witness William Rastell: 'I pray God save the king and the realm, and hold his holy hand over it, and send the king a good counsel.'[90] Yet as he had told Cromwell, in the last resort he had to obey a higher loyalty than that he owed Henry: 'as I will answer before God, I would not in any manner of point offend his grace, my duty saved unto God, whom I must in everything prefer'.[91]

8 The Cardinal

as much as he flees glory, so much does it pursue him[1]

The modern statue of John Fisher outside St George's Cathedral, Southwark depicts him carrying rather than wearing a cardinal's hat; an allusion to the fact that Fisher, created cardinal in May 1535, never received the red hat, and indeed went to his death the following month. Fisher's elevation to the purple has tended to be treated as a coda to his career: the highest honour the Roman Church could bestow on a faithful son; allegedly the direct cause of his martyrdom; but a matter significant only in terms of his personal glory or tragedy, with little importance for the reformation in general. Indeed, it is often forgotten that Fisher was the English cardinal between Wolsey and Pole. Consequently Fisher's cardinalate has been bereft of all significance. In reality, it had far-reaching consequences for anglo-papal relations and for the course of ecclesiastical history in England.

On 15 June 1535 Bernardino Sandro, writing to Thomas Starkey from Padua, remarked that people in England must have heard of the recent creation of cardinals without money changing hands ('*senza dinari*'). Among them was Fisher, and all of them were by the universal voice of great probity, learning and holy life.[2] The polished phrases of the papal bureaucracy notwithstanding, men were rarely made cardinals for their virtue, sanctity, learning or integrity. These might be incidental factors, but other considerations weighed more tellingly.

Most cardinals were members of Roman and other Italian princely houses, or relatives and favourites of the current pope. A minority of cardinals would be foreigners promoted for diplomatic reasons. English cardinals were either statesmen or members of noble families. Politics often played a direct part, as for example, when Henry VIII tried unsuccessfully to persuade Clement VII to promote Ghinucci, bishop of Worcester and the protonotario Casale, with the hope that they would further his divorce suit at the curia. Why, then, did Paul III bestow the red hat on the bishop of Rochester? One of the pope's motives was general rather than related exclusively to Fisher. Though Paul's concern with reform of the Church and convocation of a general council seems to have been sincere, he did not find this reform-mindedness incompatible with nepotism on the grand scale. Among the cardinals of his first creation of 18 December 1534 were two of his grandsons, aged respectively 14 and 17. Such youthful appointments were not unprecedented, and Paul was not unique in confusing the good of his family with the wellbeing of the Church.

However, and doubtless to his surprise, this blatant nepotism aroused the wrath of contemporaries. It was to obviate this scandal that the creations of May 1535 and December 1536 were to include men of outstanding religious, intellectual and moral qualities. Indeed, it would seem that the cardinals of 1535 were each selected for a specific purpose. The archbishop of Capua represented the imperial interest, Guillaume Du Bellay and Ghinucci of Worcester that of the French king. Fisher and Contarini, both reputedly learned and virtuous, were meant to counterbalance the political character of the first three appointments, while Simonetta was chosen for his knowledge of ecclesiastical law which would be useful in safeguarding the rights of the holy see in the forthcoming general council. The record of consistory proceedings merely notes that the necessity of creating cardinals was called to mind and lists the men who were to be so honoured. The French ambassador in Rome told Jean Du Bellay that Fisher and Contarini were last-minute appointments (*'faitz a l'improviste'*), and that the few people who knew they had been chosen had been commanded to silence on pain of excommunication.[3]

Dr Ortiz, imperial representative in Rome, credited the pope with an idealistic motive in promoting Fisher. Writing to the empress on 31 May 1535, he rejoiced at Fisher's elevation, thinking that before he was aware of it God would have given him the true red hat, the crown of martyrdom. He saw the creation as confirmation of Queen Katherine's rights and of the truth of the faith, and as a condemnation of King Henry and of the errors sown in his realm.[4] In fact, it would seem that Paul III did not intend Fisher's promotion as a defiance of Henry VIII. On the contrary, he was prepared to be quite disingenuous in his efforts to appease the king and help Fisher, and was shocked and dismayed at Henry's furious reaction.

On 29 May 1535 the bishop of Macon wrote to the French king of the pope's request that Francis I should use all his influence with Henry VIII in Fisher's favour. Macon himself felt that this would be of little use, as the imperialists were trying to stir Henry's suspicions of Francis by saying that Fisher had been promoted at the request of the French king. The pope, he said, was greatly distressed, and was ready to pass a formal attestation that he had not been requested by any prince to make Fisher cardinal. He had done so merely on account of Fisher's learning and virtue, and rather with the intention of pleasing Henry than from any ill will towards him.

On the same day a papal envoy recently returned from France wrote to Guillaume Du Bellay from Rome. After congratulating him on his own elevation he asked him on the pope's behalf to use his authority with the French king so that he would intercede for Fisher with the king of England. The pope wanted Francis to explain to Henry that Fisher's promotion 'was made not only for the virtue and singular learning of that lord and for the present needs of the Church and council, but also in honour of that king and his kingdom'. Paul III was even more disingenuous in his dealings with Gregorio da Casale, Henry's agent. He told him that Francis had written of his own desire to see Henry satisfied in his marriage case, and that he thought Fisher's promotion would be pleasing to Henry and would provide a fit instrument for treating of these matters.[5] This seems a little strange, given Fisher's persistent defence of the Aragon marriage.

Paul's own deliberate obfuscations notwithstanding, it is clear that he had two chief motives in promoting Fisher, one connected with the latter's political plight, the other with his status as one of Catholic Europe's foremost theologians. On the first point, Paul hoped – even expected – that if Fisher were made a prince of the Church Henry VIII would be shamed into releasing him from prison. He hoped to use Francis I to put pressure on the English. He did not write directly to Henry about Fisher's elevation, and Fisher himself was to be sent only a formal brief identical to those issued to the other new cardinals. But the pope wrote to Francis I in May 1535 asking his intercession with Henry on Fisher's behalf, and to the admiral of France, the new cardinal of Paris and his own nuncio at the French court to urge them to intercede with Francis.[6]

The pope's griefstricken and angry brief to the French king of 26 July 1535 expressed outrage that his expectations had not been met.

Whereas we were daily waiting to hear of the liberation of John, cardinal of Rochester of blissful memory, since we had most instantly recommended his cause to your majesty, and expected no less a result from your surpassing uprightness and your influence with Henry king of England; lo suddenly we were smitten with the terrible news that the said cardinal had been condemned and submitted to the last punishment by that selfsame Henry, by whom he had long been kept in chains.[7]

Paul's wish to secure Fisher's release was not based solely on humanitarian considerations; he had work for him to do. Up to the year 1521 Fisher was scarcely known to the curia; he had performed his *ad limina* visits by proxy, and though he had twice been appointed one of Henry VIII's ambassadors to the fifth Lateran council, he had never reached Rome.[8] In 1521 Richard Pace sent Leo X a copy of his own Latin translation of Fisher's sermon against Luther. The accompanying letter made the preacher and his learning known to the pope.[9]

Fisher's reputation certainly increased after 1521. He preached and wrote prolifically against the reformers, and his books – notably the *Confutation* of 1523 against Luther and the defence of the Eucharist against Oecolampadius of 1527 – ensured him international fame as a controversial theologian. Some of his works, devotional as well as polemical, were translated into various vernacular languages including German, Hungarian and Czech, and he was cited as an authority by Cochlaeus and other Catholic divines. From 1527 he was known as one of Katherine of Aragon's most steadfast supporters in England, and he wrote, spoke and preached in her favour. Fisher's importance as a writer is underlined by an anonymous seventeenth-century account of his martyrdom and More's, now in the Vatican archive, which stresses that Henry was careful to call in and destroy Fisher's works. This assertion is confirmed by a royal proclamation of December 1535 which ordered the surrender of a number of books, including the 1521 sermon against Luther. This proclamation was ordered to be read from every parish pulpit in London, and then to be set up in all the churches.[10]

In 1535 Paul III was contemplating seriously the calling of a general council, and he wanted Fisher to attend. The red hat, he expected, would both effect Fisher's release from prison and give him status at the forthcoming council. (However holy or learned its incumbent might be reputed, Rochester was an extremely minor diocese in the Church universal.) The task proposed for Fisher in May 1535 is clearly stated in the briefs Paul sent to Francis I, the admiral of France and Cardinal Du Bellay, while he told the nuncio Carpi to use his influence with the French king, cardinal and admiral so that Fisher would be released to attend the council against the Lutherans.[11]

On 2 June 1535 the pope's secretary advised Carpi of the imminent despatch of another nuncio with the red hats for Du Bellay and Fisher. Carpi was to work on the French king (*'faccia opera con la maestà del re'*) so that he would secure Fisher's freedom. On 1 July – actually after Fisher's execution – the secretary sent Carpi explicit notice of the pope's wishes and intentions.

> his holiness above all things desires his liberation, so that he can be of account in the business of the council, and because he is such a singular person, and of such learning and such holy life; and so as much as his most Christian majesty and the most reverend Du Bellay make difficulties, so much the more must your lordship insist, making them listen . . . so that the most Christian uses all his authority and makes the impossible possible in order to liberate him.[12]

In explaining and excusing Fisher's promotion to Henry's agent Gregorio da Casale, Paul himself adduced the general council. He needed an Englishman, he said, because a certain constitution ordered cardinals of all nations to be present at a council. He had not thought of Fisher more than of anyone else, he protested; but when he heard of the estimation in which he was held in Germany and Italy, and how Cardinal Campeggio and others praised him, it seemed a good idea to make him cardinal, which the pope thought would please Henry. Casale, who had already told those cardinals friendly to Henry's case that Fisher was extremely old and unequal to the task for which they thought him apt, warned the pope not to send the red hat without hearing from England.[13] From all accounts, then, it seems that Fisher's elevation was not to be a stick with which to beat Henry VIII, but the means by which Fisher contributed his notable learning and talent to the council which was to shape the future of the Church.

If Paul III was sanguine that the red hat would save Fisher for the general council, others were more worried about Henry VIII's reaction to the honour accorded his recalcitrant subject. Cardinal Du Bellay was fearful that his promotion would make a martyr of Fisher, while Carpi exclaimed, 'As God is my witness, I would rather see Rochester in Rome than be cardinal myself.'[14] Two remarks on the matter are attributed to Henry VIII: one, that he would send Fisher's head to Rome for the hat; the other, that if the hat were sent to England Fisher would have to wear it on his shoulders, 'for head he shall have none'. These brutal words were not just the expression of ill-tempered sadism. The reasons for Henry's violent reaction were quite complex.

Naturally the king was outraged that the sole English bishop to defy him over the divorce and royal supremacy should have been honoured by the supreme pontiff – or, as Henry saw it, the bishop of Rome. On 10 August 1535 Conrad Goclenius sent news of the deaths of Fisher and More to Erasmus. On Fisher he said, 'for no other reason the king's fury was unleashed with more violence against him because he had been chosen cardinal by the pope'. Erasmus himself reported from Basle: 'There is a persistent rumour here, probably true, that when the king discovered that the bishop of Rochester had been appointed to the college of cardinals by Paul III, he speedily had him led out of prison and beheaded. In this fashion did the king bestow upon him the red hat.'[15]

Henry VIII needed wholehearted unanimity of opinion from his subjects.[16] Though official documents such as Bishop Longland's mandate to his clergy of 1535 spoke of the 'whole consent and agreement' of the bishops and the rest of the clergy to royal supremacy, Fisher and the other prisoners in the Tower were a reminder of the hollowness of this supposed clerical unanimity.[17]

Henry required total submission. This was why he rejected Cranmer's intelligent suggestion that Fisher and More should be allowed to swear to the act of succession but be spared the preamble, which was offensive to them. This would have made it seem that they had submitted wholly to Henry: 'And if the king's pleasure so were, their said oaths might be suppressed, but when and where his highness might take some commodity by the publishing of the same.' Cranmer saw that the apparent acquiescence of Fisher and More would weaken the position of Queen Katherine, Princess Mary and their supporters abroad.

> hereby shall be a great occasion to satisfy the princess dowager and the lady Mary, which do think they should damn their souls, if they should abandon and relinquish their estates. And not only it should stop the mouths of them, but also of the emperor, and other their friends, if they give as much credence to my lord of Rochester and Master More, speaking or doing against them, as they hitherto have done and thought that all other should have done, when they spake and did with them.

There would also be a good effect on the domestic opposition: 'per-adventure it should be a good quietation to many other within this realm, if such men should say that the succession, comprised within the said act, is good and according to God's laws: for then I think there is not one within this realm that would once reclaim against it'.[18] But real, not apparent surrender was essential to Henry. Cromwell told Cranmer that 'the king's highness . . . in no wise willeth but that they shall be sworn as well to the preamble as to the act'.[19]

On 16 June 1535 the imperial ambassador Chapuys reported that news of Fisher's promotion by the pope had quickened Henry's anger against both himself and More. As soon as he heard the news, Henry declared in anger several times that he would give Fisher another hat to wear and send his head to Rome for the cardinal's hat. Immediately he had sent some of his council to the Tower to tell Fisher and More that if they did not accept royal supremacy they would be dead by St John's day.

The news from Rome, said Chapuys, had also provoked a number of anti-papal measures. The king, out of hatred for the holy see, had sent mandates and letters patent to all bishops, curates and preachers to denounce the papacy, and to schoolmasters to instruct their scholars to revile apostolic authority on pain of rebellion. The title of pope was to be erased from all missals, breviaries and books of hours, and the gospel was to be preached in churches in the vernacular. Preachers had also been set to attack Fisher and More from the pulpit. Moreover, Henry was seeking to use Fisher's pro-motion to destroy him, trying to find out whether he had petitioned for the red hat and, it was said, taking prisoner many of his rela-tions and those who guarded him in prison.[20]

Chapuys' report is largely confirmed by the royal proclamation against the pope's authority of 9 June 1535. This ordered the eras-ure of the pope's title from all service books. Bishops were to set forth the king's title every Sunday and high feast day, while the pope was to be denounced from the pulpit once a year.[21] Interrog-ation of Fisher and More was stepped up after the news of Fisher's elevation reached England, and pressure was put on them either to incriminate themselves or to conform.

Records of examinations in the Tower of servants and gaolers of Fisher and More also confirm Chapuys' report. Indeed, they show how painstaking Henry's servants were in trying to discover who had spread the news about Fisher's promotion. George Golde, a servant of the lieutenant of the Tower, deposed that it was he who had told Fisher himself the news. He had heard it from one John, a former servant of Fisher's, who had heard it on London bridge from Andrew and Noddy, servants of Antonio Bonvisi. Andrew was questioned, and admitted that he had first heard the news from Florens Voluzenus when he was a guest at Bonvisi's table; Voluzenus had first heard it at the French ambassador's house. Andrew had since heard the news from several other people, though he could not remember who.

Meanwhile, William Thornton when first questioned deposed that he had got the news from Edward White, Fisher's half-brother; but on reflection he thought he had really heard it from 'the falconer that serves the said Master Fisher of his meat'. This man, John Pewnoll alias Falconer, seems to have been the 'John' who first told George Golde the news, since he was questioned about his conversation with the lieutenant's servant. Falconer said that it was Golde who had told him the news. William Thornton when examined afresh said he had first heard the news from Master Thomas, the earl of Wiltshire's steward, and that on the same day or the next Golde and Falconer had told him the same news, one in the morning and the other in the afternoon. A servant of More's deposed that he had heard the news from Margaret Roper. Clearly, the honour paid to Fisher by Rome irked Henry sufficiently to merit such a meticulous investigation.[22]

One facet of the situation which must have incensed Henry was that Fisher's promotion emphasised England's ecclesiastical and diplomatic loneliness. On the one hand, it must be remembered that Paul III's predecessor had recently and belatedly given sentence in favour of Katherine of Aragon's marriage, in 1534. On the other hand, according to English law the Church in England had no connection with the bishop of Rome or his college of cardinals. Paul's honouring of Fisher, however, underlined the papal view that England was merely in temporary schism, and indeed was unable to secede from the Church universal. Henry was also acutely aware that the long-desired Boleyn marriage was not respected abroad. Moreover, it had so far failed to produce the male heir which, Henry believed, God had only denied him previously because of his incestuous union with the emperor's aunt, and whose birth would justify his proceedings. All this contributed to Henry's diplomatic and dynastic insecurity.

Much information about the diplomatic atmosphere comes from the correspondence of the papal nuncio in France, Rodolfo Pio di

Carpi, Bishop of Faenza. Carpi was intelligent and informed. A reform-minded prelate with a distinguished career before him, he was particularly sympathetic to the case of Fisher and worked hard to fulfil his commission to persuade Francis I to intercede with the English king.[23]

On 6 June 1535 Carpi wrote to the pope's secretary Ambrogio: 'I told his majesty at length of the desire of his holiness concerning the most reverend of Rochester, the honour and glory which his majesty would gain in liberating him, the utility that Christendom could expect from such a great deed, that man [Fisher] being the ark of all virtue.' However, though Carpi pleaded with the king 'with all the strength of my heart', and though Francis appreciated Fisher's value as a divine, the king was pessimistic about the chances of moving Henry VIII.

> He told me that there was no need to speak of the virtues of Rochester, and as for his books, no one had written better against the Lutherans than he, and in other matters his virtues were innumerable. However, though his holiness could be absolutely certain that he would do all he could more than willingly for his liberation, he doubted very much if he could do any good, and rather thought this hat would harm Rochester.

Francis then made some very revealing remarks about Henry, and about his own diplomatic difficulties.

> The king of England is the hardest friend in all the world to bear: sometimes so unstable that it is a great business [to deal with him]; at other times so pertinacious and fiercely proud that it is almost impossible to bear with him; at other times so high and mighty that he treats me like one of his subjects . . . in fact, he is the most strange man in the world, and I do not believe I can ever do any good with him; but I need to bear with him, because it is not the time for me to lose friends.[24]

The mood at the French court was not favourable to the English, though diplomatic considerations made a complete rupture impossible. Tales circulated there about Henry's cruelty to the English religious, the discontent and ambition of the Duke of Norfolk, and above all, the king's wicked behaviour towards Fisher. From the other side of the Channel Chapuys reported that Henry was greatly provoked not only against Fisher but against Du Bellay, in whom he had reposed great confidence because he had seemed to be a bad papalist ('*mauvais papiste*') before his own creation as cardinal.

The council was perhaps the crux of Henry's attitude to Fisher as cardinal, though even before news of Fisher's elevation reached England Cromwell told Chapuys that his king would never submit to a council. Henry feared the convocation of a body which might pass censures on him, and he certainly did not want his antagonist Fisher among its doctors. On 21 June Carpi reported a conversation with the admiral of France, who feared for Fisher.

> He told me that he feared greatly for the life of that good lord, because it had been greatly broadcast in England that his holiness says in the brief that he had created him cardinal to do service in the council: as the king of England knows how constantly this man has always opposed his opinion, one would believe that in a council he would want to maintain the same, which would be totally contrary to the deliberation of that king.

Carpi also reported indignantly that the English were saying that Fisher would not live a month, being extremely ill and 90 years old. Carpi feared that he would be murdered in prison.[25] Certainly he was aware that Fisher's age, as he said, had been inflated by 25 years, but neither he nor the pope was conversant with the real state of Fisher's health. In early summer 1535 the humanist doctor John Clement, who prescribed medicines for him, said that Fisher's liver was wasted and that he suffered from other ailments.[26] Conditions in the Tower cannot have helped his health. None of this, however, was known at the curia. It would seem that Fisher was regarded as a robust prelate who could go straight from prison to a council across the Alps.

Henry's angry decision to precipitate the trial and execution of Fisher provoked an equally furious reaction in Rome: Paul III decided to deprive Henry of his kingdom. The bull of deprivation of September 1535 states specifically that the death of Fisher – 'whom for his constancy of faith and sanctity of life we had promoted to the dignity of cardinal' – had decided the issue. Fisher's execution is given first place among Henry's many crimes. In July 1535 Paul wrote to the princes of Catholic Europe – the emperor and the kings of Bohemia, Poland, France, Scotland and Portugal – demanding that they pursue what his secretary called a 'just and honourable vendetta' against Henry VIII. These papal briefs highlight two important aspects of Fisher's death: his enemy had not respected his standing as a cardinal; and he had died a martyr for the Church universal.[27]

Both these points had momentous consequences for anglo-papal relations. Paul wrote to Charles V that Henry, 'to whom we do not refer without the greatest sorrow', had publicly, shamefully and wickedly put to death 'this same Rochester – outstandingly holy, famous in learning, venerable in age, a priest who was the brightness and adornment of that kingdom and the whole world'. Fisher was not merely a bishop but a cardinal of the holy Roman Church, and thus great violence had been done to the holy see. Paul tried to goad Francis I into action by saying that he had no doubt that the French king had done his utmost for Fisher's liberation; but not only had he not been set free, he had been put to death! Again he stressed the crime of killing a man who was innocent and holy, famed throughout the world for his learning in Catholic faith, and a bishop and a cardinal to boot. Fisher had died for God, for the Catholic religion, for justice and for truth. Similar motifs occur in the letter to Ferdinand of Bohemia.

Mention was also made of the martyrdom of Becket, a reference which was amplified in the brief to the king of Scots. The pope repeated his earlier assumption that promotion to the purple would have secured liberation and wellbeing to Fisher rather than harm, and went on to compare the English king with his 'progenitor' Henry II, and Fisher with Becket.

The eighth Henry had outdone the second in impiety. He had killed many, where his ancestor had only killed one; Becket had died for his own church in England, Fisher for the universal Church; Becket was an archbishop, Fisher a cardinal; Becket was sent into exile, Fisher was put in prison; Becket was struck down by assassins, Fisher violently executed; while Henry II had at least repented and purged himself before the pope.

Paul III was evidently struck by the idea that Fisher was a greater martyr than Becket. On 21 November 1535 Carpi reported that Stephen Gardiner had asked the admiral of France whether the pope intended to proceed against Henry VIII. The admiral replied that he did not know,

but that he had heard that his holiness indeed wished to canonise Rochester: if St Thomas of Canterbury had been canonised and venerated by all England because he had died defending his own particular church, then Rochester, having wished to die for the universal Church, should be placed within that number [of martyrs] and also venerated by the whole Church.[28]

On 28 July 1535 Gregorio da Casale told Cromwell of the pope's incredible indignation at the fate of Fisher and More. Casale had heard on good authority that the curia would proceed to the utmost extremities against the English. The pope seemed resolute, and had said that he would sooner have seen his two grandsons killed than Fisher and More. Ortiz told the empress that the executions, especially that of Cardinal Fisher, had so incensed the pope and cardinals against Henry VIII that they were preparing to deprive him of his kingdom.[29]

The reaction of the pope and of European opinion in general obliged Henry to justify himself through his agents abroad. Cardinal Du Bellay complained to Casale that Henry had promised the French king not to put Fisher to death, 'and yet in a morning the contrary was resolved and carried out'. Casale replied that he believed Francis would have done the same in matters that touched his honour and the interests of state, adding that Henry was not cruel but mild, and had only proceeded out of necessity. Quite mendaciously, he also said that Fisher and More had long been condemned to death by order of parliament, which the king could not and would not go against; though in his great goodness and mercy he had done everything possible to keep them alive. He added that it was not true that the king had put Fisher to death because he had been made cardinal, as they were saying in Rome; the king took little account of what the pope might do for England in creating bishops or cardinals, as all his doings were not enough to move a straw without the king's licence, and from this came the judgement on Fisher according to the order of parliament.[30]

Cromwell replied to this letter, informing Casale that Henry approved his line of reasoning with Du Bellay, and once more justifying the executions as an internal matter. Henry was surprised at the indignation of the pope and cardinals, and though he was not bound to give an account of himself to anyone but God, Cromwell would explain the matter so as to avoid calumny.

Though the king had ended his marriage case with the approval of the most learned men, Fisher and More attempted to oppose him as he tried to provide for the quiet and good of the kingdom and to correct men's morals. Though Henry had proof of their crimes he took no notice, hoping they would return to soundness of mind. Secretly they tried to undermine the work of parliament, and organised a conspiracy against the king.

Reluctantly, Henry had to send them to prison to stop the contagion spreading, and there they were treated more gently than they deserved. But so confident were they of the king's mildness that they persisted in guilt. When certain laws were passed by parliament – with no opposition – as beneficial to the realm and in accordance with true religion, these two alone opposed them and tried to refute and evade them by fallacious arguments. Finally, they were openly tried and convicted of high treason; their punishment was milder than the law prescribed, and their awful example had made many return to their loyalty. Thus, anyone of sound judgement could see how hasty the pope and cardinals had been to take offence.[31]

Similar arguments about the treason of Fisher and More were to be used by other royal agents and envoys. In his instructions to Sir John Wallop, ambassador in France, Cromwell put less emphasis on Henry's remarkable mildness and more on the horrible crimes of the two traitors: 'their treasons, conspiracies and practices, secretly practised as well within the realm as without, to move and stir dissension, and to sow sedition within the realm, intending thereby not only the destruction of the king, but also the whole subversion of his highness' realm . . . they having such malice rooted in their hearts against their prince and sovereign'.[32]

Edward Foxe, Henry's envoy to the German states, was instructed to stress Fisher's and More's conspiracy in the Tower.

when they were, for certain their untrue and false dealings towards his grace and crown, captives and in prison, they yet following their wretched determination and villainous affection that way, ceased not when they were in strait keeping, having nevertheless the prison at their liberties, both to practise an insurrection within the realm and also to use all the devices to them possible in outward parts, as well to slander and defame his majesty and his most virtuous doings and proceedings as also to procure the empechement and utter destruction of his most royal person.[33]

To aid Foxe in any arguments with the princes he was also sent a copy of Stephen Gardiner's tract justifying Fisher's execution, which had been intended primarily for distribution at the French court. One of the objects of this exercise was to salvage anglo-French relations by blaming the pope for stirring up trouble between the two kings through claiming falsely that Francis I had tried to intercede for Fisher's life. Gardiner, too, stressed the legality of Fisher's execution, 'which hath suffered the pain due unto him by the law', and expressed pious indignation that Rome 'bewaileth now the death justly executed upon a traitor: this holy see bitterly weepeth for the death of evil men, and rejoiceth for the death of good men'. What is more, Fisher's death had been merciful; he had not been poisoned, hanged, burned, boiled in lead or tortured, but despatched with a 'sudden stroke of the sword'.

Most interestingly, Gardiner pretended that Fisher's elevation to the purple was posthumous. Somewhat inconsistently, however, he denied that Fisher's death had been hastened by his promotion; said that even if cardinals had privileges it would be wrong to bestow the red hat in order to purchase immunity for a criminal; and declared that the honour of the pope and curia had been compromised by the appointment of a traitor to the college of cardinals. Moreover, the papacy had not bothered to reward Fisher for his services until recently.

> In time past, when Rochester did write many things against the adversaries of that see (without giving occasion for any complaint), he then lived miserably at home, like a man little known and little spoken of. And then this was allowed for good reason of that holy see, 'What have we to do with these rude and barbarous ultramontanes?' But now in the last end of his life, when he against all laws as well of God as of man resisted his prince and the ordinance of God, and being also a traitor was imprisoned therefore, he was then incontinently esteemed of that holy see worthy to be a cardinal.

Fisher himself, if dead men could speak, might complain to the holy see of his elevation.

> I have bestowed my felicity in time past in the defence of thee, and thou to the contrary hast abused my misery to thy own pleasure. For thou didst load me with that odious title of a cardinal at such time as not only the prison, but my offences also, had taken all honour from me.... Thou has given to me in my miserable afflictions (it may be to other a laughing game, but to me it is too earnest) that same reward for my labours which Leo X was wont in sport to give to his fool, that he should be a cardinal after his death, by writing the title of a cardinal upon his grave.[34]

A letter of John Whalley to Cromwell, written at Dover on 1 September 1535, shows both the strength of Catholic Europe's reaction to the deaths of Fisher and More, and the fact that their treatment had disturbed many of Henry VIII's subjects.

I hear say of truth, that an excommunication is come into Flanders from that authority of Rome against our sovereign lord and his realm, so that they have sent to the emperor to know his pleasure. Moreover a great obsequy hath been done at Paris six days together for late the bishop of Rochester and Sir Thomas More, and at Rome a month together. God forgive them their offences. They be well rid; for their long keeping of them did much hurt the conscience of many persons.[35]

It is well known that, for all Rome's fulminations, the bull of deprivation was never put into effect by a Catholic invasion of England. Execution of the pope's desire was fraught with difficulties, as is shown by a memorandum on the subject prepared for Charles V. If action were taken against Henry VIII, he might treat Queen Katherine as he had Cardinal Fisher. There was also the question of whether the kingdom would devolve to the apostolic see or to Princess Mary, and of whether the latter would be put in personal danger by any such settlement. Moreover, her case might be prejudiced if the deprivation were founded on heresy or treason. The memorandum concluded that all courses would be dangerous, and that it was hoped the emperor would decide what had to be done.[36]

Diplomatic considerations meant that nothing was done. The two major princely sons of Rome, the holy Roman emperor and the most Christian king of France, were in a state of armed truce when they were not openly at war; and who knew when either of them might need to negotiate with Henry VIII for an alliance or at least benevolent neutrality?[37] Added to the diplomatic uncertainties of the second half of the decade were the deaths in quick succession of Katherine of Aragon and Anne Boleyn, and the apparently contradictory attempts to formulate a religious settlement for the English Church. To foreign observers it might well seem that a return to the Roman fold might not be ruled out entirely. Indeed, even Paul III's sentence of deprivation was not finally pronounced, the king being given successive time limits in which to recognise the error of his ways.[38]

But if there were to be a return to Rome, it would have to be on Rome's terms. Henry had laid sacrilegious hands on a Roman cardinal; regardless of the schism that cardinal would have a successor, and one, moreover, who would be particularly aggravating to Henry VIII. As early as 4 July 1535 Carpi was writing warmly of the qualities of Reginald Pole, whom he had known in his student days at Padua. If it should 'please his holiness, to give him the hat of that good martyr' it would encourage the people of England to undertake a laudable and Christian vendetta against Henry.[39]

The new English cardinal was a particularly appropriate choice. Reporting on their discussions to Cromwell, Thomas Starkey said that he could not see that Pole's opinion of royal supremacy had been any different from his own; 'but after when he saw More and Rochester defend the cause with the shedding of their blood' he thought again.[40]

Pole himself took a high view of the status of cardinals, and a low one of Henry's pretensions to ecclesiastical authority. In his book on the unity of the Church he reproached the king with the death of Fisher, a holy man and a prince of the Church.

> Who... does not acknowledge the hand of God beyond nature that lengthened his life to your shame that he might perish by the sword, and allowed him to be enrolled in the number of cardinals, that it might be known to the whole world that you had slain not merely an excellent bishop, against whom you had no just cause, but a cardinal over whom you had no authority?[41]

Pole's attitude was that Henry was a sulky, refractory son of the Church universal, not the source of independent ecclesiastical authority. This was naturally the line that Rome continued to take towards England.

The raising of Fisher to the purple and his consequent death by order of the king thus constituted a watershed in the English reformation. As Paul III emphasised, Fisher died for the unity of Christendom, and therefore Henry, until such time as he should repent, was cast out as schismatic, heretic and rebel. One might argue that financial considerations, as well as later matrimonial complications, did not dispose Henry to abandon royal supremacy and accept the papal yoke again. But in any case, Henry had no way back to Rome unless he submitted humbly to the pope and confessed his past errors. As this was something of which he was incapable, his execution of Fisher can be seen as the turning-point for Henry's ecclesiology. However much he might abhor the 'heretics' among his subjects and seek to protect his Church from what he regarded as the most pernicious of their doctrines, Henry was bound irrevocably to a course of schism.

John Fisher was notoriously indifferent to worldly honours and advancement; otherwise he would not have remained bishop of Rochester for more than 30 years, but would have sought a richer and more prestigious see. What, then, was his attitude to his promotion to the rank of prince of the Church?

One of the questionnaires which furnished information for the Elizabethan biography of Fisher noted that when Cromwell asked him in the Tower whether he would receive the red hat if the pope so honoured him, Fisher replied, 'Yea, that I would, upon my knees with all humility and honour'. George Golde testified that when he informed Fisher that he would be made cardinal, 'the said Master Fisher answered and said that he set as much by that as by a rush under his foot.' Perhaps Fisher was being careful in speaking to a servant of the king's lieutenant. Fisher himself admitted under interrogation that he had said 'that if the cardinal's hat were laid at his feet he would not stoop to take it up, he did set so little by it'.[42]

Fisher's Victorian biographer Father Bridgett tried somewhat ingeniously to harmonise these two alleged attitudes: 'For the sake of the personal honour he would not stoop to pick up the hat; for the duties attached to it, and the honour of the sovereign pontiff, he would receive it on his knees.' Yet another source, now in the Vatican archive, has Fisher welcoming his elevation to the purple because it was the colour of faith and of blood.[43]

Fisher's attitude to the papal curia was far from uncritical. Apostrophising Luther in the *Confutation* of 1523 he declared:

If the Roman pontiffs, laying aside pomp and haughtiness, would but practise humility, you would not have a word left to utter against them. Yes, would that they would reform the manners of their court, and drive from it ambition, avarice and luxury. Never otherwise will they impose silence on revilers like you.[44]

Fisher had never seen Rome, but would doubtless have heard about it from friends who had, such as Tunstal and Erasmus. Tunstal in a later sermon recalled his revulsion at the arrogance of the papacy.

I see myself, being then present thirty-four year ago, when Julius, then bishop of Rome, stood on his feet, and one of his chamberlains held up his skirt, because it stood not as he thought with his dignity that he should do it himself, that his shoe might appear; whiles a nobleman of great age did prostrate himself upon the ground, and kissed his shoe; which he stately suffered to be done as of duty.[45]

Tunstal's disgust, however, did not prevent his sending a some-what fulsome letter of congratulation to Clement VII on his accession to the chair of St Peter in 1524.[46]

It is most interesting that a former chaplain of Fisher's turned to the reformed religion as a consequence of visiting Rome after his master's death. George Bowker alias Adam Damplip travelled to the eternal city, 'where he thought to have found all godliness and sincere religion, in the end he found there (as he confessed) such blasphemy of God, contempt of Christ's true religion, loose-ness of life, and abundance of all abominations and filthiness, that it abhorred his heart and conscience any longer there to remain'.[47] Though Cardinal Pole requested him to be a lecturer in his house and offered him ample remuneration, Damplip left Rome. Ironi-cally, he was later arrested for heresy under the act of six articles but was actually executed for treason, because he had taken money for his homeward journey from the arch-traitor Pole. Henry's *ani-mus* against Rome was thus as strong as his hatred of heresy.

It seems reasonable to suppose that, health permitting, Fisher would have welcomed the chance to take a hand in reform of the Church universal, and to use the general council as a means to coerce his king back to obedience. Fisher had spoken and written copiously on the authority of councils. In the sermon against Luther, for example, he alluded to the Holy Spirit's guidance of the Church.

> it is not to be doubted but in . . . holy bishops and doctors of the Church the Holy Ghost doth speak, but much rather in councils when many of them were assembled together. For ever as the storms and tempests of heresies did arise, so they were at length oppressed and convinced by this Holy Spirit, speaking in the mouths of the fathers and doctors of the Church; sometime by general councils and assemblies of many bishops together.[48]

Doubtless he hoped to see pope, council and emperor acting in concert to save Christendom from schism and heresy, besides purging the Church of her faults. Doubtless, too, had circumstances permitted, he would have been glad to participate in such an undertaking.

Notes

INTRODUCTION

1. Bodleian Library, Rawlinson MS.C 155, fo.327, Thomas Baker to John Lewis.
2. For the full titles and publication details of lives of Fisher, see Conventions, pp. x–xv, above.
3. The exception to this pattern is Rouschausse, who devotes more space than other writers to Fisher's career.
4. *Early Life*, I pp. 165, 166, *Informations B*. '*Informations*' indicates that the source is one of the questionnaires sent out by the biographer.
5. *Early Life*, II p. 215.
6. *Early Life*, II p. 213.
7. 'Observations on the Circumstances which occasioned the Death of Fisher, Bishop of Rochester', *Archaeologia*, 25 (1834) 61–99.
8. Foxe, V, p. 99. For Foxe's allegations of cruelty against Fisher, see Chapter 5, below.
9. Cf. Bradshaw, in Bradshaw and Duffy, pp. 1, 17.
10. *God Have Mercy, The Life of John Fisher of Rochester*, Ottawa, 1969, especially pp. 22–3.
11. Surts, *Works and Days of John Fisher*, Cambridge, Mass. 1967; Rex, *The Theology of John Fisher*, Cambridge, 1991.
12. Initially, Fisher was buried in the graveyard of All-Hallows-By-The-Tower. The *Greyfriars Chronicle* states that he was disinterred after More's execution and buried with him in the Tower. Unsubstantiated tradition has it that Margaret Roper obtained custody of both corpses and reburied them in More's tomb in Chelsea old church.
13. *Life of Fisher*, p. 254.
14. The oft-quoted story of Fisher's retreating from his festive household at Christmas in order to pray comes, not from the authentic *Early Life*, but from Bayly's embellished version.
15. *Early Life*, I p. 171, *Informations D*; I p. 167, *Informations B*; I p. 268.

1 CAMBRIDGE

1. A.B. Emden, *A Biographical Register of the University of Cambridge to 1500*, Cambridge, 1963, pp. 229–30; Damian Riehl Leader, *A History of the University of Cambridge, Volume 1, The University to 1546*, Cambridge, 1988, pp. 229–30.
2. *Early Life*, I p. 162, *Informations A*.
3. PRO, SP1/239, fos 223–24 (L & P, Add. App. I i, no. 1024), John Bouge to Katherine Mann, 1535.
4. Translated in Bridgett, *Life of Fisher*, p. 12.

5. William Melton, *Sermo exhortatorius*, London, c.1510.
6. *Testamenta Eboracensia*, vol. 5, Surtees Society, London and Edinburgh, 1884, pp. 251–2.
7. A.E. Stamp, *Michaelhouse*, London, 1924, pp. 50, 35–7. There are similar foundations by Robert Doket and Dame Joan Rokeby of Beverley.
8. *Early Life*, I p. 208.
9. *Early Life*, II p. 129.
10. Michael K. Jones and Malcolm Underwood. *The King's Mother: Lady Margaret Beaufort, Countess of Richmond and Derby*, Cambridge, 1992, p. 214.
11. W.G. Searle, *History of the Queens' College*, 2 vols, Cambridge, 1867–71, I pp. 133–4; Jones and Underwood, *The King's Mother*, p. 214. The fellows' letter to Wilkinson is printed in Lewis, *Life of Dr Fisher*, II p. 260.
12. John Twigg, *A History of the Queens' College, 1448–1986*, Woodbridge, 1987, pp. 18–19; Fisher's itinerary, in Bradshaw and Duffy, pp. 236–7.
13. For examples, BL, Harleian MS 7048, fos 9^v–10, 10^v–11.
14. CUL, QC Bk I, 'Journale' of Queens' College, Book I fo.286^v.
15. Jones and Underwood, *The King's Mother*, p. 215.
16. Bodleian Library, Rawlinson MS. C 155, fo.316^v. For other correspondence relating to Fisher's resignation and his succession by Robert Bekensaw, ibid. fos 316, 317; also in BL, Harleian MS. 7048, fos 11^v–13.
17. *Grace Book B, Part I, 1488–1511*, ed. Mary Bateson, Cambridge Antiquarian Society, Cambridge, 1903, p. 168.
18. Jones and Underwood, *The King's Mother*, pp. 257 and 249, this last quoting Fisher's work against Oecolampadius of 1527.
19. SJC, D91.20, fo.179.
20. *The Eagle*, XVI no. 93 (Dec.1890), 6, Hornby to Fisher; Jones and Underwood, *The King's Mother*, p. 249; Reynolds, *Life of Fisher*, pp. 145–6; BL, Additional MS. 12,060, fos 20^v–21.
21. *Erasmi Epistolae*, no. 3036.
22. Jones and Underwood, *The King's Mother*, pp. 205, 167–70.
23. SJC, D91.20, fos 37, 46, 147 (account of Margaret's cofferer); Leader, *Cambridge*, pp. 276–7; Jones and Underwood, *The King's Mother*, pp. 206–9.
24. Jones and Underwood, *The King's Mother*, pp. 210–11; Leader, *Cambridge*, p. 281.
25. *The King's Mother*, pp. 223, 224 and n., 227.
26. CUL, MM2, fos 47^v–8.
27. CUL, MM2, fo.36.
28. *The Eagle*, XVI no. 93 (Dec. 1890), 8–9.
29. CUL, MM24, fos 36^v, 48^v–9.
30. SJC, D94.507, Sharpe to Metcalfe; CUL, MMv 47, fos 29, 35, 35^v, payments for Fisher's anniversary; Jones and Underwood, *The King's Mother*, p. 227.
31. *Early Life*, I p. 241, editor's note.
32. SJC, C7.11, fos 38–40. Printed in Fisher, *Funeral Sermon of Lady Margaret*, ed. J. Hymers, Cambridge, 1840, pp. 195–203 and in *The Eagle*, XXXVII no. 138 (Dec. 1905), 8–12.

33. Jones and Underwood, *The King's Mother*, p. 235.
34. *The Eagle*, XVI no. 9 (Dec. 1890), 3–4.
35. *The Eagle*, XVI no. 9 (Dec. 1890), 2; Jones and Underwood, *The King's Mother*, pp. 243–4.
36. *The King's Mother*, pp. 241–7.
37. SJC, D106.3, fo.11.
38. SJC, D106.11, fo.43; cf. *The Eagle*, XXXI no. 152 (June 1910), 328.
39. SJC, D106.11, fos 107, 119, 136ᵛ, 144, 16.
40. SJC, C7.11, fo.200; SJC, C7.2, fos 43–5. For Katherine of Aragon, Maria Dowling, *Humanism in the Age of Henry VIII*, London, 1986, pp. 25, 26.
41. Jones and Underwood, *The King's Mother*, p. 247.
42. I am grateful to Malcolm Underwood, who is working on the early benefactors of St John's, for confirmation of this point.
43. The whole quarrel is summarised by Underwood, 'John Fisher and the Promotion of Learning', in Bradshaw and Duffy, pp. 38–9; Fisher's letter to Croke is printed in Hymers, *Funeral Sermon*, pp. 210–16.
44. *Early Statutes of the College of St John the Evangelist*, ed. J.E.B. Mayor, Cambridge, 1859, pp. 238–44; trans. Bridgett, *Life of Fisher*, pp. 32–4.
45. SJC, C7.2, fos 208–219.
46. *Early Statutes of Christ's College, Cambridge*, ed. H. Rackham, London, 1927.
47. Quoted in John Peile, *Christ's College*, London, 1900, p. 1.
48. See note 44, above.
49. *Early Life*, I p. 244.
50. *Early Life*, II p. 168. The anonymous author may have been a St John's man.
51. *Early Life*, I p. 166, *Informations B*. Edward Plankney and the more famous Richard Morison were scholar-clients of Cromwell.
52. Thomas Baker, *History of the College of St John the Evangelist, Cambridge*, ed. J.E.B. Mayor, 2 vols, Cambridge, 1869, I document 89.
53. *Early Life*, I p. 165, *Informations B*.
54. SJC, D106.4, fos 16, 32ᵛ, 33ᵛ, 40, 45, 51ᵛ, 63.
55. *Early Life*, I p. 165, *Informations B*.
56. Bodleian Library, Rawlinson MS. C 155, fos 328ᵛ, 329, Baker-Lewis correspondence.
57. Jones and Underwood, *The King's Mother*, p. 235 and note.
58. Jones and Underwood, *The King's Mother*, pp. 246, 247.
59. SJC, C7.2, fos 43–5.
60. Cf. Leader, *Cambridge*, p. 313. For references to receipt of rent for Linacre's London house, pensions and rewards to his sisters, and Day's wages as Linacre reader, SJC, D106.11, *passim*.
61. Paul Lawrence Rose, 'Erasmians and Mathematicians at Cambridge in the Early Sixteenth Century', *Sixteenth Century Journal*, 8 no. 2 (1977), 47ff.; Leader, *Cambridge*, pp. 311–12.
62. For example, SJC, D106.11, fos 72ᵛ, 78, 117.
63. Mayor, *Early Statutes*, pp. 104–16, 119, 244, 245, 250, 251, 311–13, 375–6.
64. *Erasmi Epistolae*, no. 948. For Fox and Corpus Christi, Dowling, *Humanism*, pp. 27–32.

65. SJC, D106.4, fos 1, 2, 1^v.
66. SJC, D106.11, fo.141; D57.33, fos 1^v, 2^v; D106.6, fos 40^v, 45, 46, 46^v, 49, 52, 54, 55.
67. David McKitterick, 'Two sixteenth-century catalogues of St John's College library', *Transactions of the Cambridge Bibliographical Society*, VII part 2 (1978), 139; Emden, *Cambridge to 1500*, pp. 229–300.
68. *The Eagle*, VIII no. 100 (March 1893), 11, 12.
69. Reynolds, *Life of Fisher*, p. 3.
70. Dowling, *Humanism*, p. 116.
71. Lawrence V. Ryan, *Roger Ascham*, Oxford, 1963, p. 29; SJC, C7.2, fos 65–7^v, 69, 255. Watson it was who preserved Fisher's statute book for St John's from destruction; *Early Life*, II pp. 134–5.
72. *The Eagle*, XVI no. 93 (Dec. 1880), 7–8.
73. SJC, D56.9, D56.15, D56.25.
74. *Miscellaneous Writings and Letters of Thomas Cranmer*, ed. J.E. Cox, Parker Society, Cambridge, 1846, p. 279.
75. *The Eagle*, XXXII no. 154 (March 1911), 392–3.
76. Venn, *Alumni Cantabrigienses*, vol. 3 p. 346.
77. Lewis, *Life of Dr Fisher*, I p. 54.
78. *Early Life*, II pp. 133–35 for the delegation to the Tower; this account is corrected by the editor's note. For payments for Fisher, SJC, D106.11, fos 155^v–61.
79. Lewis, *Life of Dr Fisher*, II pp. 147–50.
80. *Grace Book B*, p. 250 for gifts from the university to Fisher in 1510–11. Letters concerning the chancellorship in 1514 are in *Original Letters Illustrative of English History*, ed. Sir Henry Ellis, 3rd series, vol. I (London, 1846), pp. 168, 170.
81. *Early Life*, I p. 216.
82. *Early Life*, I p. 228.
83. Christopher N.L. Brooke, 'The University chancellor', in Bradshaw and Duffy, p. 60.
84. BL, Additional MS. 59,899 fo.37^v.
85. Bodleian Library, Bodley MS. 13 B, fos 22–31^v. A fine manuscript in the hand of the famous scribe Pieter Meghen, this was possibly a presentation copy given to the king. For its date and authorship, Underwood in Bradshaw and Duffy, p. 29 and p. 43 n.22.
86. CUL, MM2.24, fos 8^{v}ff.
87. *The Will of King Henry VII*, London, 1775, pp. 27–9.
88. *St Thomas More: Selected Letters*, ed. E.F. Rogers, New Haven and London, 1961, no. 30.
89. Leader, *Cambridge*, pp. 297–8, 300.
90. Dowling, *Humanism*, pp. 27, 72n.27. For Wakefield, see Chapters 2 and 7, below.
91. Dowling, *Humanism*, p. 89.
92. Cf. Leader, *Cambridge*, p. 331.
93. Brooke, in Bradshaw and Duffy, p. 49.

2 THE HUMANIST

1. Fisher, *Treatise of Prayer*, p. 82.
2. Cf. Bradshaw and Duffy, pp. 1–2. Writers who do not see Fisher as a humanist include E.A. Benians, *John Fisher*, Cambridge, 1935, and Michael Macklem, *God Have Mercy, The Life of John Fisher of Rochester*, Ottawa, 1969. Cf. G.R. Elton, *Reform and Reformation*, London, 1977, p. 76 and n..
3. E.L. Surtz, 'John Fisher and the Scholastics', *Studies in Philology*, 55 no. 2 (April 1958), 142, 145, 146; *Early Statutes of the College of St John the Evangelist*, ed. J.E.B. Mayor, Cambridge, 1859, p. 250.
4. Cf. Roberto Weiss, *Humanism in England During the Fifteenth Century*, 3rd edn, Oxford, 1967.
5. *Erasmi Epistolae* (Toronto trans.), no. 229; cf. no. 227.
6. *Erasmi Epistolae* (Toronto trans.), no. 237.
7. H.C. Porter, 'Fisher and Erasmus', in Bradshaw and Duffy, p. 87.
8. *Erasmi Epistolae* (Toronto trans.), no. 278; Richard Rex, *The Theology of John Fisher*, Cambridge, 1991, pp. 54–5.
9. *Erasmi Epistolae* (Toronto trans.), no. 413.
10. *Erasmi Epistolae* (Toronto trans.), no. 432.
11. *Erasmi Epistolae* (Toronto trans.), no. 452.
12. *Erasmi Epistolae*, no. 481.
13. *Erasmi Epistolae* (Toronto trans.), no. 520.
14. *Erasmi Epistolae* (Toronto trans.), no. 540.
15. *Erasmi Epistolae* (Toronto trans.), no. 592.
16. *Erasmi Epistolae*, no. 653.
17. *Erasmi Epistolae* (Toronto trans.), no. 784.
18. *Erasmi Epistolae* (Rouschausse trans.), no. 1030.
19. *Erasmi Epistolae*, nos 1323, 1571; cf. no. 1581.
20. Rex, *Theology*, p. 152; cf. Bradshaw and Duffy, pp. 7–8, 59.
21. *Erasmi Epistolae*, no. 290.
22. *Erasmi Epistolae* (Toronto trans.), no. 300.
23. *Erasmi Epistolae* (Toronto trans.), no. 324.
24. *Erasmi Epistolae* (Toronto trans.), no. 432.
25. *Erasmi Epistolae* (Toronto trans.), no. 457.
26. *Erasmi Epistolae* (Toronto trans.), no. 471; cf. no. 457.
27. *Erasmi Epistolae* (Toronto trans.), nos 543, 545.
28. *Erasmi Epistolae* (Toronto trans.), no. 562.
29. *Erasmi Epistolae* (Toronto trans.), no. 592. For Colet's keeping the book, no. 653.
30. *Erasmi Epistolae* (Rouschausse trans.), no. 1311.
31. *Erasmi Epistolae* (Toronto trans.), no. 593 from Colet. For Colet, Fisher and the cabbala, Brian Gogan, *The Common Corps of Christendom*, Leiden, 1982, pp. 314–15.
32. *Erasmi Epistolae*, no. 967.
33. Rex, *Theology*, p. 58.
34. Letter printed in Fisher, *Funeral Sermon for Lady Margaret*, ed. J. Hymers, Cambridge, 1840, p. 209.
35. E.L. Surtz, *Works and Days of John Fisher*, Cambridge, Mass., 1967,

pp. 143–5; *Erasmi Epistolae*, no. 1311; Rex, *Theology*, p. 58.

36. Letter to Henry VIII, dated 1527, printed in Wakefield, *Kotser codicis*, London, c.1534. For Wakefield's profits from his change of allegiance, Dowling, *Humanism*, pp. 46–7.
37. Lewis, *Life of Dr Fisher*, I pp. 18–19; Surtz, *Works and Days*, pp. 146, 147.
38. Surtz, *Works and Days*, p. 147.
39. Rex, *Theology*, pp. 81–2 for the commentary on the psalms; for Lefèvre, see Chapter 5, below.
40. This controversy was discovered and interpreted by Rex, *Theology*, pp. 148–61.
41. Surtz, *Works and Days*, pp. 148–53, 141.
42. Surtz, *Works and Days*, p. 147.
43. *De veritate corporis et sanguinis Christi in eucharistia*, Cologne, 1527, p. 172. Quoted and translated in Surtz, 'Fisher and the Scholastics', p. 146.
44. *Early Life*, I p. 166, *Informations B*.
45. Rex, *Theology*, pp. 192–203.
46. G.J. Gray, 'Letters of Bishop Fisher', *The Library*, 3 series (1913), 134–5, 143–4.
47. A.B. Emden, *A Biographical Register of the University of Cambridge to 1500*, Cambridge, 1963, p. 230; Michael K. Jones and Malcolm Underwood, *The King's Mother: Lady Margaret Beaufort, Countess of Richmond and Derby*, Cambridge, 1992, p. 227.
48. SJC, D106.4, fo.1; D106.6, fos 40^v, 46^v, 49, 52, 54; David McKitterick, 'Two sixteenth-century catalogues of St John's College library', *Transactions of the Cambridge Bibliographical Society*, VII part 2 (1978,), 139; Fisher, *Funeral Sermon*, pp. 207–9.
49. Damian Riehl Leader, *A History of the University of Cambridge, Volume 1, The University to 1546*, Cambridge, 1983, p. 285; *Early Life*, I p. 165, *Informations B*.
50. BL, Additional MS. 5846, fo.46.
51. Bodleian Library, Rawlinson MS. c 155, fos 328^v, 329, Baker-Lewis correspondence.
52. I am grateful to James David Draper of the Metropolitan Museum of Art, New York, for information about the bust. For Fisher's dealings with Torrigiano, *The Eagle*, XVIII no. 105 (Dec. 1894). 5–9; XXXI no. 151 (March 1910), 288.
53. Face-pattern described by Roy Strong, *Tudor and Jacobean Portraits*, 2 vols, London, 1969, I pp. 119–21.
54. Gray, 'Letters of Fisher', p. 136.
55. *Erasmi Epistolae* (Rouschausse trans.), no. 1489.
56. Germain Marc'hadour, 'Erasme et John Fisher', *Colloquia Erasmiana Turonensia*, ed. J.-C. Margolin, 2 vols, Toronto, 1972, II pp. 771–80.
57. H.C. Porter, 'Fisher and Erasmus', in Bradshaw and Duffy, pp. 81–101.
58. All the surviving letters are conveniently edited by Jean Rouschausse, *Erasmus and Fisher: Their Correspondence*, Paris, 1968.
59. *Erasmi Epistolae* (Rouschausse trans.), no. 936, whence come the following quotations.

60. *Erasmi Epistolae* (Rouschausse trans.), no. 1068.
61. *Erasmi Epistolae* (Rouschausse trans.), no. 1030.
62. Mentioned in PRO, SP1/93, fos 52–62 (L & P, VIII, no. 856), interrogations in the Tower.
63. Maria Dowling, 'Cranmer as Humanist Reformer', in Thomas Cranmer, *Churchman and Scholar*, ed. Paul Ayris and David Selwyn, Woodbridge, 1993, p. 102.
64. Bradshaw and Duffy, p. 1; E.L. Surtz, 'More's Friendship with Fisher', *Moreana*, no. 15 (1967), 116, 118, 120–1.
65. *St Thomas More: Selected Letters*, ed., E.F. Rogers, New Haven and London, 1961, p. 94; original Latin text in *The Correspondence of Sir Thomas More*, ed., E.F. Rogers, Princeton, 1947, p. 111.
66. *Correspondence of Sir Thomas More*, pp. 520–1.
67. See Chapter 1, above.
68. ASV, *Archivum Arcis*, no. 4050, Pace to Leo X, 1 June 1521.
69. See Chapter 5, below.
70. Printed in Bridgett, *Life of Fisher*, p. 297.
71. Rex, '*Christianae Fidei Corroboratio*: the Theology of John Fisher', unpublished PhD thesis, Cambridge University, 1988, pp. 45–6.

3 THE BISHOP

1. *Songs, Carols, and other Miscellaneous Poems, from the Balliol MS 354, Richard Hill's Commonplace Book,* ed. Roman Dyboski, EETS extra series (1904), pp. 81–2.
2. I Timothy 3:1–7; Titus 1:7–9.
3. Printed in Caroline A. Halsted, *Life of Margaret Beaufort*, London, 1839, p. 221. For an account of Henry VII's religiosity (which, however, makes no mention of his promotion of Fisher), Anthony Goodman, 'Henry VII and Christian Renewal', *Religion and Humanism, Studies in Church History 17*, ed. Keith Robbins, Oxford, 1981, pp. 115–26.
4. Printed in *Letters of Richard Fox*, ed. P.S. and H.M. Allen, Oxford, 1929, pp. 152–6. Translation in Bridgett, *Life of Fisher*, pp. 25–6.
5. *Early Life*, I pp. 212, 214; cf. BL, Sloane MS 1898, fo.9ᵛ. Ann Brown calls Rochester 'The poorest see in England' because of both its temporal endowment and the paucity of archival material concerning it. 'The Lands and Tenants of the Bishopric and Cathedral Priory of St Andrew, Rochester, 600–1540', unpublished PhD thesis, London University, 1974, p. 1.
6. *The Early Statutes of the College of St John the Evangelist*, ed. J.E.B. Mayor, Cambridge, 1859, pp. 238–44. Translation in Bridgett, *Life of Fisher*, pp. 32–4.
7. Bridgett, *Life of Fisher*, p. 26.
8. Bradshaw and Duffy, Appendix 3. Cf. Stephen Thompson, 'The Pastoral Work of the English and Welsh Bishops, 1500–1554', unpublished DPhil thesis, Oxford University, 1984, p. 16, table I.
9. Thompson, 'Pastoral Work', pp. 230–3; cf. his essay and itinerary for Fisher in Bradshaw and Duffy, pp. 71, 236–47.

10. *Calendar of the Patent Rolls preserved in the Public Record office: Henry VII*, 2 vols, London, 1916, vol. 2, p. 388; W.H. Dunham, 'The Members of Henry VIII's Whole Council, 1509–1527', *English Historical Review*, 59 (1944), 208.

11. ASV, *Brevia ad Principem*, Arm. 39, vol.22, fo.442ᵛ, brief of Julius II to Margaret, mother of the king of England; cf. E.E. Reynolds, 'St John Fisher and the Lady Margaret Beaufort', *Moreana*, no. 22 (August 1969), 32–3.

12. BL, Additional MS. 12060, fo.23ᵛ.

13. BL, Harleian MS. 3504, fo.255 (L & P, I, no. 20).

14. L & P, I, nos 153, 2243; II, no. 1652. For the sermon after Flodden, *Holinshed's Chronicles of England, Scotland, and Ireland, Volume III*, London, 1808, p. 583. For Fisher's presence at Windsor in 1506, SJC, D105.162.

15. Documents calendared in L & P, I, nos 1048, 1067, 1083, 3495; II, pp. 1454, 1466 (king's book of payments). See also *Lewis, Life of Dr Fisher*, I pp. 43–4.

16. *The Life of Cardinal Wolsey by George Cavendish*, ed. Samuel Weller Singer, London, 1827, pp. 522–55 (L & P, II, no. 1153).

17. L & P, II, no. 4333; IV, no. 614.

18. *The Eagle*, 16, no. 93 (Dec.1890), 12–13; L & P, II, no. 4348; BL, Cotton MS. Vitell. B XX, fo.285 (L & P, III, no. 3373).

19. SJC, D.105.53, printed in *The Eagle*, 17, no. 100 (March 1893), 15–16; *Arch. Cant.*, 6 (1866), 49, 17 (1887), 71.

20. *Early Life*, I p. 258.

21. ASV, *Diversa Cameralia*, vol. 57 fo.203ᵛ, vol. 59 fo.97, vol. 63 fo.258.

22. PRO, SP46/123, fo.83A, 'Fisher's installation speech'; cf. *Early Life*, I p. 216.

23. Thompson, 'Pastoral Work', pp. 83, 94, 190; Thompson, 'The Bishop in his Diocese', in Bradshaw and Duffy, p. 74; Margaret Bowker, *The Henrician Reformation: the Diocese of Lincoln under John Longland, 1521–47*, Cambridge, 1981, p. 56; G.M. Arnold, 'Gravesend in Days of Old', *Arch. Cant.*, 11 (1877), xlvii–xlviii.

24. Thompson, 'The Bishop in his Diocese', p. 76 and Bradshaw and Duffy, Appendix 5, p. 253; Bowker, *Diocese of Lincoln*, p. 39; cf. Reynolds, *Life of Fisher*, p. 117n.

25. Reynolds, *Life of Fisher*, p. 66; Thompson, 'Pastoral Work', p. 117.

26. Thompson, 'Pastoral Work', pp. 145, 152–53; Stanford E. Lehmberg, *The Reformation of Cathedrals*, Princeton, 1988, pp. 40, 41; *Early Life*, I p. 163n. Unfortunately little detailed evidence survives of Fisher's relations with the cathedral; cf. note 6, above.

27. Thompson, 'Pastoral Work', pp. 152–3; Reynolds, *Life of Fisher*, pp. 120–1. For Wakefield's tuition of Fisher in Hebrew, see Chapter 2, above.

28. Thompson, 'Pastoral Work', pp. 153, 155, 145, 144; Reynolds, *Life of Fisher*, pp. 100, 117–18; Episcopal Register, fo.112ᵛ.

29. A.F. Allen, 'Higham Priory', *Arch. Cant.*, 80 (1965), 195, quoting Fisher's act book.

30. Charles Seymour, *A New Topographical, Historical and Commercial Survey of Kent*, privately printed, 1776, pp. 460–2.

31. *The Eagle*, 17 no. 101 (June 1893), 11–17.
32. Sidney Kilworth Keyes, *Dartford: Some Historical Notes*, Dartford, 1931, p. 23; Bridgett, *Life of Fisher*, p. 315 for their charge of children.
33. Ino Dunkin, *History and Antiquities of Dartford*, London, 1844, pp. 161–2.
34. *Early Life*, I p. 162; Giovanni Michele Piò, *Delle Vite Degli Uomini Illustri Di San Domenico*, Bologna, 1607, cols 377–80; cf. Dom David Knowles, *The Religious Orders in England, Volume Three, The Tudor Age*, Cambridge, 1959, p. 441 and n.
35. Thompson, 'Pastoral Work', pp. 192, 44.
36. *Early Life*, I p. 224.
37. Bridgett, *Life of Fisher*, pp. 32–4.
38. *Early Life*, I p. 171, *Informations D*; II p. 129; I p. 166, *Informations B*.
39. *Early Life*, I p. 169.
40. Thompson, 'Pastoral Work', p. 47.
41. L & P, IV, no. 5095, Fox to Wolsey; Episcopal Register, fo.150^r; Thompson, 'Pastoral Work', pp. 35, 36; Peter Heath, *The English Parish Clergy on the Eve of the Reformation*, London and Toronto, 1969, p. 41.
42. Heath, *Parish Clergy*, p. 81.
43. Lehmberg, *Cathedrals*, p. 238.
44. Bradshaw and Duffy, p. 251, Appendix 4.
45. C.H. and Thomas Cooper, *Athenae Cantabrigienses*, 2 vols, Cambridge, 1858, 1861, I p. 68.
46. A.B. Emden, *A Biographical Register of the University of Cambridge* to *1500*, Cambridge, 1963. pp. 520–1.
47. Leland L. Duncan, 'The Renunciation of the Papal Authority by the Clergy of West Kent, 1534', *Arch. Cant.*, 22 (1897), 304–5.
48. Emden, *Cambridge to 1500*, pp. 191 for Doket, 525–6 for Shorton.
49. Episcopal Register, fos 36^v, 55^r.
50. Duncan, 'The Renunciation of the Papal Authority' pp. 293–309.
51. Emden, *Cambridge to 1500*, p. 403.
52. Foxe, V, pp. 498–9; *The Lisle Letters*, ed. Muriel St Clare Byrne, 6 vols, Toronto and London, 1981, vol. 5 pp. 153–67, 151–2, vol. 6 pp. 107–8.
53. Bowker, *Diocese of Lincoln*, p. 45.
54. Bowker, *Diocese of Lincoln*, pp. 43 and n., 45, 44; cf. Heath, *Parish Clergy*, p. 56.
55. ASV, *Brevi Clemente VII*, Arm. 40, vol. 30, fo.215 for Cranmer's dispensation; ASV, *Brevi Giulio II*, Arm. 39, vol. 26, fo.540 for Tunstal's. Cf. Diarmaid MacCulloch, *Thomas Cranmer, A Life*, New Haven and London, 1996, p. 49 and note. For a discussion of pluralism and other clerical abuses, Maria Dowling, 'Cranmer as Humanist Reformer', in *Thomas Cranmer Churchman and Scholar*, ed. Paul Ayris and David Selwyn, Woodbridge, 1993, pp. 103–8; cf. Bowker, *Diocese of Lincoln*, p. 45.
56. Episcopal Register, fos 24^v, 57^r, 116^r.
57. Episcopal Register, fo.30^r.
58. Episcopal Register, fos 45^r, 141^r.
59. Thompson, 'The Bishop in his Diocese', p. 75; W. Shrubsole and

S. Denne, *The History and Antiquities of Rochester and its Environs*, Rochester, 1772, p. 84.
60. Episcopal Register, fo.110^r.
61. Episcopal Register, fo.146^r.
62. Episcopal Register, fos 150^r–150^v.
63. Printed in Bridgett, *Life of Fisher*, p. 315.
64. G.M. Arnold, 'Gravesend in Days of Old', *Arch. Cant.*, 11, (1877), xlvii–xlviii. For Browne and Hitton, see Chapter 5, below.
65. Thompson, 'The Bishop in his Diocese', p. 68.
66. *Epistolarum Reginaldi Poli*, 5 vols, Farnborough, 1967, vol. I pp. 94–6 (L & P, XIV i, no. 200).
67. *Early Life*, I pp. 216, 217–18, 219.
68. Episcopal Register, fo.121^v.
69. Episcopal Register, fo.141^r.
70. Episcopal Register, fos 37^r–37^v; Dunkin, *Dartford*, pp. 191–3.
71. Will printed in Scott Robertson, 'Peche of Lullingstone', *Arch. Cant.*, 16 (1886), 235–7.
72. *The Eagle*, 17 no. 100 (March 1893), 7.
73. *Early Life*, I pp. 171, 348.
74. *Early Life*, I p. 225.
75. *The Eagle*, 17, no. 100 (March 1893), 6.
76. *Early Life*, I p. 223.
77. *The Eagle*, 16, no. 93 (Dec. 1890), 14.
78. *The History of Parliament: the House of Commons, 1509–1558, part 2, Members D-M*, ed. S.T. Bindoff, London, 1982, p. 136.
79. *Early Life*, I pp. 222–3.
80. *Early Life* , I p. 223, taken from *Informations D*, p. 171.
81. *Early Life*, I p. 220, taken from *Informations D*, p. 171. For other bishops who fed the poor, Thompson, 'Pastoral Work', p. 203.
82. *Early Life*, I pp. 221–2.
83. PRO, SP1/83, fos 176–81 (L & P, VII, no. 557).
84. I owe this sugggestion to Dr Edmund Green. *Early Life,* I pp.349–50 has a curious story about the theft of Fisher's plate, part of which was found abandoned in a wood.
85. Cf. Thompson, 'The Bishop in his Diocese', p. 75.
86. For modern assessments, Reynolds, *Life of Fisher*, p. 30; Thompson, 'The Bishop in his Diocese', p. 77–8.
87. Rouschausse, *Vie et Oeuvre*, p. x.
88. *Early Life*, II p. 130.
89. *Early Life*, II p. 210.
90. Pole, *De Unitate Ecclesiae*, quoted and translated in *Early Life*, II p. 219.

4 THE PREACHER

1. Quoted in G.R. Owst, *Preaching in Medieval England*, Cambridge, 1926, pp. 2–3.
2. Owst, *Preaching*, p. 8n; D.L. D'Avray, *The Preaching of the Friars, Ser-*

mons Diffused from Paris before 1300, Oxford, 1985, p. 15; Richard G. Davies, 'The Episcopate', in *Profession, Vocation and Culture in Later Medieval England, Essays Dedicated to the Memory of A.R. Myers*, ed. Cecil H. Clough, Liverpool, 1982, pp. 79–80; Stephen Thompson, 'The Pastoral Work of the English and Welsh Bishops, 1500–1554', unpublished D Phil thesis, Oxford University, 1984, p. 167. Brendan Bradshaw (Bradshaw and Duffy, p. 4) notes Fisher's outstanding zeal for the preaching ministry. For Fisher's own rebuke to non-preaching bishops, *English Works*, pp. 76–7.

3. Cf. *Erasmi Epistolae*, no. 1333.
4. *Erasmi Epistolae*, no. 1489.
5. *Erasmi Epistolae*, no. 3036.
6. Erasmus, *Ecclesiastes, sive De Ratione Concionandi*, Basle, 1535.
7. 1526 Sermon, sig.Di.
8. *Annals of Cambridge*, ed. C.H. Cooper, 2 vols, London and Cambridge, 1908, I p. 260; Reynolds, *Life of Fisher*, p. 17.
9. Cooper, *Annals*, I pp. 273–4; Reynolds, *Life of Fisher*, pp. 15–16.
10. Quoted in E.L. Surtz, *Works and Days of John Fisher*, Cambridge, Mass., 1967, p. 192.
11. *Early Statutes of the College of St John the Evangelist*, ed. J.E.B. Mayor, Cambridge, 1859, pp. 377–8, 313–16.
12. For the preacher-fellows, Malcolm Underwood, 'John Fisher and the promotion of learning', in Bradshaw and Duffy, p. 34.
13. *Early Life*, I pp. 245–47.
14. 'A Sermon of Henry Golde, Vicar of Ospringe, 1525–27, Preached Before Archbishop Warham', *Arch. Cant*, 57 (1940), 33–43. For St John's acquisition of Ospringe, see Chapter 1, above.
15. *Erasmi Epistolae*, no. 2157.
16. Thompson, 'Pastoral Work', p. 47.
17. Episcopal Register, fo.141[r].
18. *Early Life*, I pp. 219, 221, 348.
19. Reynolds, *Life of Fisher*, pp. 17–18.
20. *Original Letters Illustrative of English History*, ed. Sir Henry Ellis, 3 series, London, 1824, vol. 1, pp. 180–4, Longland to Wolsey; *Early Life*, I pp. 252, 263–7.
21. Vienna, England, Karton 5 (1532), fo.73[v] (L & P, V, no. 1109).
22. *English Works*, p. 211.
23. *English Works*, pp. 11, 12, 127.
24. *English Works*, pp. 17–18, 204.
25. *English Works*, p. 60.
26. *English Works*, pp. 66–7, 85.
27. *English Works*, p. 27.
28. *English Works*, p. 117.
29. 1526 Sermon, sigs Fiv[v], Aii[v].
30. *Two Fruitful Sermons*, sig.D1.
31. *English Works*, p. 402.
32. *Two Fruitful Sermons*, sigs A2–A2[v].
33. *Two Fruitful Sermons*, sigs A3[v]–B1.
34. *Two Fruitful Sermons*, sig.B1[v].

35. *Two Fruitful Sermons*, sigs B2ᵛ–B3.
36. *English Works*, p. 78.
37. *English Works*, pp. 145–6.
38. English Works, pp. 269–70.
39. *English Works*, pp. 305–6.
40. *English Works*, p. 240.
41. *English Works*, p. 92.
42. *English Works*, p. 305.
43. *English Works*, p. 178.
44. *English Works*, pp. 54–5.
45. *English Works*, pp. 421–5.
46. *English Works*, pp. 426, 425.
47. *English Works*, p. 49.
48. *English Works*, p. 37.
49. *English Works*, p. 8.
50. *English Works*, p. 82.
51. *English Works*, pp. 230, 227, 258.
52. *English Works*, p. 411.
53. Quoted in Owst, *Preaching*, p. 308.
54. *Prayers and Other Pieces by Thomas Becon*, ed. J. Ayre, Parker Society, Cambridge, 1844, p. 234. Quoted in Helen Leith Spencer, 'English Vernacular Sunday Preaching in the Late Fourteenth and Fifteenth Century, with Illustrative texts', unpublished DPhil thesis, Oxford University, 1983, p. 295; and *English Preaching in the Later Middle Ages,* Oxford, 1993, p. 324 and n.. *Dormi Secure* were books of ready-made homilies which enabled preachers to 'sleep soundly' on Saturday nights.
55. For medieval preaching, Spencer, 'English Vernacular Sunday Preaching'; D.L. D'Avray, 'The Transformation of the Medieval Sermon', unpublished DPhil thesis, Oxford University, 1976, and *The Preaching of the Friars*, Oxford, 1985. Fisher's preaching style is discussed in context, though with some odd criticism, in C.S. Lewis, *English Literature in the Sixteenth Century Excluding Drama*, Oxford, 1954; J.W. Blench, *Preaching in the Late Fifteenth and Sixteenth Centuries*, Oxford, 1964. See also William S. Stafford, 'Repentance on the Eve of the English Reformation; John Fisher's Sermons of 1508 and 1509', *Historical Magazine of the Protestant Episcopal Church*, 54 (1985).
56. Cf. Margaret Bowker, The Henrician Reformation: *the Diocese of Lincoln under John Longland, 1521–1547*, Cambridge, 1981, pp. 8–12.
57. '*Docere, delectare et movere*'; cf. Blench, *Preaching in England*, p. 71. Reynolds notes that Fisher's sermon-cycle on the Penitential Psalms is similar in form to Augustine's *Enarrationes in Psalmos*; *Life of Fisher*, pp. 17–18.
58. 1526 Sermon, sig.Fi.
59. Lewis, *English Literature*, p. 164; 1526 Sermon, sig.Givᵛ.
60. Reynolds, *Life of Fisher*, p. 36; 1526 Sermon, sig.Aiv.
61. Owst, *Preaching*, pp. 173–4; cf. Spencer, 'English Vernacular Sunday Preaching', pp. 1–2.
62. Episcopal Register, fo.30ʳ.

63. STC, nos 10891, 10892, 10892.4, 10892.7, 10894, 10894.5, 10895, 10896, 10897, 10898, 10900, 10901, 10902, 10903, 10903.a, 10904, 10905, 10906, 10907, 10908, 10909.
64. *Two Fruitful Sermons*, sig. A2.
65. PRO, SP1/239, fos 181–82 (L & P, Add. App. I ii, p. 229).
66. William Tyndale, *Doctrinal Treatises*, ed. Henry Walter, Parker Society, Cambridge, 1848, p. 221.
67. Hall's Chronicle, fo. cxlvi^b.
68. *Tudor Royal Proclamations, Volume 1, The Early Tudors*, ed. Paul L. Hughes and James F. Larkin, New Haven and London, 1964, pp. 235–7.
69. Printed in John Strype, *Ecclesiastical Memorials*, 3 vols, Oxford, 1830–40, I ii, p. 229. Quoted in Reynolds, *Life of Fisher*, p. 288 and n, who thought this might be the sermon of 1532 in favour of the queen, or another, later sermon.
70. *English Works*, p. 362.
71. 1526 Sermon, sigs Bij^v, Hiij^v.

5 HERESY

1. 1526 Sermon, sigs Aiij^v–Aiv.
2. *English Works*, p. 344.
3. 1526 Sermon, sigs Hij^v–Hiij.
4. Hall's Chronicle, pp. clxxxviiib–clxix.
5. 1526 Sermon, sig.Aij.
6. 1526 Sermon, sig.Biv^v.
7. 1526 Sermon, sig.Ci.
8. Cf. Rouschausse, *Vie et Oeuvre* pp. 213–14, paraphrasing Fisher.
9. 1526 Sermon, sig.Aiv.
10. *Early Life*, I p. 263, based on Fisher's dedicatory preface to his *Confutation*.
11. Cf. Bridgett, *Life of Fisher*, p. 217 and n.
12. The whole story is in Foxe, IV, pp. 181–2.
13. William Tyndale, *Expositions and Notes on Sundry Portions of the Holy Scriptures, together with The Practice of Prelates*, ed. Henry Walter, Parker Society, Cambridge, 1849, p. 340; Charles C. Butterworth, *The English Primers (1529–1545)*, Philadelphia, 1953, p. 12n; *The Complete Works of St Thomas More, volume 8, The Confutation of Tyndale's Answer*, ed. Richard C. Marius, James P. Lusardi, Richard J. Schroeck, New Haven and London, 1973, pp. 14–16; Foxe, VIII, pp. 712–15 and IV, 619.
14. Episcopal Register, fo.24^v.
15. The summary which follows is of necessity brief and simplified. For the more detailed and more erudite discussions of Fisher's theology, see C.H. Duggan, *The Church in the Writings of St John Fisher*, Napier, 1953; E.L.Surtz, *Works and Days of John Fisher*, Cambridge, Mass., 1967; Brian Gogan, *The Common Corps of Christendom*, Leiden, 1982; Richard Rex, *The Theology of John Fisher*, Cambridge, 1991.
16. John Fisher, *The Defence of the Priesthood*, trans. P.E. Hallett, London, 1935, pp. 19–20.

17. *Confutatio*, translated in Bridgett, *Life of Fisher*, pp. 118–19.
18. Bridgett, *Life of Fisher*, pp. 128–9.
19. Controversy neatly summarised in Rex, *Theology*, pp. 66–7; for Fisher's arguments against Lefèvre, pp. 67–77. See also Anselm Hufstader, 'Lefèvre d'Etaples and the Magdalen', *Studies in the Renaissance*, 16 (1969), 31–60; Rouschausse, *Vie et Oeuvre*, pp. 58–67; Richard Cameron, 'The Attack on the Biblical Work of Lefèvre d'Etaples', *Church History*, 38 (1969), 9–24.
20. Cf. Rex, *Theology*, p. 68; Lewis, *Dr John Fisher*, I pp. 77–8; Rouschausse, *Vie et Oeuvre*, p. 59. Modern biblical scholarship would favour Lefèvre over Fisher, but the latter's pastoral concern is of interest here.
21. 'The Sermon Against the Holy Maid of Kent and her Adherents', ed. L.E. Whatmore, *English Historical Review*, 58 (1943), 470, 471 and n.
22. *English Works*, pp. 311–12.
23. *English Works*, pp. 321, 322.
24. *English Works*, p. 328.
25. *English Works*, pp. 332–4.
26. *English Works*, p. 337.
27. *English Works*, p. 336.
28. *English Works*, p. 340.
29. Foxe, V, pp. 418–19.
30. 1526 Sermon, sig.Biij.
31. 1526 Sermon, sigs Cij, Bij^v.
32. 1526 Sermon, sig. Dij.
33. 1526 Sermon, sig. Diij.
34. 1526 Sermon, sigs Div–Ei.
35. 1526 Sermon, sigs Ei–Ei^v.
36. I owe this plausible suggestion to Dr Edmund Green.
37. 1526 Sermon, sigs Aij, Aiv.
38. G.J. Gray, 'Letters of Bishop Fisher, 1521–3', *The Library*, 3 series (1913), 136.
39. ASV, *Archivum Arcis*, no. 4050, Pace to Leo X, 1 June 1521.
40. Gray, 'Letters of Bishop Fisher', p. 136.
41. Rex, *Theology*, p. 80. Cf. J.J. Scarisbrick, 'The Conservative Episcopate in England, 1529–1535', unpublished PhD thesis, Cambridge University, 1955, pp. 340–1 and n.
42. Rex, *Theology*, pp. 103–4 for a succinct discussion of Fisher's work against Velenus.
43. Rex, *Theology*, pp. 86–7.
44. See especially Surtz, *Works and Days*, pp. 348, 388.
45. I owe this reference from the Utrecht archives to the kindness of Dr Stuart Moore.
46. *St.P*, VI, pp. 311–13 (L & P, IV, no. 435), Clement VII to Wolsey; BL, Cotton MS. Vitell. B VIII, fo.21^v (L & P, IV, no. 1868), ——to Wolsey.
47. Letter printed and translated in Bridgett, *Life of Fisher*, pp. 114–16.
48. Rex, *Theology*, pp. 83, 85; Rex, 'The English Campaign Against Luther in the 1520s', *Transactions of the Royal Historical Society*, fifth series 39 (1989), 101.

49. See Martin Spahn, *Johannes Cochlaeus, Ein Lebensbild Aus Der Zeit Der Kirchenspaltung*, Berlin, 1898.
50. Rex, *Theology*, pp. 83, 85–6 and 'Campaign', pp. 102–5; Rouschausse, *Vie et Oeuvre*, p. 218.
51. Quoted in Reynolds, *Life of Fisher*, pp. 104–5.
52. Rex, 'Campaign', pp. 96–7.
53. Cf. Maria Dowling, *Humanism in the Age of Henry VIII*, London, 1986, p. 38 and p. 69, n.3.
54. Charles Sturge, *Cuthbert Tunstal, Scholar, Statesman, Administrator*, London, 1938, p. 137.
55. SJC, D106.11 (Metcalfe's rough book), fo.72^v.
56. Foxe, IV, p. 624; Dowling, *Humanism*, p. 77; Sturge, *Tunstal*, pp. 137–8.
57. Carl Trueman, *Luther's Legacy, Salvation and the English Reformers 1525–1556*, Oxford, 1994, pp. 49ff.
58. *The supplication of Dr Barnes unto the most gracious prince King Henry VIII*, London, 1550?, sig.fii.
59. The remark about Fisher's age appears only in the first edition, of c.1531.
60. Foxe, V, p. 99; *Early Life*, I pp. 348–9 and n.
61. *A Disputation of Purgatory made by John Frith*, London, 1533?, part 3. For More on Frith, cf. *The Confutation of Tyndale's Answer*, p. 35.
62. *Early Life*, I pp. 229–35; Damian Riehl Leader, *A History of the University of Cambridge, Volume 1, The University to 1546*, Cambridge, 1988, p. 321 and n.
63. Leader, *Cambridge*, p. 320; Rex, 'Campaign', pp. 87–9 and 91–4.
64. Lamb, *Cambridge Documents*, pp. 14–15. Cf. Foxe, VIII, p. 451.
65. For Cambridge and the royal divorce see Chapter 7, below.
66. Lamb, *Cambridge Documents*, p. 27.
67. Susan Wabuda, 'Equivocation and Recantation during the English Reformation: the 'Subtle Shadows' of Dr Edward Crome', *Journal of Ecclesiastical History*, 44 no. 2 (April 1993), 229–30.
68. Wabuda, 'Equivocation', p. 231; cf. Reynolds, *Life of Fisher*, p. 185, L & P, V, no. 928.
69. Bowker, *Diocese of Lincoln*, p. 104.
70. ASV, *Brevi Clemente VII*, Arm. 40, vol. 24, fo. 248, no. 264; vol. 46, fo. 264, no. 454. As Fisher had published nothing against heresy since 1527, it is reasonable to suppose that he had requested the original dispensation at an earlier date.
71. Rex, *Theology*, p. 80.
72. *Early Life*, I p. 220; cf. BL, Sloane MS. 1898, fo. 10.

6 THE DEVOTIONAL WRITER

1. Fisher, *Treatise of Prayer*, pp. 39–40.
2. Besides the works discussed in this chapter there exists a fragment of a devotional work on the Eucharist in manuscript: PRO, SP6/9, fos 159–64. The document is a much-corrected draft and is mutilated; thus it will need expert editing before Fisher's devotional attitude to the sacrament can be fully known.

3. Printed in Reynolds, *Life of Fisher*, pp. 297–9. See also n.50, below.
4. I am grateful to Prof. Christopher Harper-Bill for much discussion on Fisher's place in the late medieval pietistic tradition. See Jonathan Hughes, *Pastors and Visionaries: Religion and Secular Life in Late Medieval Yorkshire*, Woodbridge, 1988.
5. The two Tower works were apparently first published, with Fisher's sermon on the Passion, as *A spiritual consolation, written by John Fisher bishop of Rochester, to his sister Elizabeth*, London, 1578.
6. *English Works*, p. 352.
7. *English Works*, pp. 353–4. This passage carries resonances of Erasmus' colloquy 'The Shipwreck'.
8. *English Works*, p. 360.
9. *English Works*, pp. 362–3.
10. Erasmus, *Preparation to Death*, London, 1541, sigs cij–ciij. (Latin original edition published at Basle, 1534.)
11. Printed in *The English Works of Sir Thomas More volume I*, ed. W.E. Campbell and A.W. Reed, London and New York, 1931, pp. 459–99.
12. Richard Whitford, *A daily exercise and experience of death*, ed. James Hogg, *Salzburg Studies in English Literature, Elizabethan and Renaissance Studies*, 89 vol. 5 (1979), p. 93.
13. *English Works*, p. 362.
14. *English Works*, p. 364.
15. *English Works*, pp. 367–68.
16. *English Works*, pp. 370, 371.
17. Whitford, *A daily exercise*, p. 99.
18. *English Works*, p. 376.
19. *English Works*, p. 377.
20. *English Works*, pp. 381, 382.
21. *English Works*, pp. 382–3.
22. *English Works*, pp. 377, 370.
23. *English Works*, p. 386.
24. *A godly treatise declaring the benefits, fruits, and great commodities of prayer*, London 1563. A Latin text is printed in *Opera Omnia*. The present writer has used a later translation, *A Treatise of Prayer and of the Fruits and Manner of Prayer*, trans. R.A.B., Paris, 1640 (reprinted Menston, 1969), as it is more common than the earlier edition.
25. *Treatise of Prayer*, pp. 15, 17, 16.
26. *Treatise of Prayer*, pp. 19, 20–1, 23–4, 26. The language here is reminiscent of Bernard's treatise, *De Diligendo Deo*. See *St Bernard on Loving God*, trans. William Harman van Allen, Tenby, 1909.
27. *Treatise of Prayer*, p. 30.
28. *Treatise of Prayer*, pp. 42, 43.
29. *Treatise of Prayer*, pp. 48, 50, 51. Lack of humility and overconfidence in his own learning were faults which Fisher attributed to Luther.
30. *Treatise of Prayer*, p. 67.
31. *Treatise of Prayer*, p. 76.
32. *Treatise of Prayer*, p. 83.
33. *Treatise of Prayer*, p. 89.

34. *Vives and the Renascence Education of Women*, ed. Foster Watson, London, 1912, p. 89.
35. *Giovanni Pico della Mirandola: His Life by his Nephew Giovanni Francesco Pico: also Three of His Letters; His Twelve Rules of a Christian Life; His Twelve Points of a Perfect Lover; and his Deprecatory Hymn to God*. Translated from the Latin by Sir Thomas More, ed. J.M. Rigg, London, 1890, p. 35.
36. *Treatise of Prayer*, p. 93.
37. *Treatise of Prayer*, p. 95.
38. *Treatise of Prayer*, pp. 95–6.
39. *Treatise of Prayer*, pp. 214–15.
40. *Treatise of Prayer*, pp. 218, 219–20.
41. *Pico della Mirandola: His Life*, p. 35.
42. *Treatise of Prayer*, p. 223.
43. Richard Whitford, *A work for householders*, London, 1533, sigs aij–aiij, biij–cj.
44. Erasmus, *Modus Orandi Deum*, Basle, 1524.
45. *English Works*, p. 387.
46. *English Works,* pp. 385–6.
47. *Opera Omnia*, cols 1769–72.
48. I am grateful to Dr Josef Hejnic for information about the Czech translation. The Hungarian version survives apparently in one badly-damaged copy of one edition, formerly in the library of the Unitarian college at Cluj, now in the Romanian Academy. I am deeply indebted to Ms. Penka Peykovska for her assistance with the Hungarian edition.
49. Franklin B. Williams, 'Surreptitious London Editions of Fisher and More', *Moreana*, 17 (1980), 113–15.
50. Printed in Reynolds, *Life of Fisher*, pp. 297–9. The original manuscript in Fisher's hand, in the PRO, London, was only identified as his work in the 1950s. In the sixteenth century Robert Parkyn copied it into a manuscript collection with an attribution to More. Thus it was published by A.G. Dickens as 'A New Prayer of Sir Thomas More', *Church Quarterly Review*, 247 (1937), 224–37.
51. *Treatise of Prayer*, pp. 238–9.

7 THE DISSIDENT

1. *English Works*, p. 327.
2. Cf. Michael Macklem, *God Have Mercy, the Life of John Fisher of Rochester*, Ottawa 1969; J.J. Scarisbrick, 'Fisher, Henry VIII and the Reformation crisis', in Bradshaw and Duffy.
3. For Fisher's relations with the court, see Chapter 3, above.
4. CSP, IV ii, no. 931; cf. II ii, no. 571.
5. L & P, IV, no. 3140.
6. L & P, IV, no. 3148, trans. in Reynolds, *Life of Fisher*, pp. 131–2. (Also in Bridgett, *Life of Fisher*, pp. 150–1.)
7. Reynolds, *Life of Fisher*, pp. 151–6 for a summary of the *libellus*. For

Fisher's letter to the queen, Garrett Mattingly, *Catherine of Aragon*, Boston, 1941, p. 192.

8. Guy Bedouelle and Patrick Le Gal, *Le 'Divorce' Du Roi Henry VIII: Etudes, et Documents, Travaux d'Humanisme et Renaissance*, ccxxxi, Geneva, 1987, pp. 348–9; Rouschausse, *Vie et Oeuvre*, pp. 249–50.
9. St.P., I, pp. 196–204 (L & P, IV, no. 3231).
10. Letter printed in Wakefield, *Kotser codicis*, London, c.1534, with date 1527.
11. Gilbert Burnet, *History of the Reformation of the Church of England*, ed. Nicholas Pocock, 7 vols, Oxford, 1865, vol. 4, pp. 57–58, Stafileo to Wolsey (L & P, IV, 3820). For Stafileo, Henry Ansgar Kelly, *The Matrimonial Trials of Henry VIII*, Stanford, 1976, 157–8; Bedouelle and Le Gal, *Le Divorce*, pp. 422–3.
12. L & P, IV, no. 4899; cf. Reynolds, *Life of Fisher*, p. 143.
13. L & P, IV, no. 3232; Kelly, *Matrimonial Trials*, p. 83.
14. George Cavendish, *The Life of Cardinal Wolsey*, London, 1852, pp. 133–4.
15. PRO, E 30, no. 1471. Reynolds (*Life of Fisher*, p. 151) does not think that this is the instrument mentioned by Cavendish because of the difference in date and because there is nothing in the text to which Fisher would have objected. The present writer wonders whether the missing seal does not suggest an attempt at forgery, as a false or different one attached by Warham would have been noticeable.
16. Cavendish, *Wolsey*, pp. 134–5.
17. Printed and translated in Reynolds, *Life of Fisher*, p. 153 (cf. Bridgett, *Life of Fisher*, pp. 170–2); original Italian and Latin text in *Early Life*, I p. 313n.
18. PRO, SP1/54, fos 166–214. For what follows, cf. the summary in Kelly, *Matrimonial Trials*, pp. 98–100.
19. *Early Life*, I pp. 337–43; Hall's Chronicle, fos clxxxvii–clxxxix. Cf. Stanford E. Lehmberg, *The Reformation Parliament 1529–1536*, Cambridge, 1970, pp. 87–9.
20. *Early Life*, I p. 341 and n, where the editor prefers Hall's account as probably more accurate.
21. J.A. Guy, *The Public Career of Sir Thomas More*, New Haven and London, 1980, pp. 121–2.
22. CM, no. 831, Scarpinello to Francesco Sforza, 20 Oct. 1530; CV, IV, no. 629, Falier to the Signoria, 29 Oct. 1530; Lehmberg, *Reformation Parliament*, p. 108. Fisher's indictment for *praemunire* is PRO, Controllment Roll, KB 29/162, Trinity term (22 Henry VIII), ro.12 a–b; reproduced in J.J. Scarisbrick, 'The Conservative Episcopate in England, 1529–1535', unpublished PhD thesis, Cambridge University, 1955, pp. 115–17.
23. Lehmberg, *Reformation Parliament*, pp. 113–15, largely following the *Early Life*.
24. Vienna, England Varia, 2/1 (1531), fos 17–18. Discovered by Scarisbrick and cited by him in *Henry VIII*, London, 1968, pp. 277–8.
25. PRO, SP1/125, fos 247–56; printed in Guy, *More*, pp. 207–12.
26. Lehmberg, *Reformation Parliament*, p. 150.

27. BL, Harleian MS. 7032, fos 141ᵛ–144ᵛ (L & P, VI, no. 311 (3)).
28. For Chapuys, Garrett Mattingly, 'A Humanist Ambassador', *Journal of Modern History*, 4, no. 2 (June 1932).
29. Vienna, England, Karton 5 (1531), fo. 12ᵛ (L & P, V, no. 62; CSP, IV ii, no. 615).
30. Vienna, England, Karton 5 (1531), fos 18–23 (L & P, V, no. 112; CSP, IV ii, no. 641).
31. Charles Sturge, *Cuthbert Tunstal, Churchman, Scholar, Administrator*, London, New York and Toronto, 1938, p. 181.
32. Vienna, England, Karton 5 (1531), fos 13–15 (L & P, V, no. 120; CSP, IV ii, no. 646).
33. CV IV, no. 668; *Chronicle of the Grey Friars of London,* ed. John Gough Nichols, Camden Society, London, 1852, pp. 35, 102–3.
34. *Early Life*, I pp. 344–7.
35. There seem to be two possibilities. Either Fisher and his servants in their panic jumped to the conclusion that the gun had been fired from Boleyn's house; or, as Dr. Edmund Green suggests, the idea that the gunshot came from that house was attached to the tale later.
36. L & P, V, no. 472; CSP, IV ii, no. 805.
37. Vienna, England, Karton 5 (1532), fos 5–7 (L & P, V, no. 707; CSP, IV ii, no. 863).
38. Vienna, England, Karton 5 (1532), fo. 8 (L & P, V, no. 737; CSP, IV ii, no. 888).
39. Vienna, England, Karton 5 (1533), fos 38–40 (L & P, VI, no. 296; CSP, IV ii, no. 1057).
40. Vienna, England, Karton 5 (1533), fos 43–45 (L & P, VI, no. 324; CSP, IV ii, no. 1058).
41. Lamb, *Cambridge Documents*, pp. 14–15.
42. Bridgett, *Life of Fisher,* Appendix 457; Richard Rex, 'The English Campaign Against Luther in the 1520s', *Transactions of the Royal Historical Society,* fifth series, 39 (1989), 93; Maria Dowling, *Humanism in the Age of Henry VIII*, London, 1986, p. 91; L & P, VII, no. 805, John Gowgh to Cromwell, 1534.
43. Lamb, *Cambridge Documents*, pp. 23–5; cf. Bedouelle and Le Gal, *Le Divorce*, pp. 62–4, 70–75. For Cambridge opponents of the divorce and royal supremacy, many of whom were associates of Fisher, Maria Dowling, 'Humanist Support for Katherine of Aragon', *Bulletin of the Institute of Historical Research* 57 (1984), 46–55; Rex, 'Campaign', p. 93.
44. CSP, IV ii, no. 241.
45. Vienna, England, Karton 4 (1530), fos 284–5 (L & P, IV, no. 6199).
46. Cf. L & P, IV, 6596.
47. Vienna, England, Karton 4 (1530), fos 355–7 (L & P, IV, no. 6738).
48. L & P IV, no. 6757.
49. CSP, IV i, no. 547.
50. BL, Cotton MS. Otho C X, fo. 160 (L & P V, App. 9).
51. CSP, IV i, no. 547. The case seems to have been debated on one occasion between Stokesley and Longland on the king's side and Standish and Clerk on the queen's, but Fisher played no part in this. In any

case, 'silence was enjoined on all parties'. CM, no. 861, Scarpinello to Francesco Sforza, 20 April 1531.

52. PRO, SP1/93, fos 63–77 (L & P, VIII, no. 859), several copies of the interrogatories. The Latin version of this damaged document is translated and printed in large part in Reynolds, *Life of Fisher*, pp. 228–37; the quotations here are from pp. 233–4.
53. Vienna, England, Karton 5 (1531), fos 65–6 (L & P, V, no. 460).
54. Vienna, England, Karton 5 (1531), fo. 75 (L & P, V, no. 546).
55. Vienna, England, Karton 5 (1531), fos 69–70 (L & P, V, no. 478; CSP, IV ii, no. 808). For Moscoso, Bedouelle and Le Gal, *Le Divorce*, pp. 380–1.
56. Vienna, England, Karton 5 (1532), fos 72–4 (L & P, V, no. 1109; CSP, IV ii, no. 962). The treatise on clerical liberty exists in fragments as PRO, SP6/11, fos 38–40ᵛ, 215–23. For a full discussion, Scarisbrick, 'Reformation Crisis', in Bradshaw and Duffy, pp. 163–5.
57. St.P., VII, pp. 489–92 (L & P, VI, no. 934).
58. L & P, V, nos 207, 342; cf. no. 378. The best reconstruction of Fisher's writings is in Bedouelle and Le Gal, *Le Divorce*, pp. 345–50.
59. Printed in Reynolds, *Life of Fisher*, p. 230. Cf. note 61, above.
60. Reynolds, *Life of Fisher*, pp. 235, 230–1.
61. PRO, SP1/142, fos 201–2 (L & P, XIV i, no. 190).
62. Printed in Reynolds, *Life of Fisher*, p. 232.
63. Reynolds, *Life of Fisher*, p. 233.
64. Reynolds, *Life of Fisher*, p. 236.
65. BL, Cotton MS. Cleop. E VI, fo. 168, Bedyll to Cromwell, 28 July 1535.
66. Vienna, England, Karton 5 (1533), fo. 118 (L & P, VI, no. 1164; CSP, IV ii, no. 1130).
67. Vienna, England, Karton 5 (1533), fo. 122 (L & P, VI, no. 1249; CSP, IV ii, no. 1133).
68. Cf. BL, Cotton MS. Titus B I, fos 478–79 (L &P, VI, no. 1381 (2)).
69. L & P, VI, no. 1468.
70. BL, Cotton MS. Vesp. F XIII, fo. 1540 (L & P, VII, no. 116); printed in John Bruce, 'Observations on the Circumstances which Occasioned the Death of Fisher, Bishop of Rochester', *Archaeologia*, 25 (1834), 89.
71. BL, Cotton MS. Cleop. E VI, fo. 155 (L & P, VII, no. 136); Bruce, 'Observations', pp. 89–90.
72. Burnet, *Reformation*, vol. 4, pp. 195–201 (L & P, VII, no. 238).
73. BL, Cotton MS. Cleop. E VI, fos 156ff. (L & P. VII, no. 239); Bruce, 'Observations', pp. 90–3.
74. *Original Letters Illustrative of English History*, ed. Sir Henry Ellis, 3 series, London, 1846, pp. 289–95 (L & P, VII, no. 240).
75. Reynolds, *Life of Fisher*, p. 89. The bill of attainder was agreed in the lords on 12 March, sent to the commons and passed immediately on 17 March.
76. L & P, VII, no. 246; CSP, V i, no. 22.
77. Vienna, England, Karton 5 (1534), fos 96–106 (L & P, VII, nos 490, 690; CSP, V i, no. 45).
78. BL, Cotton MS. Cleop. E VI, fo. 165 (L & P, VII, no. 498).

79. *Miscellaneous Writings and Letters of Thomas Cranmer*, ed. J.E. Cox, Parker Society, Cambridge, 1846, pp. 285–6 (L & P, VII, no. 499).
80. PRO, SP1/83, fo. 98 (L & P, VII, no. 500).
81. PRO, Parliament Roll C65, 143, m.2–3, attainder of Fisher and others.
82. Cf. Lehmberg, *Reformation Parliament*, pp. 203–4.
83. Printed in Bruce, 'Observations', pp. 93–4 (L & P, VII, no. 1563).
84. See Chapter 8, below.
85. PRO, SP1/93, fos 52–62 (L & P, VIII, no. 856). This series of documents is badly faded, mutilated and out of sequence.
86. BL, Cotton MS. Cleop. E VI, fos 165ff. (L & P, VIII, no. 858); printed in Bruce, 'Observations', pp. 95–9.
87. Printed in Bruce, 'Observations', p. 95.
88. *Early Life*, II pp. 161, 172–76, 256. For opinions on the veracity of the story, Reynolds, *Life of Fisher*, p. 259n.
89. Vienna, England Karton 7 (1535), fos 32–5 (L & P, VIII, no. 876; CSP, V i, no. 174).
90. *Early Life*, II p. 265.
91. Bruce, 'Observations', p. 93.

8 THE CARDINAL

1. ASV, *Archivum Arcis*, no. 4050, Richard Pace to Leo X, 1 June 1521, describing Fisher.
2. BL, Cotton MS. Nero B VII, fo. 109 (L & P, VIII, no. 875), Sandro to Starkey 15 June 1535.
3. ASV, *Consistoriale Acta*, Misc. 18, fo. 256; L. Dorez, *La Cour du Pape Paul III*, Paris, 1932 p. 18n.
4. L & P, VIII, no. 786; CSP, V i, no. 169.
5. L & P, VIII, no. 779, Macon to Francis I; Dorez, *Paul III*, p. 123n, Latino Giovenale de' Manetti to Du Bellay; St.P., VII, p. 604 (L & P, VIII, no. 777), Gregorio da Casale to Cromwell.
6. ASV, *Brevi Paolo III*, Arm. XL, no. 51, fo. 248, briefs to the new cardinals; fos 452–4, 456–7, briefs to the admiral of France, Francis I, Cardinal Du Bellay and the papal nuncio Carpi.
7. ASV, *Brevi Paolo III*, Arm. XL, no. 52, fo. 378.
8. For Fisher's *ad limina* visits, ASV, *Diversa Cameralia*, vol. 57, fo. 203; 59, fo. 97; 63, fo. 258. For Fisher and the Lateran council, L & P, I, nos 1048, 1067, 1083, 3495; II, pp. 1454, 1466 (king's book of payments).
9. See note 1 above.
10. ASV, *Collectanea Angliae Miscellanea*, Arm. I, vol. 15, fos 59–72, '*De Joanne Fishero episcopo Rofensi et Thoma Moro Brittanis*'; *Tudor Royal Proclamations, Volume 1, The Early Tudors*, ed. Paul L. Hughes and James F. Larkin, New Haven and London, 1964, pp. 235–7.
11. See note 7, above.
12. ASV, AA 6528, *Gallicae Nunciature sub Paulo PP II*, Vol. 1, fos 22–4, Ricalcato to Carpi, 2 June 1535.
13. St.P., VII, p. 604 (L & P, VIII, no. 777), Casale to Cromwell, 29 May 1535.

14. ASV, *Francia*, I, B, fo. 351ᵛ.
15. *Erasmi Epistolae*, nos 3037, 3048.
16. Cf. J.-P. Moreau, *Rome ou L'Angleterre?: les réactions politiques des catholiques anglais au moment du schisme (1529–1533)* Paris, 1984, p. 111: '*Pourtant, si insignifiante que puis nous apparaître l'opposition, Henri VIII en est profondement irrité. Il lui faut l'accord de* tous *les Anglais et notamment de Fisher et de More*'.
17. Susan Wabuda, 'Bishop Longland's Mandate to his Clergy, 1535', *The Library*, sixth series, 13 no. 3 (Sept. 1991), 255–61.
18. *Miscellaneous Writings and Letters of Thomas Cranmer*, ed. J.E. Cox, Parker Society, Cambridge, 1844, pp. 285–6.
19. *Life and Letters of Thomas Cromwell*, ed. R.B. Merriman, 2 vols, Oxford, 1902, I p. 381.
20. Vienna, England, Karton 7 (1535), fos 32–5 (L & P, VIII, no. 876; CSP, VI, no. 174).
21. *Tudor Royal Proclamations*, pp. 229–32; see also Wabuda, 'Longland's Mandate'.
22. PRO, SP1/93, fos 57–62 (L & P, VIII, 856), examinations in the Tower.
23. For Carpi, *Acta Nuntiaturae Gallicae 1. Correspondance des Nonces en France Carpi et Ferrerio 1535–1540*, ed. J. Lestocquoy, Rome and Paris, 1961, pp. xxxiii–xxxvi; *Dizionario Storico-Ecclesiastica*, ed. Gaetano Moroni Romano, vol. LIII, Venice, 1852, pp. 235–6.
24. ASV, *Francia*, I, B, fos 350–2.
25. ASV, *Francia*, I, B, fos 354–7ᵛ, Carpi to Ambrogio, 21 June 1535.
26. PRO, SP1/93, fo. 60 (L & P, VIII, no. 856), examination of John Falconer.
27. ASV, *Archivum Arcis*, Arm. V, no. 1588, copy of bull of deprivation (also printed in Pierre Janelle, *Obedience in Church and State*, Cambridge, 1930, pp. 12–19); *Brevi di Paolo III*, Arm XL, no. 52, fos 377–82, briefs to the Catholic monarchs.
28. ASV, AA 6528, *Gallicae Nunciature*, fos 420–36 (L & P, IX, 818).
29. PRO, SP1/94, fos 245–6 (L & P, VIII, no. 1144); L & P, IX, no. 15.
30. St.P., VII, pp. 618ff. (L & P, VIII, no. 1121).
31. St.P., VII, pp. 633ff. (L & P, IX, no. 240).
32. John Strype, *Ecclesiastical Memorials*, 3 vols, Oxford, 1830–40, I ii, pp. 247–52 (L & P, IX, no. 157).
33. PRO, SP1/96, fos 24–5 (L & P, IX, no. 213).
34. The whole tract printed in Janelle, *Obedience in Church and State*, pp. 22–65.
35. PRO, SP1/96, fos 59, 60. For a domestic sermon justifying the two deaths, given after Fisher's execution but before More's, Simon Matthewe, *A sermon made in the cathedral church of saint Paul at London*, London 1535.
36. L & P VIII, no. 1115; CSP, V i, no. 187.
37. For Francis' diplomatic use of the papal brief, Janelle, *Obedience*, p. 26n.
38. Kelly, *Matrimonial Trials*, p. 167.
39. ASV, *Francia*, I, B, fos 365ᵛ–366ᵛ (L & P, VIII, no. 986).
40. SP1/105, fo. 46 (L & P, XI, no. 73).

41. L & P, X, no. 975.
42. *Early Life*, I p. 167, *Informations B*; John Bruce, 'Observations on the Circumstances which Occasioned the Death of Fisher, Bishop of Rochester', *Archaeologia*, XXV (1834), 99.
43. Bridgett, *Life of Fisher*, p. 359; ASV, *Collectanea Angliae, Miscellanea*, Arm. I, vol. 15, fo. 62.
44. Bridgett, *Life of Fisher*, pp. 120–1, from the *Confutation*.
45. *A Sermon . . . made upon Palm Sunday*, London, 1539, sigs Bviii^v–Ci.
46. ASV, *Lettere di Principi*, vol. 2, fos 140, 145.
47. Foxe, V, pp. 498–9.
48. *English Works*, p. 335.

Bibliography

I MANUSCRIPT SOURCES

Cambridge

Cambridge University Library
MS Ff. v. 25, theological tracts
MSS mm. v. 47 and Mm. 2.24, papers relating to Christ's College
QC Bk I, 'Journale' of Queens' College

St John's College archives

Miscellaneous papers
C7.2, list of early benefactors
C7.11, old register
D91.20, Margaret Beaufort's household accounts

College accounts
D57.33
D106.3
D106.4
D106.6
D106.11

Correspondence
D56.9
D56.15
D56.25
D94.07
D105.51
D105.163

London

British Library
Additional Manuscripts 5846; 12,060; 59,899

Cotton Manuscripts Cleopatra E VI; Nero B VII; Otho C X; Titus B I; Vespasianus F XIII; Vitellius B VIII and B XX

Harleian Manuscripts 3504, 7032, 7048

Sloane MS 1898

Public Record Office

State Papers of Henry VIII (SP1)
Theological tracts (SP6)
Fisher's 'installment speech' (SP46/123)

Instrument from legatine court (E30, no. 1471)
Fisher's indictment for *praemunire* (Controllment Roll, KB29/162)
Fisher's first act of attainder (Parliament Roll C65, 143, m.2–3)

Oxford

Bodleian Library
Bodley MS 13 B, Fisher's oration to Henry VII
Rawlinson MS C 155, Baker-Lewis correspondence and papers

Vatican

Archivio Segreto del Vaticano

  Archivum Arcis
  Brevi Clemente VII
  Brevi Giulio II
  Brevi Paolo III
  Brevia ad Principem
  Collectanea Angliae Miscellanea
  Consistoriale Acta
  Diversa Cameralia
  Francia I, B
  Gallicae Nunciature sub Paolo PP III
  Lettere di Principi

Vienna

Haus,-Hof,-und Staatsarchiv

Staatenabteilungen England, England Varia

II   PRINTED PRIMARY SOURCES

Acta Nuntiaturae Gallicae 1, Correspondance des Nonces en France Carpi et Ferrerio, 1535–1540, ed. J. Lestocquoy, Rome and Paris, 1961
Ambassades en Angleterre de Jean Du Bellay. La Premiere Ambassade, Sept. 1527 à Fev. 1529, ed. V.L. Bourilly & P. de Vaissiere, Paris, 1905
Annals of Cambridge, ed. C.H. Cooper, 5 vols, Cambridge and London, 1842–1908
Guy Bedouelle & Patrick Le Gal, *Le 'Divorce' Du Roi Henry VIII: Etudes et Documents, Travaux d'Humanisme et Renaissance ccxxxi*, Geneva, 1987
John Bruce, 'Observations on the Circumstances which Occasioned the Death of Fisher, Bishop of Rochester', *Archaeologia* 25 (1834)
Catalogue of the Library of Syon Monastery, Isleworth, ed. Mary Bateson, Cambridge, 1898
'Church Authority and Power in Medieval and Early Modern Britain: The Episcopal Registers Part 8', microfilm, Brighton, 1987
A Collection of Letters, Statutes and Other Documents, from the MS Library

of Corp. Christ. Coll., Illustrative of the History of the University of Cambridge, ed. John Lamb, London, 1838

Thomas Cranmer, *Miscellaneous Writings and Letters*, ed. J.E. Cox, Parker Society, Cambridge, 1846

Early Statutes of Christ's College, Cambridge, ed. H. Rackham, Cambridge, 1927

Early Statutes of the College of St John the Evangelist, ed. J.E.B. Mayor, Cambridge, 1859

Stephan Ehses, *Römische Dokumente zur Geschichte der Ehescheidung Heinrichs VIII von England*, Paderborn, 1893

Erasmus, *Correspondence*, trans. Wallace K. Ferguson, R.A.B. Mynors, D.F.S. Thomson, Alexander Dalzell, 11 vols, Toronto, 1974–1994

Erasmus and Fisher: Their Correspondence, ed. J. Rouschausse, Paris, 1968

Erasmus, *Opus Epistolarum*, ed. P.S. & H.M. Allen, H.W. Garrod, 11 vols, Oxford, 1906–1947

Richard Fox, *Letters*, ed. P.S. & H.M. Allen, Oxford, 1929

The Register of Richard Fox While Bishop of Bath and Wells, ed. Edmund Chisholm Batten, London, 1889

Grace Book A, 1454–1488, ed. Stanley M. Leathes, Cambridge Antiquarian Society, Cambridge and London, 1897

Grace Book B Part I, 1488–1511, Part II, 1511–1544, ed. Mary Bateson, Cambridge Antiquarian Society, Cambridge and London, 1903, 1905

G.J. Gray, 'Letters of Bishop Fisher', *The Library* 3rd series (1913)

Journals of the House of Lords Beginning Anno primo Henrici Octavi, Vol. I, London, 1920

The Lisle Letters, ed. Muriel St Clare Byrne, 6 vols, London and Chicago, 1981

R.B. Merriman, *Life and Letters of Thomas Cromwell*, 2 vols, Oxford, 1902

Thomas More, *Correspondence*, ed. E.F. Rogers, Princeton, 1947

Thomas More, *Selected Letters*, ed. E.F. Rogers, New Haven and London, 1967

Notes from the Records of St John's College, Cambridge, ed. R.F. Scott, 3 series, privately printed, 1889–1913

Nuntiaturberichte aus Deutschland 1533–1559 Nebst Erganzenden Actenstucken. Erster Band, Nuntiaturen des Vergerio, 1533–1536, ed. Walter Friedenburg, Gotha, 1892

Original Letters Illustrative of English History, ed. Sir Henry Ellis, 3 series, 11 vols, London, 1824–1846

Reginald Pole, *Epistolae*, 5 vols, Farnborough, 1967

Testamenta Eboracensia, Vol. V, Surtees Society, London and Edinburgh, 1884

John Thorpe, *Registrum Roffense*, London, 1769

Three Chapters of Letters Relating to the Suppression of the Monasteries, ed. Thomas Wright, Camden Society, London, 1843

Tudor Royal Proclamations, ed. Paul L. Hughes & James F. Larkin, 3 vols, New Haven and London, 1964–69

Valor Ecclesiasticus Temp. Henr. VIII, 6 vols, London, 1810–1834

Susan Wabuda, 'Bishop Longland's Mandate to his Clergy', *The Library*, 6th series, 13 (September 1991)

The Will of King Henry VII, London, 1775

III EARLY MODERN WORKS

Thomas Abell, *Invicta Veritas*, Luneberg, 1532

Roger Ascham, *English Works*, ed. William Aldis Wright, Cambridge, 1904

Robert Barnes, *The supplication of Doctor Barnes unto the most gracious king Henry VIII*, London, 1550?

William Capon, 'The Sermon Against the Holy Maid of Kent and her Adherents, delivered at Paul's Cross, November the 23rd, 1533, and at Canterbury, December the 7th', ed. L.E. Whatmore, *English Historical Review* 58 (1943)

Catherine of Siena, *Preghiere ed Elevazioni*, Rome, 1920

George Cavendish, *The Life and Death of Cardinal Wolsey*, ed. J. Singer, EETS, London, 1959

Chronicle of the Grey Friars of London, ed. John Gough Nichols, Camden Society, London, 1852

John Dyos, *A sermon preached at Paul's Cross*, London, 1579

Erasmus, *De Conscribendis Epistolis*, Cambridge, 1521

—— *De Praeparatione ad mortem*, Basle, 1534; trans. as *Preparation to Death*, London, 1541

—— *Divi Ioannis Chrysostomi de orando deum, libri duo*, Basle, 1525

—— *Ecclesiastes, sive De Ratione Concionandi*, Basle, 1535

—— *Modus Orandi Deum*, Basle, 1534

—— *In sanctissimorum martirum Roffensis episcopi ac Thomae Mori*, Hagenau, 1536

John Fisher, *Assertionis Lutheranae confutatio*, Cologne, 1523

—— *De causa matrimonii*, Alcalà, 1530

—— *De unica Magdalena*, Paris, 1519

—— *De veritate corporis et sanguinis Christi in Eucharistia*, Cologne, 1527

—— *Defensio Regie assertionis contra Babylonicam captivitatem*, Cologne, 1525

—— *English Works*, ed. J.E.B. Mayor, EETS, London, 1876

—— *Funeral Sermon of Lady Margaret*, ed. J. Hymers, Cambridge, 1840

—— *Here after ensueth two fruitful sermons*, 2nd edn? London, 1532

—— *Opera*, Würzburg, 1597

—— *Psalmi seu Precationes*, Cologne, 1525

—— *Sacri sacerdotii defensio contra Lutherum*, Cologne, 1525; trans. by P.E. Hallett as *Defence of the Priesthood*, London, 1935

—— *Sermon... concerning certain heretics*, London, 1526

—— *A spiritual consolation... to his sister Elizabeth*, London, 1578

—— *A Treatise of Prayer, and of the Fruits and Manner of Prayer*, trans. R.A.B., Paris, 1640; facsimile reprint, Menston, 1969

Richard Fitzjames, *Sermo die lune in ebdomada Pasche*, London, 1495

John Foxe, *Acts and Monuments*, ed. S.R. Cattley, 8 vols, London, 1837

John Frith, *A Disputation of Purgatory*, London, 1533?

Stephen Gardiner, *Obedience in Church and State*, ed. Pierre Janelle, Cambridge, 1930

Edward Hall, *The Union of the Two Noble Families of Lancaster and York*, London, 1550; facsimile reprint, Menston, 1970

Nicholas Harpsfield, *A Treatise on the Pretended Divorce between Henry*

VIII and Catherine of Aragon, ed. Nicholas Pocock, Camden Society, London, 1878

Gentian Hervet, *Quaedam Opuscula*, Lyons, 1541

Holinshed's Chronicles of England, Scotland and Ireland, Volume III, London, 1808

Jacques Lefèvre d'Etaples, *Prefatory Epistles . . . and Related Texts*, ed. Eugene F. Rice, New York, 1972

Simon Matthew, *A sermon made in the cathedral church of Saint Paul in London*, London, 1535

William Melton, *Sermo exhortatorius*, London, 1510?

Thomas More, *Apology*, ed. J.B. Trapp, New Haven and London, 1979

—— *Confutation of Tyndale's Answer*, ed. L.A. Schuster, R.C. Marius, J.P. Lusardi, R.J. Schroeck, New Haven and London, 1973

—— *Dialogue Concerning Heresy*, ed. W.E. Campbell, London, 1927

—— *English Prayers and Treatise on the Holy Eucharist*, ed. P.E. Hallett, London, 1938

Giovanni Pico della Mirandola: His Life by his Nephew Giovanni Francesco Pico. . . . and his Deprecatory Hymn to God, trans. Thomas More, ed. J.M. Rigg, London, 1890

Giovanni Michele Piò, *Delle Vite Degli Uomini Illustri Di San Domenico*, Bologna, 1607

Nicolas Sander, *Rise and Growth of the Anglican Schism*, ed. David Lewis, London, 1877

Cuthbert Tunstal, *A Sermon . . . made upon Palm Sunday*, London, 1539

William Tyndale, *An Answer to Sir Thomas More's Dialogue, The Supper of the Lord, and William Tracy's Testament Expounded*, ed. Henry Walter, Parker Society, Cambridge, 1850

—— *Doctrinal Treatises*, ed. Henry Walter, Parker Society, Cambridge, 1848

—— *Expositions and Notes on Sundry Portions of the Holy Scriptures, together with the Practice of Prelates*, ed. Henry Walter, Parker Society, Cambridge, 1849

Polydore Vergil, *Anglica Historia*, ed. Denys Hay, Camden Society, London, 1950

—— *De Rerum Inventoribus*, Basle, 1532

Vie du bienheureux martyr Jean Fisher, cardinal, évêque de Rochester, ed. F. Van Ortroy, *Analecta Bollandiana*, Vols X, XII (1891, 1893)

Vives and the Renascence Education of Women, ed. Foster Watson, London, 1912

Florens Voluzenus, *De Animi Tranquillitate*, Lyons, 1543

Robert Wakefield, *Kotser Codicis*, London, 1534?

—— *Oratio de laudibus et utilitate trium linguarum Arabicae, Chaldaicae et Hebraicae*, London, 1524

Richard Whitford, *A daily exercise and experience of death*, ed. James Hogg, *Salzburg Studies in English Literature, Elizabethan and Renaissance Studies*, 89, Vol. 5 (1979)

—— *A work for householders*, London, 1533

IV SECONDARY WORKS

Margaret Aston, *England's Iconoclasts, Volume I, Laws Against Images*, Oxford, 1988

Thomas Baker, *History of the College of St John the Evangelist, Cambridge*, ed. J.E.B. Mayor, Cambridge, 1869

E.A. Benians, *John Fisher*, Cambridge, 1935

Peter G. Bietenholz & Thomas B. Deutscher, eds, *Contemporaries of Erasmus: a Biographical Register of the Renaissance and Reformation*, 3 vols, Toronto, 1985–87

J.W. Blench, *Preaching in England in the Late Fifteenth and Sixteenth Centuries*, Oxford, 1964

Margaret Bowker, *The Henrician Reformation: the Diocese of Lincoln under John Longland, 1521–1547*, Cambridge, 1981

—— *University Sermon in Commemoration of Benefactors*, Cambridge, 1990

Brendan Bradshaw and Eamon Duffy, eds, *Humanism, Reform and the Reformation: the Career of Bishop John Fisher*, Cambridge, 1989

T.E. Bridgett, *Life of Blessed John Fisher*, 2nd edn, London, 1922

—— *Life and Writings of Blessed Thomas More*, London, 1891

Ann Brown, 'The Lands and Tenants of the Bishopric and the Cathedral Priory of St Andrew, Rochester', unpublished PhD thesis, London University, 1974

A.K. Bruce, *Erasmus and Holbein*, London, 1936

Gilbert Burnet, *History of the Reformation of the Church of England*, ed. Nicholas Pocock, 7 vols, Oxford, 1865

Charles Burns, 'Papal Gifts and Honours for the Earlier Tudors', *Miscellanea Historiae Pontificae*, 50 (1983)

Cuthbert Butler, *Western Mysticism: the Teaching of SS Augustine, Gregory and Bernard on Contemplation and the Contemplative Life*, London, 1922

Charles C. Butterworth, *The English Primers (1529–1545)*, Philadelphia, 1953

Richard Cameron, 'The Attack on the Biblical Works of Lefèvre d'Etaples, 1514–1521', *Church History* 38 (1969)

Carlo Carpasso, *Paolo III*, 2 vols, Messina, 1923–24

Peter Clark, *English Provincial Society from the Reformation to the Revolution: Religion, Politics and Society in Kent 1500–1640*, London, 1977

William A. Clebsch, *England's Earliest Protestants, 1520–1535*, New Haven, 1964

Hartley Coleridge, *The Worthies of Yorkshire and Lancashire*, London, 1836

W.H. Cologan, 'Blessed John Fisher and the Royal Supremacy', Catholic Truth Society, London, 1890

Robert Cooke, *Catholic Memories of the Tower of London*, London, 1875

C.H. Cooper, *Memoir of Margaret Countess of Richmond and Derby*, Cambridge, 1874

C.H. and Thomas Cooper, *Athenae Cantabrigienses*, 2 vols, Cambridge, 1858, 1861

Richard G. Davies, 'The Episcopate', in *Profession, Vocation and Culture in Later Medieval England: Essays Dedicated to the Memory of A.R. Myers*, ed. Cecil H. Clough, Liverpool, 1982

D.L. D'Avray, *The Preaching of the Friars: Sermons Diffused from Paris before 1300*, Oxford, 1985

—— 'The Transformation of the Medieval Sermon', unpublished DPhil thesis, Oxford University, 1976

E.J. Devereux, 'More, Fisher and the Attainder Bill', *Moreana*, 16 no. 62 (June 1979)

A.G. Dickens, *Reformation Studies*, London, 1982

L. Dorez, *La Cour du Pape Paul III*, Paris, 1932

Therese Marie Dougherty, 'John Fisher and the Sixteenth-Century Eucharistic Controversy', *Moreana* no. 29 (Feb. 1969)

Maria Dowling, *Humanism in the Age of Henry VIII*, London, 1986

—— 'Humanist Support for Katherine of Aragon', *Bulletin of the Institute of Historical Research* 57 no. 135 (May 1984)

—— 'John Fisher and the Preaching Ministry', *Archiv für Reformationsgeschichte* 82 (1991)

C.H. Duggan, *The Church in the Writings of St John Fisher*, Napier, 1953

W.H. Dunham, 'The Members of Henry VIII's Whole Council 1509–1527', *English Historical Review* 59 (1944)

Ino Dunkin, *History and Antiquities of Dartford*, London, 1844

G.R. Elton, *Policy and Police*, Cambridge, 1972

—— 'Sir Thomas More and the Opposition to Henry VIII', *Bulletin of the Institute of Historical Research* 41, no. 103 (May 1968)

A.B. Emden, *A Biographical Register of the University of Cambridge to 1500*, Cambridge, 1963

Alistair Fox, *Thomas More: History and Providence*, Oxford, 1982

Paul Friedmann, *Anne Boleyn, a Chapter of English History*, 2 vols, London, 1884

Brian Gogan, *The Common Corps of Christendom*, Leiden, 1982

E.P. Goldschmidt, *The First Cambridge Press in its European Setting*, Cambridge, 1955

Anthony Goodman, 'Henry VII and Christian Renewal', in *Religion and Humanism, Studies in Church History 17*, ed. Keith Robbins, Oxford, 1981

J.A. Guy, *The Public Career of Sir Thomas More*, New Haven & London, 1980

Caroline A. Halsted, *Life of Margaret Beaufort*, London, 1839

Peter Heath, *The English Parish Clergy on the Eve of the Reformation*, London and Toronto, 1969

G.C. Heseltine, *Great Yorkshiremen*, London, 1932

Alfred Higgins, 'On the Work of Florentine Sculptors in England in the Early Part of the Sixteenth Century', *Archaeological Journal* 51 (1894)

Anselm Hufstader, 'Lefèvre d'Etaples and the Magdalen', *Studies in the Renaissance* 16 (1969)

Jonathan Hughes, *Pastors and Visionaries: Religion and Secular Life in Late Medieval Yorkshire*, Woodbridge, 1988

Pierre Janelle, 'Humanisme et Unité Chrétienne: John Fisher et Thomas More', *Etudes 223 (1935)*

Michael K. Jones and Malcolm G. Underwood, *The King's Mother: Lady Margaret Beaufort, Countess of Richmond and Derby*, Cambridge, 1992

Henry Ansgar Kelly, *The Matrimonial Trials of Henry VIII*, Stanford, 1976

Sidney Kilworth Keyes, *Dartford: Some Historical Notes*, Dartford, 1933

David Knowles, *The Religious Orders in England, Volume 3, The Tudor Age*, Cambridge, 1959

Veronica Lawrence, 'The Life and Writings of Richard Whitford', unpublished PhD thesis, St Andrews University, 1986

Damian Riehl Leader, *A History of the University of Cambridge, Volume 1, The University to 1546*, Cambridge, 1988

Stanford E. Lehmberg, *The Reformation of Cathedrals*, Princeton, 1988

—— *The Reformation Parliament 1529–1536*, Cambridge, 1970

John Le Neve, *Fasti Ecclesiae Anglicanae, 1300–1541, IV. Monastic Cathedrals (Southern Province)*, comp. B. Jones, London, 1963

C.S. Lewis, *English Literature in the Sixteenth Century Excluding Drama*, Oxford, 1954

John Lewis, *The Life of Dr Fisher*, ed. T. Hudson Turner, 2 vols, London, 1855

A.H. Lloyd, *Early History of Christ's College, Cambridge*, Cambridge, 1934

William E. Lunt, *Financial Relations of the Papacy with England*, 1327–1534, Cambridge, Mass. 1962

Diarmaid MacCulloch, *Thomas Cranmer: a Life*, New Haven & London, 1996

Michael Macklem, *God Have Mercy: the Life of John Fisher of Rochester*, Ottawa, 1969

David McKitterick, 'Two sixteenth-century catalogues of St John's College Library', *Transactions of the Cambridge Bibliographical Society*, 7 pt 2 (1978)

Margaret Mann, *Erasme et les Debuts de la Réforme Française*, Paris, 1934

Garrett Mattingly, *Catherine of Aragon*, Boston, 1941

—— 'A Humanist Ambassador', *Journal of Modern History* 4 no. 2 (June 1932)

Carl S. Meyer, 'Henry VIII Burns Luther's Books, 12 May 1521', *Journal of Ecclesiastical History* 9 no. 2 (Oct. 1958)

Germain Marc'hadour, 'Erasme et John Fisher', in *Colloquia Erasmiana Turonensia*, ed. J.-C. Margolin, 2 vols, Toronto, 1972

J.-P. Moreau, *Rome ou Angleterre?: les réactions politiques des catholiques anglais au moment du schisme (1529–1533)*, Paris, 1984

James Bass Mullinger, *St John's College*, London, 1901

Clare Marie Murphy, 'St John Fisher and the Field of Cloth of Gold', *Moreana* 23 no. 89 (Feb. 1986)

Virginia Marie Murphy, 'The Debate over Henry VIII's First Divorce: an Analysis of the Contemporary Treatises', unpublished PhD thesis, Cambridge University, 1984

G.D. Nicholson, 'The Nature and Function of Historical Argument in the Henrician Reformation', unpublished PhD thesis, Cambridge University

G.R. Owst, *Preaching in Medieval England*, Cambridge, 1926

K.T. Parker, *The Drawings of Hans Holbein in the Collection of His Majesty the King at Windsor Castle*, Oxford, 1945

John E. Paul, *Catherine of Aragon and Her Friends*, London, 1966

John Peile, *Biographical Register of Christ's College, 1505–1905*, 2 vols, Cambridge, 1910

—— *Christ's College*, London, 1910

Richard Rawlinson, *History and Antiquities of the Cathedral Church of Rochester*, London, 1723

P. Remington, 'A Portrait of an English Ecclesiastic of the Sixteenth Century', *Bulletin of the Metropolitan Museum of Art* 13 no. 11 (1936)

Richard Rex, 'Christianae Fidei Corroboratio: the Theology of John Fisher', unpublished PhD thesis, Cambridge, 1988

—— 'The English Campaign against Luther in the 1520s', *Transactions of the Royal Historical Society*, fifth series, 39 (1989)

—— *The Theology of John Fisher*, Cambridge, 1991

E.E. Reynolds, 'A Portrait of St John Fisher', *Moreana* no. 4 (1964)

—— *Saint John Fisher*, London, 1955

—— 'St John Fisher and the Lady Margaret Beaufort', *Moreana* no. 22 (1969)

Paul Lawrence Rose, 'Erasmians and Mathematicians at Cambridge in the Early Sixteenth Century', *Sixteenth Century Journal* 8 no. 2 (1977)

Jean Rouschausse, *La Vie et Oeuvre de Jean Fisher*, Nieuwkoop, 1972

Marie-Claude Rousseau, 'Echoes de Rome . . . More et Fisher', *Moreana, Gazette Thomas More 1* (1979)

Joycelyne G. Russell, *The Field of Cloth of Gold: Men and Manners in 1520*, London, 1969

Lawrence V. Ryan, *Roger Ascham*, London, 1963

J.J. Scarisbrick, 'The Conservative Episcopate in England, 1529–1535', unpublished PhD thesis, Cambridge University, 1955

Bob Scribner, Roy Porter, Mikuláš Teich, eds, *The Reformation in National Context*, Cambridge, 1994

W.G. Searle, *History of the Queens' College*, 2 vols, Cambridge, 1867, 1871

Charles Seymour, *A New Topographical, Historical and Commercial Survey of Kent*, privately printed, 1776

W. Shrubsole and S. Denne, *The History and Antiquities of Rochester and its Environs*, Rochester, 1772

David M. Smith, *Guide to Bishops' Registers of England and Wales, A Survey from the Middle Ages to the Abolition of Episcopacy in 1646*, London, 1981

Preserved Smith, 'Luther and Henry VIII', *English Historical Review* 25 no. 100 (Oct 1910)

Martin Spahn, *Johannes Cochlaeus, Ein Lebensbild Aus Der Zeit Der Kirchenspaltung*, Berlin, 1898

Helen Leith Spencer, 'English Vernacular Sunday Preaching in the Late Fourteenth and Fifteenth Century, with Illustrative Texts', unpublished DPhil thesis, Oxford University, 1983

—— *English Preaching in the Later Middle Ages*, Oxford, 1993

William S. Stafford, 'Repentance on the Eve of the English Reformation: John Fisher's Sermons of 1508 and 1509', *Historical Magazine of the Protestant Episcopal Church*, 54 (1985)

A.E. Stamp, *Michaelhouse*, London, 1924

Roy Strong, *Tudor and Jacobean Portraits*, 2 vols, London, 1969

John Strype, *Ecclesiastical Memorials*, 3 vols, Oxford, 1820–40

Charles Sturge, *Cuthbert Tunstal, Churchman, Scholar, Statesman, Administrator*, London, 1938

Edward L. Surtz, 'John Fisher and the Scholastics', *Studies in Philology* 55 no. 2 (April 1958)

—— 'More's friendship with Fisher', *Moreana* no. 15 (1967)

—— *The Works and Days of John Fisher*, Cambridge, Mass. 1967

Margaret E. Thompson, *The Carthusian Order in England*, London, 1930

Stephen Thompson, 'The Pastoral Work of the English and Welsh Bishops, 1500–1554', unpublished DPhil thesis, Oxford University, 1984

Arthur Tilley, 'Greek Studies in England in the Early Sixteenth Century', *English Historical Review,* 53 (1938)

Carl Trueman, *Luther's Legacy: Salvation and the English Reformers, 1525–1556*, Oxford, 1994

John Twigg, *A History of the Queens' College*, Woodbridge, 1987

Malcolm G. Underwood, 'The Lady Margaret and her Cambridge Connections', *Sixteenth Century Journal*, 13 no. 1 (1982)

—— 'Politics and Piety in the Household of Lady Margaret Beaufort', *Journal of Ecclesiastical History*, 31 no. 1 (Jan. 1987)

J. & J.A. Venn, *Alumni Cantabrigienses*, 4 vols, Cambridge, 1922–27

Susan Wabuda, 'Equivocation and Recantation during the English Reformation: the "Subtle Shadows" of Dr Edward Crome', *Journal of Ecclesiastical History*, 44 no. 2 (April 1993)

Roberto Weiss, *Humanism in England During the Fifteenth Century*, 3rd edn, Oxford, 1967

Paul A. Welsby, 'Saint John Fisher, Bishop of Rochester', Church Literature Association, London, 1978

Westminster Cathedral, 'More and Fisher Martyrs: a Commemoration', London, 1985

Franklin B. Williams, 'Surreptitious London Editions of Fisher and More', *Moreana* 17 nos 65–66 (June 1980)

Glanmor Williams, 'Two Neglected London–Welsh Clerics: Richard Whitford and Richard Gwent', *Transactions of the Honorable Society of Cymmrodorion*, pt 1 (1961)

Browne Willis, *A Survey of the Cathedrals Vol. III* (London, 1742)

Michael L. Zell, 'The Personnel of the Clergy in Kent in the Reformation Period', *English Historical Review*, 89 (1974)

Index